*More Praise for Sarah McBride's*

## Tomorrow Will Be Different

"Sarah McBride's memoir is a must-read, offering encouragement while showing that the fight for equality is just getting started."

—*Paste*

"Whatever the idea of a memoir from a still fresh-faced adult might connote, McBride subverts it: The past few years of her life contain more human experience than many lifetimes. . . . The tumult of these years—the affirming highs and the devastating lows—are chronicled in her vital and powerful new memoir, *Tomorrow Will Be Different*."

—*San Francisco Chronicle*

"Sarah McBride is a force to be reckoned with. . . . And now, McBride is detailing her history-making journey in her new memoir, *Tomorrow Will Be Different*."

—*HuffPost*

"*Tomorrow Will Be Different* is a book about falling in love, being true to yourself, and creating change. Sarah's journey is as relatable as it is inspiring—a powerful, compelling story, beautifully told by a fearless activist who has only just begun to make her mark on the world."

—Cecile Richards, *New York Times* bestselling author of *Make Trouble* and former president of Planned Parenthood

# Tomorrow Will Be Different

# Tomorrow Will Be Different

LOVE, LOSS, AND THE FIGHT
FOR TRANS EQUALITY

## Sarah McBride

THREE RIVERS PRESS
NEW YORK

Library of Congress Cataloging-in-Publication Data
Names: McBride, Sarah, 1990– author.
Title: Tomorrow will be different : love, loss, and the fight for trans
 equality / Sarah McBride.
Description: New York : Crown Archetype, [2018]
Identifiers: LCCN 2017040046 (print) | LCCN 2017049458 (ebook) |
ISBN 9781524761493 (e-book) | ISBN 9781524761479 (hardcover) |
ISBN 9781524761486 (trade pbk.)
Subjects: LCSH: McBride, Sarah, 1990– | Transgender people—
United States—Biography. | Transgender people—Civil rights—
United States. | Transgender people—Identity.
Classification: LCC HQ77.8.M387 (ebook) | LCC HQ77.8.M387 A3 2018 (print) |
DDC 306.76/8092 [B] —dc23
LC record available at https://lccn.loc.gov/2017040046.

ISBN 978-1-5247-6148-6
Ebook ISBN 978-1-5247-6149-3

Printed in the United States of America

Cover design by Rachel Willey

10 9 8 7 6 5

First Paperback Edition

*For Andy*

# CONTENTS

# Foreword by Joe Biden

I remember the first time I heard about Sarah McBride.

It was 2006 and my son Beau was running in his first election for attorney general of Delaware. We often talked about the issues, fund-raising, and ads. But second only to our family, he talked most of all about the people he met—nurses, longshoremen, the single mom working the diner, the children and seniors needing protection from predators, the teachers paying out of pocket for supplies for their students. He knew the campaign was about them—and the people who worked for him and shared his belief that his grandfather first taught me, that everyone is entitled to be treated with dignity and respect.

That's when Beau told me about a smart, sharp teenager who was volunteering on the campaign, knocking on doors, making phone calls, and doing the hard work of democracy.

It was in one of those conversations that Beau gave Sarah his highest praise, telling me she was "going to change the world."

That's how I first heard about Sarah.

But it was only in 2012, when, like most everyone else, we learned who she really was when she came out as transgender. I read her powerful coming-out essay in American University's student newspaper, where she didn't just speak her truth, she put a face, name, and voice to an identity that is too often caricatured and demonized.

She was honest and heartfelt. Even at that young age, she was a leader. Not because she thought she was better than anyone else, but because she treated everyone as equals. She was a Biden even then.

Despite her internal struggle, Sarah would be the first to say she was the lucky one and that she stands on the shoulders of famous advocates and everyday activists who marched and fought to create a world where a story like hers might be possible.

She'd remind us of all the people who came before her who lived their secrets until death, or risked their jobs, careers, and sometimes their physical safety when they came out, who never received the acceptance she did from her family and friends.

My admiration for her sense of perspective and purpose grew when she interned at the White House, becoming the first transgender woman to ever do so and giving meaning to what Harvey Milk once said: "Hope will never remain silent."

By then, the administration had ended the discriminatory law known as "Don't Ask, Don't Tell" so our gay service members could openly serve the country they love without hiding who they love. President Obama announced that our government would no longer defend the Defense of Marriage Act—and just a few days after Sarah wrote her coming-out essay, I went on *Meet the Press* and told America that love is love is love.

During Sarah's time in the White House, she saw how every issue we cared about—delivering affordable health care to millions of people, creating good-paying middle-class jobs, keeping our country safe, addressing climate change, and, yes, advancing equality for LGBTQ Americans—all came down to that basic belief held since our founding, that we are all created equal, endowed with basic unalienable rights of life, liberty, and the pursuit of happiness.

After her White House internship ended, she worked to secure those rights back home in Delaware. I'd read the local papers to learn how she testified in front of the General Assembly on the need for hate-crimes legislation protecting LGBTQ Delawareans. Beau, Delaware's attorney general, would tell me how she organized grassroots efforts to help him and Governor Jack Markell enact a law protecting those same Delawareans from being denied housing, employment, or public accommodations.

She was just out of college and she had already changed the world.

It was also around this time when her world changed once again, in the most human, universal, and most cruel way. She fell in love and married a good, decent, honorable man only to watch cancer take his life and love away from her.

For those of us who know, such a loss leaves a black hole in your heart. It wounds your soul. The pain never really goes away. But as the seasons pass, you remember how your loved one would have lived—and that picks you up and keeps you going. You think about all the people who have suffered the same as or more than you, but with a lot less help or reason to get through—and that picks you up and keeps you going.

For Sarah, she has gotten up and kept going with Andy still in her heart and soul. And she continues to be there for every transgender person still rejected by their families and friends. For the one in five who will be fired from their jobs because of who they are. For the transgender women of color who continue to live in an epidemic of violence. For the young transgender student bullied and harassed in schools or homeless on the streets. She is there for every transgender American targeted by state legislators and their "bathroom bills" that serve only to prey on people's fears.

And as this book is being published, she is there for every transgender service member under attack by a president who lacks the moral clarity of the nation in abundance of it because of people like Sarah and everyone Barack, Michelle, Jill, and I met in our lives and while we were in office. In their homes, on our staff, on the front lines of war, and in houses of worship, we have known, stood with, and supported countless gay, lesbian, bisexual, and transgender Americans and their families, who are just like us.

I'm proud to have been a part of an administration that spoke out and stood up for transgender Americans. But despite that progress, I left the vice presidency knowing that much of the hardest work remains ahead of us in building a more perfect union for all Americans, no matter their sexual orientation or gender identity.

The history of civil rights in America reminds us that progress is precious and can never be taken for granted. In the face of hateful rhetoric or divisive legislation, we cannot remain silent. That's why Jill and I are proud that our foundation will focus on LGBTQ equality along with other causes that are near and dear to our hearts, from ending violence against women to finding a cure for cancer.

In doing this work, I return to the most important lesson my father taught me and my children, the same principle that animates courageous advocates like Sarah McBride: that all people are entitled to be treated with dignity and respect.

It's a simple proposition, but one that too often gets lost in the political noise.

As a country, we need to reject the false distinction between social inequality and economic inequality, for any barrier to good jobs, safe schools, or basic health care is inequality one and the same.

As a nation, we must continue to ensure that the American Dream is available to all people. Our LGBTQ fellow citizens are service members and factory workers, teachers and doctors. They are patients and caregivers, family members and friends. Equality is not a matter of "identity politics," it is a human right, and an economic necessity for many of the most vulnerable in this nation, people whose lives, dignity, and security are on the line.

We are at an inflection point in the fight for transgender equality, what I have called the civil rights issue of our time. And it's not just a singular issue of identity, it's about freeing the soul of America from the constraints of bigotry, hate, and fear, and opening people's hearts and minds to what binds us all together.

And that's what makes Sarah's book so powerful. If you're living your own internal struggle, this book can help you find a way to live authentically, fully, and freely. If you're a parent or a teacher of a transgender child, it will help you see the world through their eyes. Most of all, if you have never known a transgender person, or have genuine questions about who they are, let this book be an opportunity to learn and put your mind at ease.

Let it show that we all have hopes and dreams and experience joy and sorrow.

Let it show that we are all created equal and entitled to be treated with dignity and respect.

In July 2016, ten years after I first heard her name, Sarah delivered an impassioned speech at the Democratic National Convention in Philadelphia and spent the subsequent weeks on the campaign trail doing the hard work of democracy she once did as a high school student. A few months later, in December, Jill and I hosted our last holiday party at the Naval Observatory, and even if the festive mood was dampened by the electoral loss, we enjoyed the evening with our closest friends, who made the previous eight years an experience of a lifetime.

Sarah and her family were there. On their way out, I stopped to thank her for everything she did for Beau. Her response brought me to tears.

"It was an honor to know your son. He embraced me without hesitation and helped make it possible for me to live my dreams and return to my family and home."

I know Beau was proud to have known Sarah. Jill and I share his pride.

After reading her story, I hope you do, too.

*Joe Biden*
*Wilmington, Delaware*
*September 2017*

# This is the world we will help build.

It's rare to know in real time that what you are about to do will define the course of the rest of your life. But as I sat at my laptop in the small office I had been given as student body president at American University, I knew that my world was about to turn upside down. I was about to reveal my deepest secret and take a step that just a few months before would have seemed impossible and unimaginable.

My hand hovered over the keypad of my laptop, ready yet reluctant to click "post" on a Facebook note that would change my life forever. I could almost hear the responses I feared would come.

*What a freak.*

*Ew.*

*This is disgusting.*

And probably the most biting, because I was afraid it was true: *Well, there goes any life and future for that kid.*

Throughout my whole life until this point, it had always seemed that my dreams and my identity were mutually exclusive. My life had been defined by a constant tension between the two: the belief—as certain as the color of the sky—that it was impossible for me to have a family, a career, fulfillment, while also embracing the truth that I am a transgender woman.

For the first twenty-one years of my life, my dreams—the possibility of improving my world and making my family proud—had won out over my identity. But the older I got, the harder it became to rationalize away something that had become clear was the core of who I am. And by college, it had enveloped my whole being. It was present every second of my life.

I no longer had a choice. I couldn't hide anymore. I couldn't continue living someone else's existence. I needed to come out. I needed to tell the world that I was transgender. I needed to live my own life as me.

A little over a year before, I had been elected student body president at American University. AU, nestled between suburban neighborhoods in northwest Washington, D.C., is one of the most politically active schools in the country and boasts a rich history of political milestones. It was the site where John F. Kennedy called for "not merely peace in our time, but peace for all time" months after the Cuban Missile Crisis, and the home of the younger Ted Kennedy's pivotal endorsement of then-senator Barack Obama in the 2008 Democratic primary.

I had always loved politics, advocacy, and government. They had seemed like the best way to improve my community and leave a lasting impact on the world. From the ages of six and seven, after discovering the White House and learning about all of the history that occurred within its walls, I knew that politics would be my life's calling.

When I served as student body president at AU and began working on the issues I had always cared about—gender equity, racial justice, opportunity regardless of economic background, and, yes, LGBTQ equality—it became clear that making a difference in the world wouldn't diminish or dilute my own pain and incompleteness.

I had come out to my parents over winter break in the middle of my yearlong term. Since then, I had come out to my closest friends, and as I woke up on the morning of April 30, 2012, my last day as student body president, I was resolved to announce to the world that I was really Sarah McBride.

It was a beautiful spring day without a cloud in the sky. I crossed the bustling, open quad at the center of campus, my heart pounding, and made my way to the student center, where the student government offices are located.

In 2011 and 2012, transgender issues and identities had not burst onto the national scene like they would in the years following. Most people I knew had never even considered the possibility of someone in their life being transgender when I came out to them. I was likely the first transgender person they had ever met—at least as far as they knew.

AU is a progressive campus. And I knew that the students were, by and large, good, compassionate people. I knew the school was generally inclusive and welcoming of gay students, but I had no chance to see how the campus as a whole would respond to a transgender student, let alone a transgender student body president.

Sitting at my desk, I opened my laptop, clicked on Facebook, and reviewed an open letter that I had drafted and redrafted and redrafted several times during the previous few weeks.

"This note has been a long time coming, 21 years, actually," the post started.

Today, I ended my term as AU's student body president. Being president has been an unbelievable privilege for me. I have learned and grown so much over the last year, both personally and professionally. As proud as I am of all of the issues we tackled together as a campus community, the biggest takeaway, for me, has been the resolution of an internal struggle. You see, for my entire life, I've struggled with my gender identity.

And it was only after the experiences of this year that I was able to come to terms with what had been my deepest secret: I'm transgender.

For me, it is something I've always known but had never accepted. It's been present my whole life, from as early as I can remember.

As I reread the note one last time, I was dead certain that I needed to do this, but I knew there was absolutely no going back after I clicked "post." I was about to jump feetfirst into a world that I wasn't sure I was prepared for. You don't resist something so all-encompassing because you think it's going to be all sunshine and rainbows on the other end.

There were few high-profile trans success stories at the time. The percentage of Americans who said they knew someone who was transgender was in the single digits, a number that has since risen dramatically. Laverne Cox had yet to grace the cover of *Time* magazine and Caitlyn Jenner was still the clumsy stepparent in *Keeping Up with the Kardashians.* For closeted young people, the Internet had been a critical outlet and a window into the lives of the few trans people whose stories or profiles were available. But it also gave me an unvarnished glimpse into the challenges and barriers.

A year earlier, a startling report by the National Center for Transgender Equality and the National LGBTQ Task Force had been published. Titled "Injustice at Every Turn," the survey was sobering:

One in four transgender people in the report had been fired from their job because they were transgender.

One in five had been homeless.

And 41 percent had attempted suicide at some point in their lives. Nearly half had tried to end their lives, in many cases because the world was too hateful to bear.

Still, after two decades, I knew that nothing—not even my biggest dreams—would make the pain worth it. Now, sitting there, my hand on my mouse, I took a deep breath and posted the message.

The die was cast and there was nothing more I could do about it. My secret was out there.

It didn't take long for the news to spread like wildfire. Comments came flooding in, not just from my friends but also from classmates whom I barely knew. Miraculously, every single one of the messages was full of love and support.

One student commented, "If you ever begin to feel that your ambitions and determination to live openly as yourself cannot coexist, please remember this moment. This is leadership. I've never been more proud to have you as our president."

Another student wrote, "This is one of those times when I'm incredibly proud to go to AU and be a part of such an accepting community. The world just became a bit more tolerant and a bit more open today with your help."

"AU takes Pride in McBride," a classmate posted.

I leaned back in my chair, overcome with the relief at the responses. They were nothing like I had feared. A weight had lifted from my shoulders. I was out and the world had not collapsed. Fear of the unknown no longer stood in the way of completeness. I felt free.

My amazement was interrupted by three knocks on the door. I wiped the tears that had begun to fill my eyes, walked over, and opened the large glass door that led into the executive suite. Standing in the hall was a line of seven men, most of them wearing shirts stamped with a jumble of Greek letters.

They were *my* fraternity brothers. I had joined a year earlier after some pressure from a few friends and one last-ditch attempt at trying to prove to myself that I was someone I knew I wasn't.

The brothers outstretched their arms and, one by one, stepped up to give me a hug. They knew I had just amicably disaffiliated for obvious reasons and they wanted to make clear, in person, that they were still there for me. That I may not be their fraternity brother anymore, but that I'd always be their sister.

As they left, the editor of the school newspaper, *The Eagle*, made his way to my office. Zach, an AU sophomore with a full dark beard, thick head of hair, and wire-rimmed glasses, looked the part of an aspiring newspaper editor. He had just taken over the paper for the coming year and he came with a question and a request.

"We have several pieces in tomorrow's paper that reference you and your time in office. Would you like us to change your name and pronouns in the pieces to reflect your note?" he asked.

"Absolutely," I responded, thankful for his thoughtfulness in his approach to my news and his new job.

He cleared his throat for the next question. It was clear he was worried it would be invasive or inappropriate.

"Would you be interested in publishing your coming-out note in tomorrow's paper?"

I had actually thought about asking *The Eagle* to publish my note but almost immediately dismissed it as a self-indulgent exercise. But when Zach asked, I thought: *Maybe this isn't actually self-indulgent. Maybe this is an opportunity to educate. Maybe my journey, as limited as it is, deserves to be heard.* I couldn't pass up the opportunity to humanize trans identities—to humanize myself—for whoever would read my piece. I hoped that perhaps my words could provide an entry point for my peers and maybe even a few strangers to tap into the most powerful human emotion: empathy.

"I think that would be great, yes," I responded.

"Great. That's great. One thing, though . . ." He hesitated for a moment. "It's a little long. We'd need to cut it down to around six hundred words."

We made our way down the hall toward the student newspaper offices so I could work with him to cut my twelve-hundred-word announcement in half. When I walked into the bustling, cramped, on-deadline, and completely filled newsroom, the space fell silent. I had just walked into a room where everyone had clearly been talking about me. I worried that this awkward moment would represent the rest of my life. Or, at least, for the year that I had left at AU.

I walked through the open space and into a small room with a single computer in the back. I sat there with Zach, cutting and adjusting. Each word, each thought, felt critically important, but column inches supersede all.

An hour later, we had whittled it down to just about six hundred words. By now my phone had started to blow up with texts, calls, and emails, many from the media outside of AU. I prepared to walk into the newsroom again.

As I opened the door, a hush fell back over the room. But this time, the atmosphere felt different. Everyone was smiling. And not in the "we're laughing at you" kind of way that I'd feared. Their smiles contained a sense of pride. A simple look of "good job" coupled with a nod. A few even stood up from their desks and shook my hand.

I had spent the previous year telling AU students, who were often more interested in interning on Capitol Hill than in improving their own campus, that they should not ignore the opportunities for change right in front of them. I told them that our campus should reflect the world we want to build in ten or fifteen years. After all, we were a student body uniquely skilled in political change, and we should invest some of our talents in our campus. I'd ask them, "If we cannot change our college, then how can we expect to change our country?"

And in the hours after posting my note on Facebook—and with the newspaper preparing to publish my piece—you could feel the buzz on campus. My post was already being shared throughout campus and beyond. And it was being met not with jokes and mockery but instead with celebration and excitement. That night, one student commented that the reaction from the student body to my news was like "we had won a sports championship." A total and overwhelming outpouring of love and joy.

As the news spread beyond our campus, American University was readying to make a statement to the country: that while we may just be starting to learn about transgender identities, this is how you react—with love, kindness, and dignity. And that through AU's example, this is the world we will help build.

Together, on that night, it felt like our campus was sending a small but powerful message: that for transgender people, tomorrow can be different.

It doesn't always get better. Sometimes it is a step back; it's the loss of a life, an act of hate, or the rescinding of rights in states like North Carolina and in the military. It's the perpetuation of a status quo in which a majority of states and the federal government still lack clear protections from discrimination for lesbian, gay, bisexual, transgender, and queer people; where too many remain at risk of being fired from their job, denied housing, or kicked out of a restaurant simply because of who they are.

But increasingly, it's a step forward. The growing ranks of allies around the country; the cities and states that are stepping up to protect their LGBTQ residents from discrimination and violence; the increasing power of our voices that are, collectively, enacting change in homes and in schools, in city halls, and in the halls of Congress.

When I came out, I never anticipated just how far the LGBTQ community and movement would come in so short a time. Inheriting a legacy of advocates, activists, and everyday people who, through the flames of violence and the ashes of hatred, toiled and fought for a different world, we've grown into one of the most effective movements for social justice in history. And even as we've faced some crushing defeats, transgender people—and all LGBTQ individuals—have made historic advancements.

I've seen this progress firsthand in my own life and my own work. I saw it while fighting for equality in my home state of Delaware and in the transforming love of a husband who helped make my life possible even while he was losing his own. I saw it onstage at the Democratic National Convention and I continue to see it every day traveling around the country to stand with a community that is finally being seen and affirmed in our beauty and authenticity.

After a decade of unprecedented progress, the knowledge that change is possible, the hope of a better day, is the fuel that drives us. We strive toward a world where every person can live their life to the fullest. While the progress is uneven and can come in fits and starts, I still know today—years after that night at American University— that, with hard work and compassion, we can make more tomorrows better than today.

# "I'm transgender."

Growing up, the TV was always on in my house.

So it was fitting that the first time I heard the word "transgender," I was ten years old and watching television.

The den on the second floor of our home was totally dark except for the light from *Just Shoot Me!*, a weekly television show about a women's fashion magazine, when a guest character named Brandi—played by the beautiful Jenny McCarthy—appeared on the screen. Brandi had been the best friend of one of the show's main characters, played by David Spade, in elementary school. But the story came with a twist: Spade had known Brandi only as a boy, but now here she was, a beautiful woman.

Cue the laugh track.

I turned to my mom, a warm and friendly woman around the age of fifty at the time, who was sitting across from me in a recliner. I gulped and asked her, "Can people really change their gender?"

I worried that even asking the question would raise questions about me. In the moments since Brandi's twist was revealed, I had quickly convinced myself that this was a possibility that existed only in the world of television.

My mom responded nonchalantly, still focused on the show. "Yes, they're called transgender. Or something like that."

*Oh my God, that's me,* I thought. The show wasn't particularly disrespectful by the standards of late-1990s/early-2000s television, but the joke was clearly that Brandi, a transgender woman, was of even passing interest to other human beings. It was *hilarious* that people were attracted to her. The audience's laughter built up every time someone commented on her looks, not knowing that she was really trans.

Representation in popular culture is key. It is often the first way many of us learn about different identities, cultures, and ideas. That evening's episode had offered me the life-affirming revelation that there are other people like me and that there was a way for me to live my truth. But it did so in a way that made clear that, should I take that path, I'd be risking pretty much everything, from finding someone who would love me as me to being taken seriously by the broader world.

Ten-year-olds don't know a lot, but they know that they don't want to be a joke. Looking at my mom, that realization sank in. *I'm going to have to tell her this someday, and she is going to be so disappointed.*

Watching this sitcom wasn't the beginning of this struggle for me. For as long as I can remember, I've known who I am. For the first ten years of my life, I didn't know there was anything I could do about it or that there were other people like me, but I knew who I was. It wasn't that I knew I was different. I knew, specifically, that I was a girl.

When the boys and girls would line up separately in kindergarten, I'd find myself longing to be in the other line. The rigid and binary gender lines are made abundantly clear to all of us at a young age, from the color-coded clothing to "boy's toys" and "girl's toys." For a five-year-old, the distance between the two gendered lines in kindergarten might as well be a mile apart. It was clear: There was no crossing of the divide, under any circumstances.

• • •

I grew up on a picturesque block of large homes in west Wilmington, Delaware, a beautiful tree-lined street of three-story, symmetrical houses built in the 1920s. The neighborhood was filled with young families of lawyers, doctors, and accountants. The kids, all roughly my age, would meet every night for a game of tag or capture the flag. While it was the 1990s, the atmosphere could have been the 1950s. It could have been *Leave It to Beaver*.

Just across the street from us was the home of two girls, Courtney and Stephanie, a year younger and a year older than me. Their house became my escape. In the playroom, located away from all the parents, they'd let me put on their different Disney princess dresses. My favorite was a shiny blue Cinderella dress. Putting it on and looking down, I felt the longing go away. A completeness instantly came over me, and a dull pain that I didn't fully understand was gone.

But every time, as I'd play in the Cinderella dress, the proverbial stroke of midnight would arrive. I'd have to take it off and return to playing the part that I'd already learned was more than just expected of me—it was "me" to everyone else in my life. I was playing an extended game of dress-up, a part society had thrust on me that, it seemed, I had no choice but to follow.

All of this was four or five years before I saw that sitcom with my mom. Convinced that there was no way out, I'd dream of the universe intervening. I'd lie in bed each night and pray that I'd wake up the next day and be myself, for my closet to be filled with dresses, and for my family to still love me and be proud of me.

By the time I had "officially" learned about transgender people at the age of ten, I'd already grown a deep interest in politics. As a young kid, I loved building blocks and constructing elaborate houses out of them. By six, I'd spend nights and weekends building detailed re-creations of the White House in my bedroom. Nerdy, I know.

The first books I started to read were, naturally, about the building and the history within it. Soon, I was voraciously reading about the presidents and gaining a profound love of history. In elementary school, my teachers and other parents had already started calling me "the little president."

*Me, my endless smile, and the best blue-blazer imitation suit jacket a seven-year-old could muster.*

As a young person first gaining a fuller perspective on the size of the world, the scope of the social change I read about fascinated me. I devoured books about Franklin Roosevelt, his New Deal, and World War II. I became obsessed with Lincoln.

But nothing inspired me more than the fights for equal rights at the center of our history. Each generation, it became clear, was defined by whether they expanded equality, welcoming and including people who had once been excluded or rejected.

And as I began to understand that there was something about me that society disapproved of, I became drawn not just to the history, but also to the possibility of politics as a means of fixing society. Of creating a world that was a little more loving and inclusive. Even if I couldn't fix it for myself, I thought that fixing it for others could make my life worthwhile.

Being me appeared so impossible that changing the world seemed like the more realistic bet. And the thought of doing both at the same time was, in a word, incomprehensible. Something became abundantly clear to me as I read my history books: No one like me had ever made it very far. Or, at least, no one who had come out and lived their truth.

At an early age, I was very aware of just how lucky I was. As we drove across town to my elementary school, the privilege that my family enjoyed was clear. I knew just how fortunate I was to have the opportunities that I did, but I still felt alone. And more than anything else, I felt resigned to a life that required me to choose between who I am and the kind of life I hoped for.

Politics seemed, comparatively, so attainable and tangible. Growing up, I personally knew more U.S. senators than transgender people. With Delaware as small as it is, a state of less than a million people, we'd routinely see our elected officials at the grocery store or the gym. And to any young person remotely interested in politics in Delaware in the early 2000s, one man stood above the rest. At eleven years old, I met my political idol.

Joe Biden was a towering figure to me. Even before he was selected as Barack Obama's running mate, he was the hometown kid who had made it big, the Delawarean who had become a national figure with presidential ambition and buzz. When I first met him at a local pizza shop while eating with my parents, I was star-struck. Here was the guy I had seen on the news—*right in front of me*.

He had just gotten off the Amtrak from D.C. and was meeting his wife, Jill, for dinner. They sat right next to our table. And knowing how much it would mean to me, my parents introduced me as he walked over.

I was speechless. I just stared up at him, barely able to introduce myself.

He kneeled down, ripped out his schedule for the day from his briefing book, and pulled out a pen.

"Remember me when you are president," he wrote, followed by his signature.

I stared at the page for the remainder of dinner and, when we got home that night, promptly hung it in my bedroom next to my Little League trophies. The February 1, 2002, Joe Biden schedule became my prized possession as a kid.

And in early 2004 I got my first real taste of Delaware politics. My dad, a compassionate, intellectually curious, and hardworking attorney, told me that his colleague Matt Denn had decided to run for insurance commissioner, a statewide position charged with overseeing the insurance industry in Delaware that, for some reason, is elected in our state.

Perhaps doing my father a favor because he knew how much I loved politics, Matt graciously allowed me and my friends, some of whom were equally interested in politics, to travel around with him as he campaigned. Most of the time, we'd hand out campaign literature or make phone calls on his behalf, but since we had started developing a strong interest in film as well, we also trailed the candidate with a big video camera for a documentary on his race.

It was on the trail in 2004 that I met an elected official named Jack Markell. Jack was in his early forties and serving his second term as Delaware's state treasurer. Prior to entering politics, Jack had been a successful businessman, helping to lead the cell-phone company Nextel and working as an executive at Comcast. In 1998, he dove into politics and was elected state treasurer. To an intimidated thirteen-year-old, he was one of the most approachable of the statewide politicians, almost always sporting a big, warm smile.

In a crowded lobby of a hotel hosting the state Democratic Party convention, my friends and I approached Jack and asked him for an interview for our documentary. Either because we sensed that he was going to run for higher office someday or because we didn't know what we were doing (as much as I still wish it was the former, it was probably the latter), we started lobbing controversial policy questions at him that were totally unrelated to his role and our film: "What's your position on marriage equality?" "Where do you stand on the death penalty?"

He probably thought, *Who the hell are these kids and why are they asking me questions when I just sign the damn checks for the state?* Either way, he was gracious, and at each campaign event that year he would always come up to us and seemed genuinely interested in how we were doing. He made an impression on me; he was an adult politician who cared about what I was doing and what I thought. Like the Joe Biden note, Jack made me feel like I mattered in politics, even though I was only thirteen.

I was excited when I learned that Jack was rumored to be considering running for governor in 2008, when the sitting governor would be term-limited. Before he could do that, though, Jack would need to win reelection as state treasurer in 2006. And when my parents hosted a small campaign event for him two years after we had first met, I had the chance to introduce the man who had become my friend on the trail.

After doing a good enough job with the speech at my parents' house, Jack asked me to introduce him at an event where he would officially launch his reelection campaign as state treasurer. It was just fifty people in the back of a restaurant, but to my sixteen-year-old self, it felt like I had made the big time.

Soon, I was introducing Jack everywhere, beginning a three-year ride of opening for him at various events and functions as he sought and eventually won the governor's office. Speaking as a fifteen-, sixteen-, seventeen-, and eventually eighteen-year-old about what Jack Markell meant to me, I would frequently say that "whenever I'm asked who my role models are, after my parents, but before presidents, I always say Jack Markell."

After he announced his candidacy for governor in the spring of 2007, I went to work for his campaign, first as an intern and then, during the summer of 2008, as a field organizer, my first paid job in politics. I spent the lead-up to the primary organizing volunteers in the state representative district where I grew up, knocking on doors and registering voters. It was a tough race. Jack was the underdog as he battled it out with the heir apparent, the sitting lieutenant governor, John Carney.

Throughout the campaign, the speeches continued. At fund-raisers and campaign events across the state, I'd be Jack's opening act, speaking about his intelligence, accomplishments, and, most of all, his heart. It was a routine that, following a monumental wave of door knocking, phone banks, canvass organizing, volunteer calls, and speeches, culminated in Jack and his wife, Carla, asking me to introduce him on primary night, effectively the general election in our deeply blue state.

The vast majority of elected officials had endorsed our opponent, and the party machine was out in force for its preferred candidate. But in the end Jack would triumph by fewer than two thousand votes. A close margin to be sure, but even winning an election by one vote feels like a massive victory.

It was one of the best nights of my life. I believed in Jack and he believed in me. Standing in front of a big blue curtain and before news cameras, reporters, and hundreds of cheering supporters, I introduced the soon-to-be-governor on the biggest night of his political life. It was surreal.

"I don't think I've ever seen a presumptive governor introduced on his victory night by an eighteen-year-old," observed a radio reporter covering the results as they carried my introduction live.

Jack and Carla had become like a second family to me. I was with them on Jack's inauguration day in 2009, they would attend my high school graduation with my family in June, and that summer, just before I went off to college, I would travel around the state with Jack as his personal aide, the Charlie Young to his Jed Bartlet (for fans of *The*

*West Wing*). I'd stay with them at the governor's mansion, Woodburn, sometimes as a family friend and sometimes as a staffer.

He genuinely believed that I could be governor and would give me pointers along the way. He had already fulfilled his dream but was committed to lifting others up behind him. He gave me the confidence to think big and to fight for what I know is right.

If he was struggling with a speech, he'd call me into his ornate office, step out from behind his desk, and motion for me to sit at it.

"I don't know what to say here," he'd instruct me. "Would you mind giving it a try?"

He'd walk out of the room to go to another meeting, leaving me sitting at the governor's desk to finish his speech, an overwhelming assignment for an eighteen-year-old kid. He'd frequently say things to me like "when this is your desk," "when this is your home," "when you're governor." Jack made me believe that my dreams were possible. But I still knew there was a trade-off. I had known it since childhood: I needed to hide and conform. I feared that if I deviated from the norm too much, my world would come crashing down.

But I never let that impact my values. I tried to be an ally to the LGBTQ community when so many think that the only way to prove they aren't queer is with bullying and machismo. Outwardly, I presented as a straight, cisgender—the term for people who are not transgender—boy. I dated girls throughout high school and the first part of college. I had short hair and wore traditional masculine clothing. I did all of this out of a sense of obligation that I needed to play the part that others assigned to me. I just didn't want to let anyone down. And I didn't want to let myself down.

While I appeared happy to everyone else, perpetually sporting a large smile I had become known for, I continued to carry with me the struggle of that five-year-old in her neighbor's Cinderella dress. And just as I had done as a young kid, every night as a teenager I would hope and pray that I would wake up the next day as myself.

Unable to go over to friends' houses and play "dress-up" anymore,

I'd find any excuse to wear a dress or makeup. I attended an arts middle and high school, where I focused on cinema studies. Films were an escape. They allowed me to develop plots where I would play a girl.

But they weren't the only outlet. Halloween was one of the few opportunities when it became remotely socially acceptable for me to express myself. So while every other kid was going out as someone or something else, it was one of the few opportunities that I had the chance to go out as me. Nothing fancy. In fact, pretty boring: jeans, a cute top, and a cheap wig I'd purchase at a costume store.

It wasn't until I got a computer of my own in middle school that I opened a window into trans lives. I learned that transgender people have existed throughout time and cultures. We didn't always use the same words to describe them, but there they were transgressing gender lines.

I read about the six gender identities that existed in ancient Jewish culture, including Saris, a person who was assigned male at birth but developed female characteristics later in life, either biologically or through human intervention. I found out that many Native American cultures affirmed and celebrated individuals they called Two-Spirit.

I learned about the diversity of the trans community. That it does not just include trans women and trans men, but also gender nonconforming, genderqueer, or gender-expansive people. Gender identities beyond the binary of men and women have existed and, in many cases, have been rightly celebrated throughout cultures.

I learned about our history. I came across the story of Lili Elbe, one of the first trans women to undergo gender affirmation surgery, whose story was told in the book and film *The Danish Girl*. Europe in the 1920s saw pioneering efforts in expanding the culture's understanding of sexuality and gender, progress largely wiped out with the Nazis' rise to power in Germany. I read articles from newspapers in the fifties about Christine Jorgensen, the "blond GI bombshell."

And I first learned the names Marsha P. Johnson and Sylvia Rivera, the transgender women of color who threw the first bricks launching riots protesting anti-LGBTQ police violence in New York City at a bar called the Stonewall Inn. That uprising, known as the Stonewall Riots, helped launch the modern movement for LGBTQ rights and dignity.

Late at night, I'd hop online and read about *our* identities. I'd look at pictures of those who had come out. I'd surf the Myspace and, later, Facebook pages of everyday trans people. I'd read their stories and find that many of the things they wrote about were things I was feeling or experiencing in my own life.

I knew who I was, but I still couldn't fully accept it. I'd stand in my bathroom, staring at myself in the mirror, just daring myself to say it out loud.

*Say it. Say it. Say it. Say it. You know it's true,* I'd think to myself.

"I'm transgender," I'd finally say into my mirror. "I'm a girl."

Instantly, shame would run over me. It couldn't be true. Incapable of accepting that fact, I kept trying to convince myself that it would diminish with age. Or, at the very least, that I could compensate for it. At eighteen and nineteen, I'd still try to convince myself with the same arguments I made ten years earlier.

*Maybe I don't have to live my truth if I can spend my life making the world a little fairer, if I can have a hand in making more space for other people—and future generations—to live their lives more fully.*

With the support of people like Jack Markell and others, this goal seemed within reach. At the very least, it certainly seemed possible.

But with each professional advancement, I carried with me the sinking feeling I felt when I first learned, sitting with my mom, the word "transgender." Each step forward increased the disappointment that I knew I'd be if—and, really, when—I'd come out.

I worried about disappointing people like Jack, who had invested so much time and energy in mentoring me. But most of all, I feared disappointing my parents.

I lucked out in the parent lottery. My mom, Sally, is a former guidance counselor turned stay-at-home mom, or as she refers to herself, a domestic engineer. My dad is a former antiwar protester turned corporate attorney in the capital of corporate law: Delaware. They had me eight and ten years after my brothers, Sean and Dan, and are the type of warm, generous, and intelligent parents that friends frequently adopt as their own surrogate family.

I never once heard my parents disparage a person for who they were, and I watched them seamlessly and lovingly greet the news that my brother Sean is gay with compassion and unending support.

"We all just want Sean to be happy and healthy," my parents told me when Sean sat me down in eighth grade to tell me he was dating Blake, the man who would eventually become his husband.

But even for my progressive parents, I feared my news would be too much. After all, at that point, it was still too much for me.

I also knew that if I confided in anyone, it would force me to admit it fully to myself, and I wasn't ready for that. So I kept it inside, as best I could. Increasingly, it was something I thought about every single waking hour of every single day.

In 2009, I moved down to Washington, D.C., to continue pursuing politics. I started at American University, a college consistently ranked one of the most, if not *the* most, politically active in the country.

During my sophomore year, after serving in the Student Senate, I decided, at the urging of the sitting student body president, to run for president of the AU student government. So I ran. And I ran hard. At our hyperpolitical campus, it was a coveted position.

I became the first candidate for student body president to knock on every single door in every single residence hall on the main campus: thousands of doors. I worked night and day and, in the end, won by about ten percentage points in a four-person field—a decent margin, given the number of people in the race.

It was the first time I had tested my skills outside Delaware—and outside of Jack's mentorship. I promised my parents that I would call them the moment I found out the results, which were expected to be in at about eight p.m. on a Wednesday night. I was delayed in calling them due to celebrations in the dining hall and interviews with campus media.

"Mom! Dad! I won!" I yelled into the phone when they picked up.

Ever the crier, my mom broke down and said, "Why did it take so long for you to call?! We were convinced you had lost!"

They were ecstatic when they got the news, and shortly after getting off the phone with them, I got a call from Jack.

"You kicked ass," he said, clearly having checked the results online. Jack and I had frequently talked about his own run for student body president at Brown University, which he lost. Fifth place out of five candidates.

"Thank you, but winning your student government race is a bad omen for things to come," I said, reminding him of his, and Bill Clinton's, early losses in college campaigns.

He laughed and shot back, "Well, I have a feeling you'll turn out differently than the folks who beat us."

To my surprise, the role was a full-time job and then some. It was a job you could never escape. Sitting in class on the first day of school during my term, everyone's heads would turn when the professor called out my name on the roster. People, particularly freshmen, would explode with excitement if they had a drink next to me at a party. I was a "campus celebrity," as my friends would mockingly say.

At the start, I thought I would enjoy that part, but it got old quickly. The introvert in me enjoyed my anonymity, and even the coolest parts still felt like I was living someone else's life.

The theme of my term continued my long-standing passion for inclusion and equality that I had developed as a precocious reader of history. Everything I did was about "making AU as inclusive, accessible, and open as possible." Every initiative, every policy, every speech fell within that theme, including our robust work on LGBTQ equality.

It was through this work that I gained my first experience in trans-specific advocacy by offering the student government's support to a Transgender Day of Remembrance event, a commemoration of those who had lost their lives throughout the previous year. Beyond the 41 percent of transgender people who report attempting suicide are the countless, and often unknown, individuals who take their own lives, as well as the dozens in the United States who lose their lives to violence committed at the hands of someone else.

I worked with the school administration to secure gender-inclusive housing, which would allow students of all gender identities to room with the student or students of their choice. The old policy, automatic segregation based on someone's legal gender, was rooted in the assumption that two people of different genders could never comfortably live together and that doing so would inevitably lead to attraction and, potentially, drama.

That policy, however, completely erases the reality of gay students and harkens back to a period when men and women could never just be friends. It also limited options for students who were transgender but had not yet legally changed their gender. With surprising support from the school administration, we succeeded in expanding options and creating more choice for students.

The substance of the job felt good. From big-scale issues like combating sexual assault to smaller quality-of-life issues like the construction of speed bumps in highly foot-trafficked parts of campus, getting things done and making life a little easier for others was truly just as professionally fulfilling as I imagined. But even that satisfaction could not distract me from my identity. And I finally became convinced that the reasons I used to rationalize staying in the closet wouldn't actually bring me the wholeness I hoped for. It was becoming clear that as rewarding as making a difference in my community was, it wouldn't compensate for a life in the closet. Far from it.

One day, while I was sitting in the office of our friendly director of student housing, he asked me where my passion for LGBTQ equality came from. I had been pushing gender-inclusive housing pretty hard, and people were curious where the interest originated. After all, at that point, I identified as your typical straight boy. Everyone, including straight, cisgender people, should be able to care about LGBTQ equality without others questioning their motivation, but I knew the director of student housing understood that. He was letting me know that others were curious.

"Well, it's the right thing, for one. But I think personally..." I paused. I wanted to say it. I wanted to say, "because I'm transgender."

But I couldn't.

"One of my brothers is gay," I told him. "And I want to make sure people like my brother have the same opportunities to feel safe and welcomed as every other student."

The answer was half true, of course, but it was the closest I had ever gotten to confiding in someone.

I left his office feeling like I was about to explode. By now, I had gone from thinking about my gender identity every hour to thinking about it every single minute. I could no longer compartmentalize. The only way I could get through anything was to imagine myself redoing it as a girl. Even the simplest action, like walking between classes, became unbearable unless I relived it in my own head, imagining a life that resembled my own but with one big difference: I was myself.

But even then, I was increasingly miserable. I'd still put on the smile I'd become known for, but it wasn't really there. I was lost. My aspirations had been my distraction for so long, but they no longer provided me with the hope that things would get better.

And so I gave up on them. I gave up on politics. I was so exhausted by my own internal struggle that it was clear I wouldn't have the strength for it. The tension between my dreams and my identity had always resulted in my dreams winning out.

But that wasn't the case anymore. The pain had become too much. But in a twisted way, giving up allowed me to begin to come to terms with my identity.

Sitting in a biology class one day, I started to GChat one of my best friends, Helen, who was studying abroad in South Africa at the time. I had become close friends with them in high school. We worked on Jack Markell's campaign together and started Delaware's high school Young Democrats chapter. A year after they went on to American University, I followed suit. Helen is a social activist to their core, someone our friends describe as a walking bleeding heart.

Somehow, with them in South Africa, confiding in them felt a little less real, the distance amplified by an impersonal computer screen. I told them, in a series of online conversations, that I was struggling with my gender identity, that I thought I might be transgender, and that I wasn't sure if I wanted to transition but that I had been thinking about it more and more.

Helen was nothing but supportive. They affirmed me at every step, and when I made the request that they try calling me by a different name and female pronouns, they obliged. Even in just telling Helen, I began to feel a little better.

Had they responded in any other way, I might have been scared back into the closet, confirmed in my suspicion that my world would come crashing down. Instead, their love and support made the impossible finally seem possible.

*Maybe my world won't fall apart.*

• • •

A month later, while on winter break, Helen and I sat in my parents' living room. The room was decked out for Christmas, my family's favorite holiday. My mom has perfected the excessive holiday decorations that fall just on the funky side of tacky. Over hot chocolate, curled up on an oversized chair by our fireplace, I told Helen, "I think it's only a matter of time before I come out as transgender."

Baby step by baby step, I was slowly going from hiding, to confiding, to accepting. I was still frightened. I didn't know how people would react. I feared I would be giving up the possibility of finding love—the first thing I learned about trans people was that loving us was a joke. But even with that fear, I could start to admit the reality and inevitability of my identity.

Two days later, on Christmas Eve, I sat next to my parents at a candlelight service in the beautiful stone sanctuary of our longtime Presbyterian church. The choir was singing "O Holy Night," one of my favorite Christmas hymns. And as I stared at the stained-glass window on the final night of Epiphany, I had my own realization.

*I can't do this anymore. I cannot continue to miss this beauty. My life is passing me by, and I am done wasting it as someone I am not.*

I took my cell phone out of my pocket and texted Helen. "I'm transgender and I'm going to tell my parents after Christmas."

I tossed and turned that night, unable to sleep because I knew I would be shattering my parents' sense of comfort and security for my future in just a matter of days.

Christmas morning started like all previous Christmases. I woke up and descended the stairs to see my parents ready for my brother Dan and me to open our presents. My oldest brother, Sean, was up in New York with his husband, Blake, for the holiday.

As the youngest, I usually got to open a present first, probably a vestige of my days as an impatient little kid in our family of five. This year was no different.

With my parents watching, I unwrapped what I knew was going to be clothes. I opened the box, and there, just as I had initially asked for, was a button-down shirt and a tie. As if I needed another reminder. As if I wasn't nervous enough.

The shirt and tie felt like a symbol of the stark contrast between where I was and where I wanted to be, between how I was perceived and who I knew I was, and between my parents' hopes for the future—a happy, successful child—and what I knew they would fear with my news: rejection. Rejection by friends, by neighbors, and, most certainly, by jobs.

I finished opening presents and retreated upstairs to my bedroom. About thirty minutes later, my mom walked in and sat on the edge of my bed. She's an incredibly empathetic person and could sense something was off.

"What's wrong? You've seemed down, and you never seem down," she asked me.

"It's nothing. I'm just overwhelmed at school," I responded.

I could tell she didn't believe me, but she didn't press the subject. She left and went back downstairs to begin preparing the stuffing for our traditional Christmas dinner.

*She just asked you. You have the courage to say it right now. Just do it.*

I walked downstairs and into the small sitting room, where my mom was waiting for the oven to preheat. I sat down on the other end of our large, overstuffed couch and took a very deep breath.

There was no turning back at this point. I knew that once I told them, they would ask every question and latch onto any glimmer of hope that I was mistaken. I needed to present a completely even-keeled, thoughtful, and determined certainty. I had to be as firm in my resolve to them as I was in my knowledge of who I am.

"I've been thinking a lot about my sexual orientation and gender identity," I began, throwing in "sexual orientation" because I knew she wouldn't have the slightest idea what gender identity meant, and I wanted her to know that I was about to come out as something. "And I've come to the conclusion that I'm transgender."

I paused, and she put her hand up to her now-shocked face. Through her fingers and already on the verge of tears, she asked, "So you want to be a girl?"

I was prepared for them to use inaccurate terminology and phrasing. I didn't *want* to be a girl. I *was* a girl. And I wanted to be seen as me. But now wasn't the time for those types of clarifications.

"Yes," I said as confidently as I could, knowing that I had just destroyed so much of her world.

She burst into tears. "I can't handle this! I can't handle this!" she started screaming. "I need your dad!"

She ran up to my father's third-floor study, where my dad and my brother Dan had gathered to set up his new TV. I chased after her and could see my dad's confusion and fear as she came in bawling.

"Go ahead! Tell him what you just told me!"

I repeated the same sentence to him that I had said to my mom. My dad, sitting in his desk chair, put his arms on his head and let out a long sigh of disbelief.

I stared down at the carpet, waiting for his response. He sat there for another few seconds, thinking. I knew I needed to remain calm, almost like a therapist who was helping them through their emotional processing.

Dan, a slender state prosecutor with dark hair and a closely trimmed beard, broke the silence. "Well, I have an announcement, too. I'm heterosexual," he jokingly declared, referencing the fact that he was now the only one of the three kids who was not LGBTQ.

As my parents continued to take in my announcement, Dan cut through the silence once again: "I always thought you were gay, but I guess this makes sense."

I chuckled, but I'm not sure the comment registered with my parents. Seeing my mom uncontrollably sad and confused, my dad went into calm-attorney mode and began asking questions.

Obviously the first ten questions were some version of "Are you sure?"

The answer to that question was simple.

"I've never been more certain about anything in my life. I know this as much as I know that I love you two." After all, I had spent my whole life thinking about it.

"I feel like my life is over. I feel like you are dying," my mom repeatedly cried.

I had read during my years of research online that my parents would likely feel this way. After all, I was telling them that someone they loved might soon look very different, and they must have felt as if the life they'd imagined for their child was in peril. I'd never find a partner. I'd never find a job. I'd never be welcomed back in our home state.

"I'm still the same person with the same interests, intelligence, sense of humor, and the same smile," I said, referencing my nearly constant trademark expression.

My dad asked about hormones. Not the hormone I was hoping to start taking, estrogen, but rather testosterone. What if they pumped me with testosterone, he asked, searching for a solution.

I assured him that would, frankly, make matters much worse.

As the questions went on, it became clear that my parents were struggling with the same empathy gap that I later would realize was one of the main barriers to trans equality among progressive voters: They couldn't wrap their minds around how it might feel to have a gender identity that differs from one's assigned sex at birth.

With sexual orientation it's a bit easier. Most people can extrapolate from their own experiences with love and lust, but they don't have an analogous experience with being transgender.

"The best way I can describe it for myself," I told them, "is a constant feeling of homesickness. An unwavering ache in the pit of my stomach that only goes away when I can be seen and affirmed in the gender I've always felt myself to be. And unlike homesickness with location, which eventually diminishes as you get used to the new home, this homesickness only grows with time and separation."

My dad, a longtime progressive, also said that he didn't understand how one could feel like something that is a social construct. Wasn't gender, and all the things associated with it, just a creation of society? Wasn't that what feminism had taught us?

I explained to him that, for me, gender is a lot like language. Language, too, is a social construct, but one that expresses very real things. The word "happiness" was created by humans, but that doesn't diminish the fact that happiness is a very real feeling. People can have a deeply held sense of their own gender even if the descriptions, characteristics, attributes, and expressions of that gender are made up by society.

And just as with happiness—for which there are varying words, expressions, and actions that demonstrate that same feeling—gender can have an infinite number of expressions. We can respect that people can have a very real gender identity while also acknowledging that gender is fluid and that gender-based stereotypes are not an accurate representation of the rich diversity within any gender identity.

All of these answers helped them intellectualize my news but did little to assuage their fears. What would come of my future? The only reference point my parents had for transgender people were punch lines in comedies or dead bodies in dramas. They had no references for success, something that had provided them significant comfort when my brother came out as gay.

After I went back down to my bedroom, my dad did what I had done for years: He Googled "transgender."

Over the course of his research, he came across the report that had become all too familiar to me, "Injustice at Every Turn." He saw the discrimination and violence faced by the community.

And then there was the suicide number. Forty-one percent of transgender respondents had reported attempting suicide in their lives. Forty-one percent.

I had never worried that I would be rejected by my parents or kicked out of the house. Like a lot of children, my biggest fear was much simpler. I didn't want to disappoint them. Statistically speaking, that made me very lucky.

While 41 percent of transgender people had attempted suicide, that number dropped by half when the transgender person was supported by their family. And it dropped even further when they were also embraced by their community. My parents made clear from the start that they would support me, but "Injustice at Every Turn" reinforced just how important that support would be in their child's life.

• • •

I awoke the next day at seven a.m. to my parents opening my door. As soon as I opened my eyes and saw them, I could tell that neither had slept, and that the crying, which had subsided by evening, had returned. This time, though, both of them were sobbing.

My parents walked to either side of my bed and got in with me, still crying. They both held me and pleaded again and again: "Please don't do this. Please don't do this. Please don't do this."

I let them cry and tried to tell them that it would be okay, but I couldn't provide them with the response they hoped for. I hated to see my parents cry. Nothing I had ever done had caused them so much pain, and it ate at me to know that my life was making their lives harder. But there wasn't a choice here, and I knew the alternative was far worse for all of us. I knew I had made the right choice. The only choice.

But for the next few days, I witnessed my parents mourn the "death" of their son, alternating between the different stages of grief, as my mom stared at pictures of me as a child. It was surreal, and all I could do was continue to tell them I wasn't going anywhere. I told them over and over again that they were keeping me, while gaining a daughter.

But it took my oldest brother, Sean, ten years my senior, to put things into perspective for them.

Sean had called to wish us a merry Christmas, and when my mom told him my news, he hopped in the car with his husband and made his way straight down to Delaware, frantically searching everything and anything about "transgender" along the way. Sean was always a calm voice of reason in our family and, as an openly gay man, felt like an ally in the back-and-forth with my parents.

Sitting downstairs with my mom, Sean took some of the load off me and answered some of their questions. I think he also knew that my news was so shocking that having a second person to validate what I had said would help my parents digest the reality of the situation.

"What are the chances? I mean, what are the chances I have both a gay son and a transgender child?" my mom asked Sean.

"Mom, what are the chances a parent finds out that their child has terminal cancer?" Sean, a radiation oncologist, replied. "Your child isn't going anywhere. No one is dying."

It was the response she needed. She needed someone to push back and not feel sorry for her. She needed someone to put things into perspective.

Soon enough, I hoped we would all come to the place where she could ask that same question, "What are the chances?," out of awe and not out of self-pity—a place where my parents could see that they had raised children who were confident and strong enough to live their truths and whose different perspectives enhanced our family's beauty.

But that was for another day. This was a start, and I considered myself very fortunate.

# CHAPTER 2

# "Hi, I'm Andy. . . . I think we'd get along pretty swimmingly."

Coming out to my parents was, up until that point, the hardest thing I had ever done in my life. And yet, because of my privilege, it was still relatively easy compared to many others for whom coming out means losing their job, their family, and, potentially, their life. Indeed, family rejection of a child coming out is one of the leading factors in the high rate of homelessness among LGBTQ young people, who make up as many as 40 percent of all homeless youth.

My fortune was perpetually reinforced as I came out to my friends and other family members over the coming months. Each response was different, ranging from grief to shock to excitement, but all were affirming. And all kept my secret in our circle.

Next to my parents, the hardest person to tell was Jack Markell. Jack had become like family and I was worried about disappointing him, particularly since he had spent so much time and energy mentoring me. Our relationship was also well known after my public role in his campaign a few years before, and so I even worried that our continued friendship could be a liability for him.

I had delayed telling him until a few months after coming out to my parents, but eventually it was time.

Given that he was governor, I wanted to make sure I reached out at a convenient moment. Pacing around my bedroom, I first called Jack's right-hand man, Brian Selandar, a political operative who had helped orchestrate Jack's rise to the governorship.

Brian was up in New York City with the governor when I reached him.

"I'm not sure how to say this, but I . . . uh . . . I'm transgender," I blurted out to Brian after a few pleasantries. "I'm hoping you can help me tell the governor. Maybe you can even tell him and then let him know to give me a call if he has questions? I don't want him to feel like he needs to spend a lot of time on this."

"Of course," Brian kindly responded. "He's on *Morning Joe*," referring to the MSNBC morning talk show, "but I can tell him on our way back to Delaware."

My stomach was in knots all day as I anticipated a call from Jack after he got the news from Brian. I had run up to campus for a few student government meetings, and as I walked back to my apartment building, my phone rang. It was Jack.

"Well, that's big news," he announced as I answered the phone. I could tell there was a smile on his face as he talked. *Phew.*

"Yes, Governor! It's something I've known for a really long time and I've finally come to terms with it," I replied quickly, thinking he didn't have much time to talk.

"Tell me about that. I want to hear all about it."

I recounted the journey, from self-loathing to self-acceptance to the fear for my future. The call lasted thirty minutes and Jack repeatedly reassured me. "Carla and I love you just as much," he said, referring to both he and his wife, the first lady of Delaware. "We are here for you just as much as before."

I told him that Carla should feel free to call me. And he closed by asking if he could call my parents. The answer was yes, of course.

While I talked with Carla for over an hour, Jack talked to my parents. He reached my mom first, catching her as she walked through a bustling shopping mall just outside of town.

"Sally," he began, "it's Jack Markell." He told her we had just talked and repeated the message he had expressed to me. "Carla and I love you all and we will be there for you," he told her.

Overcome with emotion, my mom fell to the ground. Sitting on the bright white tiles in the middle of the mall with shoppers walking around her, she began to cry. It was probably the first time she had cried from happiness rather than sadness in our family's still-short journey.

When I had told my mom I was trans, she confessed that she feared our small but tight-knit community would disown us, but here was our governor—the symbol of our state—standing firmly beside us. It was a sign of things to come, and it immediately became a powerful tool in our family's quest to remain an integral part of the community we so loved.

Most people are good, no doubt, but when we are faced with issues we haven't yet thought about or interacted with, we often look to one another for how we should respond. Our behavior models for others the acceptable reaction; acceptance creates an expectation, while rejection provides an excuse.

My parents knew this, and in discussing it as they sleeplessly lay in bed the night after I came out, they resolved to make crystal clear to the world that they loved and affirmed me. They created a standard for others to meet. And with Jack and Carla, we not only kept valued friends, we also gained visible allies who amplified that standard to our state.

In the weeks after I came out to Jack and Carla, we grew even closer than before. Despite being governor of an entire state, Jack would call me every two weeks to check in.

"Sarah, it's Jack," he'd start, using the name my friends and family were slowly adopting. "I just wanted to see how you were holding up."

Each time I came out, it felt like another step in becoming myself, and each step made me feel a little bit more whole. But telling people did only so much. People now knew about me, but I was still hidden.

By now, our fears of rejection were slowly diminishing, and while my parents had come to know that I wasn't going away, they were still a long way from *truly* feeling that way. With each hug, I could feel that they were squeezing just a little longer and harder. With each look, I could tell they were taking me in "one last time." And whenever I'd hang out with a different friend, my mom would ask hopefully, "You aren't going to tell them, are you?"

I thought I was done with secrets, but the secrecy had shifted to my parents, particularly my mom. The shame and fear she initially felt as I slowly shared my news was hard to bear. I had been so used to my parents being proud of me.

When I returned to Wilmington one weekend during the months between coming out to my parents and coming out publicly, I drove up wearing a women's pea coat and ring.

I called my mom in advance to prepare her. She sighed at my clothing choice.

"Pull into the back," she told me, referring to the empty and secluded alley behind our house that we never use.

They still didn't want it to be real. It had seemed like they were making progress, but now it felt like my mom couldn't even handle a jacket and a ring. What would happen when I started living every day, totally, as the woman I had always known myself to be?

These comments hurt. But honestly, I couldn't blame her. I'd had twenty-one years to overcome the shame.

I had constantly told them that I was still the same person, but I was starting to feel like I was competing with myself. The sense of living someone else's life that had become so unbearable persisted. I wanted them to love me as their daughter, not as the person they thought was their son. I wanted them to see and love me as me.

Each of us has a deep and profound desire to be seen, to be acknowledged, and to be respected in our totality. There is a unique kind of pain in being unseen. It's a pain that cuts deep by diminishing and disempowering, and whether done intentionally or unintentionally, it's an experience that leaves real scars.

Within most cultures, when a baby is born, we look at the child's external anatomy and make a determination. Anatomy that looks one way means the child is a girl and anatomy that looks another way means the child is a boy. For the vast majority of people, the assumption of their gender identity largely aligns with the reality of their gender identity, but for a portion of the population—those of us who are transgender—we are assigned a gender identity that doesn't fit.

Even for the most well-intentioned person, it may be difficult to separate an individual's gender identity from the sex assigned to them based on the appearance of external anatomy. We've been taught and raised to believe that these two concepts are inextricably joined, that one not only leads to the other, but that they are actually one and the same.

This challenge—to decouple concepts previously perceived as permanently and inalterably linked—is not a new one. In the nineteenth century, the notion of "gender roles" would have seemed redundant, as a person's sex inherently came with certain roles. In the first half of the twentieth century, the terms "straight" or "heterosexual" didn't exist because one's sex and who they loved were inseparable parts of each other. The words "straight" or "heterosexual" were unnecessary—the words "man" and "woman" covered it.

Slowly but surely we have learned to separate what was once deemed inseparable. Increasingly, we are coming to grips with the reality that the sex someone appears to be at birth does not dictate their gender identity.

It is this trend that links the fight for gender equity with the fight for gay rights with the fight for trans equality: ending the notion that one perception at birth, the sex we are assigned, should dictate how we act, what we do, whom we love, and who we are.

When we finally separate that perception from those expectations, we allow ourselves to witness the wholeness of other human beings. This effort—coupled with the overlapping fights for racial justice, disability rights, and equality for religious minorities—shares a similar thread. We are fighting to be seen in our personhood, in our worth, in our love, and as ourselves.

And while I was now out, I still wasn't *seen* by my parents, by my friends, and by the broader world. I couldn't blame them; when I looked in the mirror, even I still didn't see myself. And after finally checking off the last part of my "coming out to-do list" (telling the AU and broader Delaware communities), I was finally ready to take the steps I felt I needed to take in order to no longer feel hidden and to have my gender identity expressed to the world.

Not everyone in the trans community may know exactly what steps, if any, they need at the start of their journey. Transitioning, the term used to describe the process of having our gender identity seen by the outside world, isn't a one-size-fits-all experience. For many, this likely includes adjusting aspects of our gender expression, such as clothing and hair. For others, it may include taking hormones or undergoing different kinds of surgery.

I started hormones shortly after coming out to my parents. Slowly, they began to have an effect on things like my skin and my fat distribution, but mostly on my psyche. Even though I had started on hormones and they were having an effect, I was still presenting as someone I was not. I had held off on adjusting my gender expression until I had come out to my school and the public. Now that was done and I was ready to live as myself.

Again, it's important to note that this process looks very different for everyone. Some transgender people may already feel comfortable with how they are expressing themselves. For instance, a transgender man—a person assigned female at birth but who is and identifies as a man—may already be presenting in a more masculine way before he comes out as trans. And just as a cisgender woman may wear her hair short, many transgender people will not express their gender in strictly feminine or masculine ways.

For me, it was a rather stark and abrupt change. I had set the date that I would begin living as myself more visibly: five days after posting my coming-out note. It was a day I had looked forward to for a very long time, so I decided to throw a party and be surrounded by some of my best friends. I was starting a new wardrobe from scratch, a surprisingly significant undertaking, so I also asked friends to bring presents: an old top, a new dress, a cheap necklace. Anything that could help me fill my closet.

When the night of the party finally arrived, my new apartment in a town house in central Washington, D.C., which I had moved into a week earlier, was filled with people. They were mostly friends from college, but also many of my best friends from Delaware.

My ex-girlfriend, Jaimie, who I had dated for about a year, had remained my friend after our breakup and was there. A beautiful and smart brunette with a strong resemblance to a young Katie Holmes, Jaimie had broken up with me a few months before I came out to my parents. We were both very understanding people and never found ourselves mad at each other, but in the somewhat rocky weeks leading up to the end of our relationship, she made the apt observation that she felt more like she was dating a girl than a boy.

Our breakup was a turning point in my path toward coming out. It was the first extended period of time in years that I had been single. For a while, the presence of a girlfriend had been one of many factors keeping me in the closet. Sparing others from humiliation was a constant theme in my mind.

Jaimie and I had hung out a few times after our breakup, and so when we hung out in the days after my Christmas coming out, I told her my news. As we drove in my mom's old Toyota Highlander, I started by telling her that I was dating a boy, a classmate who had served as my chief of staff during the first half of my term as student body president. And like my gender identity, which I had known for as long as I could remember, I had always known that I liked boys. While they are two distinct concepts—sexual orientation refers to who you love, while gender identity refers to who you are—I kept both inside, knowing that grappling with the first would almost instantly precipitate the second.

"Oh my God, we'll be like Will and Grace!" she exclaimed, referencing the iconic television characters who had dated and remained best friends after Will came out as gay.

"Well," I cautioned, "I'm not gay. I'm actually transgender."

"Oh. *Oh!* Okay!" she responded, working to quickly turn her shock to excitement and then to support.

Jaimie echoed my brother Dan's comments while we were dating, adding, "I guess this makes a lot of sense. I was actually just learning about gender identity and trans issues in my gender-studies class."

Jaimie, along with a few friends from college, would help teach me to do my makeup during the following months, and she was with me in the hours leading up to my coming-out party.

As I greeted my guests in a white lace dress I had purchased online, the atmosphere at the party was euphoric. No more secrets. No more hiding. It was a pure celebration of love and authenticity, of friendship and life. I felt liberated. It was a true birth day. And my smile, which had faded over the previous year, was back in full force.

And in the weeks following the party, finally living as myself, my euphoria gave way to an almost meditative state. The constant homesickness that had cluttered my mind for years was finally gone. I hadn't come out to create a positive, but to remove a negative and to alleviate that nearly constant pain and incompleteness. Transitioning wouldn't inherently bring me happiness, but it had allowed me to be free to pursue every emotion: to think more clearly; to live more fully; to survive.

And while I had experienced fleeting moments of this freedom growing up, with the Cinderella dress or on all those Halloweens, it was now permanent. I didn't have to dread that stroke of midnight.

*This. This is what it feels like to be yourself,* I thought.

I had never felt that way before.

Coming out and transitioning was a decision that I had no choice in making. I had to do it. And while it helped me in many ways, there is no question that in living my truth, I faced a new set of obstacles. I was stepping into a world built for men as a woman.

There is no question that my path to womanhood was unique. Every woman's path is different. Each of us travels with different kinds of privileges and challenges.

I had always been someone who tried to think about the prejudice and bigotry in the world. So I thought I generally understood what to expect. But in the end, I was so focused on the transphobia I might face after transitioning that I didn't fully realize just how pervasive the sexism and misogyny would be.

And it truly was everywhere. From the subtle to the blatant, I had entered a world of impossible double standards and endless contradictions.

In exploring my own womanhood, it became clear that if I was "too feminine" I was inauthentic, a presumption in even progressive spheres that masculinity is some sort of natural state of being, a preference. But then, if I wasn't feminine enough, I wasn't a "real" woman. Television, movies, pop culture, fashion, and politics are all trying to tell us what it means to be a "real" woman.

The experience of each woman—cis or trans—is different, but a similar thread underpins it all: the policing of gender. The devaluation of lives, hopes, and one's body. The threat of violence.

It took me some time to find my own niche in the infinite ways to express one's gender. Young women and girls often work through this in middle and high school. I was doing it in my twenties. Like many young women, my first burst of individual gender expression was a kind of hyperfemininity—pink dresses, more makeup than I needed, and jewelry. Part of this was a release of the pent-up femininity that I had not felt free to express before, and part of it was the imperfect actions of an imperfect human living in an imperfect world that so often demands conformity from everyone.

Over time, though, I eventually landed in my own sweet spot: a gender expression that was my own and where I felt comfortable. Feminine, still, but more muted. But navigating my own gender expression—and all the expectations, prejudices, and double standards that come with it—only began to scratch the surface.

The first few months after coming out were a rude awakening. I could no longer merely exist in the world. Now I had to actively navigate through it, every minute of every day. Every decision carried with it a greater weight, consequences that would impact everything from my emotional well-being to my physical safety. And going anywhere new added additional stress.

Growing up, my default face had always been that smile, but now I had to consciously train myself not to smile anymore, lest I invite unwanted attention from men on the street. And I'll never forget the feeling the first time I experienced street harassment.

I never realized just how disempowering, unsafe, and unsettling it would feel to have a stranger assume they were entitled to comment on my appearance or my body. Walking by a man could elicit an unwelcome comment, an invitation for objectification for having the audacity to walk down the street. If I'm not smiling, I'm told to smile. If I am smiling, it's seen as a request for more comments. And then there was the man in an airport who repeatedly chastised me for smiling *too* much. The sexism had come full circle.

Somehow society manages to treat women like both a delicate infant and a sexualized idol in the same moment. Our thoughts are dismissed and our emotions minimized. And the mundane decisions that I never had to think about when I would wake up before I came out—the clothes I'd wear, the route I'd take, and all of the other tiny decisions one makes just merely going about their day—now became central to avoiding a thousand judgments or, worse, violence.

I finally had come out of the closet, only to find myself stuck in the kitchen.

And while the pain and mental clutter of being in the closet was gone, I also became hyperaware of my identity as a transgender person. Much like stepping into a world built for men as a woman, I was also stepping into a world built for cisgender people as a transgender person. And with each new person, I'd wonder, *What do they think of people like me?*

Walking down the street, I could feel the stares as I went to the grocery store or to my summer internship at the Victory Fund, an organization dedicated to electing LGBTQ candidates. The smirks on the faces of passersby would sometimes turn to laughter as they walked past me.

After moving into my new apartment with friends far away from campus, I found myself jumping through hoops to hide my transition from the landlord, who had first met me before I transitioned. I worried that I would become one of the many trans people—one in five—who has lost their housing due to their transgender identity. Coming home from my internship, if I saw the property manager's ominous white pickup truck in the driveway, I'd circle the block in my car for thirty minutes until he left. I'd do anything to avoid him finding out that I'm trans, a realization that leads to discrimination for so many.

And then there was the fear of violence. That nearly ever-present worry as a trans person was often wrapped up in the harassment and experiences I faced as a woman. These two identities—being a woman and being transgender—interact with each other in a way that serves to compound the animus that comes trans women's way. This reality, referred to as intersectionality, recognizes that we all live our lives with multiple identities intersecting with one another, creating a mix of privileges and challenges that all people carry with us. Race, gender, economic background, religion, immigration status, family acceptance, and so much more create a complex matrix that sometimes erects obstacles but other times ensures support in overcoming barriers put in your way.

When I faced harassment, the feelings of disempowerment and the lack of safety I felt as a woman were met with a deep fear of escalating violence due to my trans identity.

Sitting in the backseat of a taxi one day a bit later in my transition, I noticed the driver smiling at me in the mirror.

"I'll give you a free ride if you take your top off," he creepily offered.

"No. No, I'll pass," I hesitantly replied.

He kept asking, telling me it was a good deal.

When he asked what I was doing that night, I told him I was going out to dinner with friends.

"Oh, you're going to be naughty," he said through a sinister laugh. "I'll want to find you after you've had a few drinks."

When I recounted the story to friends, mostly all cisgender women, they rebuffed me for not standing up for myself and other women. I should have thought to take down his medallion number. I should have thought to rebuke him.

His actions were disgusting and I wanted to tell him off, but instead I shut up and made myself as small as possible. I didn't want to draw any more attention to myself.

As a woman, I was scared for my safety and I just wanted to get to my destination as quickly as possible. And as a trans person, I was profoundly afraid that he'd realize I was trans. There are few things more dangerous to a transgender woman than the risk of a straight man not totally comfortable in his sexuality or masculinity realizing he is attracted to her.

Transphobia tells these straight, cisgender men that being attracted to a transgender woman makes them gay (it does not). Society's homophobia tells them that being gay is bad (it is not). These prejudices mix in their mind, threatening both their sexuality and their masculinity. One step too masculine, one stride too manly, one word too deep and I risk the violence that often comes to a trans woman who commits the crime of attracting the interest of a straight, cisgender man.

But in the same way that my gender as a woman and my identity as a trans person intersect to foster discrimination or violence, my other identities combine to provide me with a cloak of privilege not offered to others.

While trans people are twice as likely to live in poverty than the general population, trans people of color are three times as likely to live in poverty. Dozens of transgender people are killed each year in the United States and every year trans women of color make up a majority of those killed, a significant overrepresentation that results from the toxic combination of racism, misogyny, transphobia, and homophobia, a blend that can have deadly consequences.

As a white person, my race provides me with certain securities that are refused to people of color. My family and friends provide support structures denied to those who are rejected by their communities. My economic security grants me resources to escape situations that would put me more at risk. And even if my landlord had found out that I was trans and responded negatively, I never feared that I wouldn't be able to land on my feet and find and afford housing that would welcome me.

Having certain privileges does not mean that your life is easy or that you do not face challenges. It just means that you don't experience specific kinds of obstacles or barriers faced by someone with a different identity or background. And our empathy should require us to acknowledge the plight of others in both its similarities to ours and in its differences.

Indeed, as lifesaving as transitioning was for me, it was also life-altering. The relief was profound when I found an affirming space. The overwhelming fear and anxiety that would fill my mind in more public spaces would wash away.

I was fortunate to have those places. American University was one of them, in large part because of the relationships I had forged as student body president.

But it was another space—an unexpected one—that quickly became a refuge in the months after I came out. It was a building that I worshipped so much throughout my childhood, the one that had sparked my initial interest in politics: the White House.

I had been on tours of the president's home while growing up, and as student body president, I had attended a small outdoor press event there; but like most people, I had never been to an event *inside*.

Three weeks after publishing my coming-out note, and the swirl of media around it, I received an email from the White House Social Office, the staff tasked with hosting events at the White House. I opened the email to see an invitation topped with the gold seal of the president of the United States. Under the seal, it read, "The President requests the pleasure of your company at a reception in celebration of LGBT Pride Month to be held at The White House."

In addition to serving as the home and office of the president and the first family, the White House's bottom two floors, known as the State Floors, serve as a large, ornate event space. Presidents traditionally host receptions and events commemorating different groups and communities, but it wasn't until President Obama that the LGBTQ community had been invited for an annual reception honoring and celebrating our lives and basic dignity.

Walking into the White House for the Pride event three weeks later was awe-inspiring. Uniformed Secret Service agents greeted guests as we made our way through the small East Wing, down a long windowed corridor, and into the central part of the White House, the famous structure that appears on the twenty-dollar bill.

Drinking from a champagne flute, I took in the grandeur of the rooms I had intensely studied as a kid. The State Dining Room, with its portrait of a thoughtful Lincoln. The oval Blue Room, constructed at the request of George Washington and the inspiration for the construction of the West Wing's Oval Office. And finally, the East Room, a large ballroom adorned with stunning gold curtains and three large chandeliers.

You could feel the history in that room. Presidents have been inaugurated there. The legendary painting of George Washington hangs on the wall. The bodies of Lincoln, Franklin Roosevelt, and Kennedy lay in state in the center of the room after their deaths. And in 1964, the Reverend Dr. Martin Luther King Jr. looked over the shoulder of President Johnson as the Civil Rights Act was signed into law there.

President Obama was scheduled to address us from a lectern placed at the far end of the ballroom, but until then, I mingled with the guests. It was the first time I had been in a space filled with this many LGBTQ people. Same-sex couples were walking around holding hands. A transgender person proposed to their significant other in the central hall. The feeling in the room was celebratory. And standing in the White House surrounded by people like me, I felt at home.

A bustling at the front of the East Room signified that the president was about to speak. As I made my way up to the front of the room, I bumped into a young man, a handsome twenty-six-year-old transgender attorney named Andrew Cray.

"Oops, I'm sorry," I apologized and moved forward as the announcer boomed, "Ladies and gentlemen, the president of the United States."

The president, greeted with rapturous applause, made his way from a side room, up onto a stage, and to a lectern marked with the seal of the office.

"Now, each June since I took office," he opened, "we have gathered to pay tribute to the generations of lesbian, gay, bisexual, and transgender Americans who devoted their lives to our most basic of ideals—equality not just for some, but for all."

I had heard the president speak at rallies and on health care, but I had never witnessed him speak entirely about LGBTQ people. It was an empowering experience, and as he spoke, it felt like he was speaking to me.

"And as long as I have the privilege of being your president, I promise you, you won't just have a friend in the White House, you will have a fellow advocate for an America where no matter what you look like or where you come from or who you love, you can dream big dreams and dream as openly as you want."

It was an affirming and memorable experience, but I didn't fully realize how pivotal the White House would become in my own journey, beginning with that young transgender man I had bumped into just before Obama's speech.

Frankly, I didn't think much about that chance encounter with Andy. It didn't really register until a message popped up on Facebook two months later.

"Hey, Sarah! So . . . I've seen you at more than a few events around D.C. But I am a little shy about introducing myself—so hi, I'm Andy," he continued. "Despite being pretty bad at introducing myself, I'm actually not that shy, and if you're interested in getting coffee or drinks or something sometime, let me know. I think we'd get along pretty swimmingly."

The message appeared in my Facebook inbox on August 14, 2012, just as I was getting ready to leave my internship for the day. I'm not usually one to fully engage with strangers on Facebook, particularly while at work, but for some reason I felt compelled to. Maybe it was the fact that we were both transgender, or maybe it was our list of mutual friends, or his adorable use of the word "swimmingly," but it was clear from the start that he was someone special.

Over the next several weeks, we chatted on and off over Facebook and by text messages. I learned he worked on LGBTQ equality at the Center for American Progress, a prominent advocacy and research institution known in D.C.-speak as a "think tank." I found out that we both loved terrible reality television, James Cameron's *Titanic*, and *Star Wars* (although his love for the trilogy was unlike anything I have ever seen!). We had both studied film earlier in our lives, I as a high school student attending a creative and performing arts school and he as a film major in college for a period of time.

After weeks of chatting and escalating flirtation on Facebook, he finally asked me to dinner. "Please don't take this as pressure, but just as a testament to how great I think you are—I haven't locked in any plans for tomorrow. Would you like to go out?"

Like any twentysomething girl, I was anxious about taking that next step, to go from flirting online to a real-life relationship. Despite how wonderful he seemed, I wasn't yet sure how I felt about him. But that wasn't why I was so nervous.

I was nervous because this would be my first *first* date since transitioning, since taking the initial steps to live as Sarah. At the time, I still worried that people—even those who hadn't known me before coming out—saw me as a walking costume.

My natural hair wasn't in a place where I felt comfortable with it, so I was still wearing a dark wig that fell to just under my collarbone. I had been on hormones for only a few months. And while none of those things should invalidate my gender identity, I worried that Andy, even as a transgender man, would be disappointed. I worried that, to him, I wouldn't be the woman I knew myself to be and the woman he had so clearly built up in his mind.

But of course I said yes.

• • •

Our first date was on an unseasonably hot early fall evening in 2012. It was a clear night and probably slightly cooler than it felt to me due to my nerves.

It was just after dusk when I stood impatiently on my front stoop waiting for Andy to pick me up. The restaurant was only about six or seven blocks from my house, but Andy, obviously wanting to make the date feel as traditional and perfect as possible, picked me up at home.

Our chance encounter at the White House Pride Reception hadn't registered with me, so I had never truly seen him in person, just in pictures on Facebook. As he stepped out of his spotless black Audi, I couldn't help but be taken aback by just how suave he seemed to be in person. He was immaculately but casually dressed, clean-shaven, and wearing square glasses with big black rims that can be described only as nerdy-chic.

He walked me to his car, and we took the short drive over to the restaurant, which actually was closer to his apartment than my house was, making his gesture to pick me up all the more ridiculous and sweet.

We parked and walked half a block to the restaurant. With every step, as with all my public adventures, it felt like a thousand eyes were staring at me, wondering the same question: *Is that a man?* Much of it was in my own mind, but some looks were undeniable.

Andy and I sat down at our table at a small tapas restaurant on the main drag of Adams Morgan, a lively, colorful D.C. neighborhood filled with restaurants, bars, and, at that time of night, young professionals beginning their drunken evening out. Our table was imperfectly situated for my insecure self, located just on the edge of the restaurant's small outdoor patio and in the line of sight of everyone tipsily walking by.

Our server approached from behind Andy, catching a glimpse of me and making a face I had grown to know all too well, a look that might as well have included the verbal confirmation "Oh, you're transgender."

The server was kind and didn't do anything out of the ordinary following the initial, subtle look, but I could tell she knew. I wondered what she thought about Andy, handsome and not "visibly transgender," clearly out on a date with me. I could imagine her inner monologue. *How disappointed this guy must be in his date.*

As proud as I had grown to be transgender, I was still struggling with the same insecurities that a lot of transgender women face. The message we so often receive from society is that to be "read," as we call it in the trans community, as transgender is an implicit and negative statement about your beauty.

Sitting there, I envied Andy. He seemed so cool and comfortable in his own skin, so unworried about the world around him. As someone much further along in his transition than I was, he carried himself with a confidence that I had not yet mastered. I did a good job of hiding the insecurity, doing my best to come off as the confident person I'd presented online to Andy.

The server took our orders and left. Andy and I continued our conversation until a few seconds later, when he stopped mid-sentence, tongue-tied, clearly overtaken by something. I braced for the worst.

"I'm sorry, but, my God, you are beautiful," he blurted out.

And with that, in that moment, my insecurities washed away.

In the three months since coming out publicly and living as my authentic self, I had never genuinely felt seen until that point. In every other interaction, I still felt as if others saw me as either the person they previously had perceived me to be or, entirely, a trans person at the beginning of my transition.

With that simple comment, Andy was the first person who seemed to see me and be interested in me as Sarah. He was the first person who showed me that in transitioning I could still be loved and could still find a partner, something I had worried was out of the question.

In that moment, Andy was the first person to make me feel genuinely, remotely beautiful in my own skin. It wasn't the validation of a man, it was the true recognition of myself by another person that felt so good.

The rest of the dinner was a blur of comfort, laughter, and good food. Following dinner, we hopped into his car and drove back to my place.

On the short drive, Andy, who had told me that he loved to make mix CDs, put on his most recent. The first song was new to me. I asked him what it was and he replied, "'Safe and Sound' by Capital Cities, and I bet it's going to be pretty popular soon." I listened to the lyrics.

*Even if we're six feet underground*
*I know that we'll be safe and sound.*

The song would eventually become our song, returning at some of the most dramatic points in our relationship, sometimes by chance and sometimes intentionally.

We pulled up to my home as the song ended. Andy quickly got out of the car and ran over to open my door. As I stepped out, I felt Andy's hand connect with mine. When I looked at him with a smirk, he appeared terrified, wondering if he had done something wrong. Andy raised his eyebrows to ask if it was okay for him to hold my hand. My smirk turned into a smile, I squeezed his hand tighter, and we walked to the door.

And that's where we first kissed, for a few seconds, then ten, fifteen, and twenty.

As we separated, trying to play it cool, I wished him a good night and thanked him for the amazing date.

"Can we do this again?" he asked with almost childlike excitement.

"I would love to, Andy."

# CHAPTER 3

# "Sarah."

A few months before coming out publicly, I had applied for a White House internship, a six-month, full-time role within the building I had worshipped my entire life. Ever since I was nine or ten years old, I had always dreamed of interning there, imagining myself walking the halls and entering the building every day for work.

I had hoped to apply for the fall semester during my senior year—the first semester following my term as student body president—but when I came out to my parents and began to quietly transition, I thought about holding off.

I knew that this White House had been supportive of LGBTQ equality, but as far as I knew, there had never been anyone like me, an openly transgender woman, in any White House position. The thought of rejection so soon after coming out frightened me, and I wanted to protect myself. Thousands of people apply for a White House internship each semester. Being accepted is a crapshoot for anyone, but if it didn't happen, I'd always worry, *Was it because I'm transgender? Did they think I'd be a liability? Or, worse, an embarrassment?*

In the end, the years of unbridled excitement I'd had since I was younger won out. I didn't want to pass up the potential opportunity to work for this president and vice president and be a part of their historic administration.

Given that the White House internship required a security back-ground check, I had to submit the application under my legal name, which was still my birth name. The application also included a box for a preferred name or a nickname. Most applicants write in a shorter version of their legal name, or maybe make clear that they go by their middle name instead. I put down "Sarah."

Sarah. It felt good to finally write my name in an official capacity, let alone an application to work at the White House. It was the first formal document to reflect the name I had adopted only a few months before.

Names are important. Not just in the transgender community but everywhere. It's the first thing a parent gives to a baby. It's how our society bestows personhood, recognizes individuality, and affirms the humanity in each one of us. That's why one of the first steps in mar-ginalizing someone is to remove their name. It communicates that you are unimportant and unseen. When governments seek to oppress, they often replace names with impersonal numbers. When an indi-vidual seeks to bully or commit violence, they replace names with dehumanizing slurs or insults.

For transgender people, our names, along with our pronouns, are often the first way we express our gender identity and the most com-mon way for society to recognize it.

There is often a curiosity about the names given to us at birth. This is a deeply personal piece of information for many of us. It may seem odd that many transgender people deem such information so sensitive. People who change their last name, for instance, don't usu-ally bristle at the question "What was your name before?"

Not every trans person is uncomfortable with saying or hearing their birth name. For many of us, though, we are reluctant to give out that information because it often becomes weaponized against us, invoked instead of our chosen name to ignore and deny our gender identity.

And even for the most well-intentioned cisgender people, when they see my old pictures or find out my birth name, I can see the wheels turning in their heads as they reconstruct an image of me, seeing me not in the present but in the past.

Every trans person's path to their own name is different. Some have just always known. Others pick a name that may share a first letter with their birth name. I know plenty of trans people whose parents helped them pick their name, and not just people who transitioned young, but also individuals who came out in their forties or fifties.

For me, like many expecting parents, I just looked at lists of names. *I can't pick that one because I know someone with that name and they were an asshole*, I'd think as I skimmed the baby names. Finally, I narrowed it down to a few, and chatting with Helen, I settled on Sarah. Yes, it might seem like a pretty generic name to some, but for me it just felt like it fit. Every Sarah I knew was smart and funny and exuded a type of casual femininity that I identified with.

I picked the name the night before I came out to my parents. I wanted everything to be as firm as possible, since I knew they'd latch onto any sense of uncertainty. It all had to feel real to them, and having a name made it real.

During the five months between coming out to my parents and coming out publicly, my friends did an amazing job of calling me "McBride" in public and "Sarah" in private. They also took the initiative, with my permission, to cover up my old name on a student government campaign poster hanging in my campus office, replacing it with "Sarah McBride for SG President."

Writing my name on that White House application felt good. But given that the name on the application effectively outed me—and I wanted to make sure they understood what the White House was getting—I also made clear in my application essays that I am transgender, information that I tried to seamlessly work into my answers, given that one of my primary motivations for wanting to be a part of the Obama administration was to contribute to its work on LGBTQ rights.

Helen had actually interned at the White House a year before in the Office of Public Engagement (OPE), a division that grew out of what had been called the Office of the Public Liaison. Ever the community organizer, President Obama expanded the small office tasked with dealing with stakeholder groups to roughly thirty staffers, with point people working with the African American community, women, Latinos, unions, small businesses, the disability community, and the LGBTQ movement, among others. While Helen's background was in gender-equity advocacy, they had been assigned to the staffer heading up LGBTQ outreach. They had an amazing experience and recommended that I list the Office of Public Engagement as my first choice on the application. So I did.

Two months after coming out, I received the news I had been hoping and waiting for: I had been accepted into the program, and in late August 2012, I prepared to walk into the White House for my first day.

In August 2012, trans equality had not yet significantly entered the national public debate like it would in the years that followed. During their first term, the Obama administration had taken several important but lower-profile steps on trans rights.

For instance, as the largest single employer in the United States, the president had instructed federal agencies and departments to begin adopting gender identity–inclusive equal employment policies. Such a development was a far cry from the days when people suspected of being LGBTQ were rooted out of their jobs in the executive branch. In fact, up until the Clinton administration, LGBTQ people were routinely denied security clearances simply because of who they were.

Perhaps the most significant action taken by 2012 had been by Secretary Hillary Clinton's Department of State, when they adopted new policies for changing the gender marker on U.S. passports, allowing people to do so even if they hadn't had gender affirmation surgery. To many, this may seem like a small, technical advancement, but in reality the change was the first major nationwide reform on behalf of transgender people ever.

According to a 2011 survey by the National Center for Transgender Equality, only 21 percent of transgender people who had transitioned had been able to update all of their identity documents to reflect their gender identity. A full third—33 percent—lacked any identity document representing their true gender.

IDs are among our most utilized documents. They are required to travel, enroll in school, obtain a job, open a bank account, and, increasingly and unfortunately, vote. There are legitimate arguments that gender is not even necessary on these documents, but so long as drivers' licenses, passports, birth certificates, and other IDs include gender markers, it remains critical for them to reflect the gender identity of the person carrying them.

Allowing transgender people to update those documents makes a profound statement that we are respected and acknowledged as who we are. They make clear how the person should be treated. Perhaps more important, identification provides a vital layer of security and protection for us. IDs that still reflect a transgender person's sex assigned at birth can out the carrier, exposing them to discrimination, harassment, and, potentially, violence. Imagine having to reveal a deeply personal piece of information that could put you in danger every single time you fly on a plane, go to a bar, or use your credit card.

Prior to the change, the State Department required that individuals undergo gender affirmation surgery in order to update their gender marker. This, unfortunately, was a common, misguided, and burdensome policy that effectively put a $20,000 (or more) charge on accurate identity documents. And that's just for those who plan on having gender affirmation surgery. Many in the community never do, because they feel like they do not need it, they can't undergo surgery for medical reasons, or they can't afford it.

So the change was a major step. Even if other forms of identification were still outdated, the updated passports provided many transgender people across the country with a usable document not just when traveling but when signing up for loans or applying for a job.

Despite the weight of the change for the community, it received little notice by the national media. And the uniqueness of the advancement underscored an early cautiousness on the part of the Obama administration on the issue of trans rights, a fact that likely reflected both the current political environment and a lack of familiarity with transgender people and our lives.

In anticipation of my time at the White House, I moved quickly to legally change my name and update my driver's license, including my gender marker. Everyone who works in the White House is issued a security badge that includes the person's legal name in big letters. The badge must be visible at all times, and I didn't want to walk around with my old name staring everyone in the face.

For the first three months after stepping into the world as myself, before I started at the White House, I had to utilize my old driver's license, with my old name, an old picture, and a big fat *M* on it. I'd avoid situations where a license was necessary, and in the few instances when I used it, my heart would race as I'd hand my license to whoever was requesting it.

"Is this a joke?" one server asked me after I handed her my driver's license while out to dinner with a friend.

Stopped for a traffic violation, a male police officer clearly felt uncomfortable interacting with me after I handed him my old driver's license.

"Umm. Ummm," he fumbled after looking down at my picture. "Hold on a second." He walked back to his car, and a female officer, who felt more comfortable talking with me, exchanged places with him.

"Just change your name," many cisgender adults would tell me. But it wasn't that easy. While many people change their name following a marriage or after a divorce, the policies for a name change outside of those contexts usually differ significantly.

Each state has slightly different rules, but in Delaware, to change my name I had to schedule a court appearance and, prior to that, post the name change in two newspapers around the state. The policies are vestiges of a pre-Internet age and seek to avoid fraud or debt avoidance. The requirements take time and, most of all, cost money. Notices in the newspapers cost a few hundred dollars. Fortunately, my parents helped with the costs, and after a few weeks of notices in two Delaware papers, I went before a judge in Wilmington, Delaware, to have my name legally changed by order of the court.

I was nervous but ecstatic for the formal name change to come. I wanted to update my ID, a perpetual asterisk on my identity. But it was deeper than that. Just as each person's love and support lifted my spirits and being seen as myself made me feel whole, the legal name change would be a clear declaration that my government sees and affirms me.

At the courthouse, most people were changing their names to nicknames they had gone by their entire lives. As the proceedings went on, it was clear I was the only person changing a name to transition.

The bailiff finally called my name and I walked slowly up to the lectern in the middle of the room right in front of the judge.

"I see you are here to change your name for the purpose of a gender transition," the judge, a young Italian woman with short dark hair, read through the glasses perched on her nose.

I could feel the fifty eyes of the audience staring at me.

"Yes, Your Honor," I sheepishly responded.

The judge looked up, began to smile, and responded, "I'm honored to be a part of such an important day for you. Congratulations. So ordered."

I turned around to head to my seat next to my mom. As I walked back into the public section of the courtroom, I kept my head down, trying to avoid eye contact until I saw a hand jut out in front of me. It was an older man offering me a celebratory handshake. Another woman leaned over and, with a big smile on her face, clapped her hands quietly. And as the hearing ended and we exited the courtroom, several other attendees came up to shake my hand and congratulate me on this step.

It was a refreshing experience, despite how nerve-racking it was. Much like Governor Markell, the judge had modeled the right response for that courtroom. I was grateful to have had such a positive experience. To this day, many transgender people face extra legal barriers to updating their names. Individual judges hostile to trans identities have been known to deny requests for a name change outright, even when they have no legal foundation for doing so.

"I will not change a name from an obvious female name to an obvious male name and vice versa," a judge told a trans man in Georgia.

"The DNA code shows God meant for them to stay male and female," another judge in Oklahoma told a trans woman seeking a name change.

I thanked my lucky stars that my judge was so supportive. And with my name change now finalized, I put together the forms to change the gender on my license, which required a letter from a health professional effectively verifying my trans identity. With just two weeks to spare before the start of my internship at the White House, I received my updated driver's license.

I couldn't stop looking at it once I had it in my hands.

"Sarah Elizabeth McBride," it read. "*F.*"

With the new ID in tow, I made my way to the White House for my first day.

The West Wing has become synonymous with the White House staff. And while the president and the most senior advisers work in the cramped extension attached to the west end of the White House, the vast majority of the staffers and all the interns are housed in a large building across an alley from the West Wing. Still within the White House grounds, the Eisenhower Executive Office Building, or EEOB in D.C. lingo, looks like a giant gray wedding cake with columns on top of columns.

Built just after the Civil War, the building served for eight decades as the headquarters for the Department of State, as well as the Departments of War and the Navy before they were merged into the Department of Defense. It's a divisive building; half of my friends think it is the most beautiful structure in D.C., while others side with Mark Twain, who called it the "ugliest building in America." Whatever you think, it's an imposing structure, and far grander than the more exclusive West Wing.

In my black dress and blazer, I entered the first security checkpoint and handed the Secret Service my new ID. They cleared me to go through, and after walking through double doors into a small corridor lined with large pictures of President Obama and Vice President Biden, I handed my ID over at a second checkpoint.

The Secret Service agent looked at my license and, handing me a temporary badge, pointed me through the doors and said, "Welcome to the White House, Ms. McBride."

*Welcome to the White House, Ms. McBride.*

# CHAPTER 4

# The People's House.

I had arrived at the White House early on that first day, about thirty minutes before I was instructed to be there.

I entered a conference room on the fourth floor of the EEOB. The towering walls were bright white, and in the center of the room was a large oak table with brown leather chairs on either side. Filling one wall were large windows that looked out over the West Wing and the White House, practically the same view I had printed out images of in middle school and hung in my bedroom.

I was the first one to arrive. Standing there alone, I looked around. Three months before, I had feared that my professional life was over. I took a deep breath and took in the moment. *I'm here. I'm about to work in the White House as myself.*

It's impossible to express the profound liberation and sensation of being able to do something as your true self when, for years, you've never been able to actually *be* yourself. That's true for the small things, but particularly so for the moments that would be exciting for anyone, such as beginning an internship at the White House. I had spent my life never truly experiencing moments like this, but now I was fully there. I was truly living.

I was also acutely aware that, as far as I knew, no one quite like me—an out transgender woman—had worked in a role like this, even as an intern. I had asked friends in the advocacy community if they knew of any other transgender people who had worked at the White House. They told me that two or three transgender men had interned during the first few years of the Obama administration, but it wasn't clear how out they were to their colleagues. And at the time, no trans person had served on staff yet, a barrier historically broken a few years later by a young transgender woman named Raffi Freedman-Gurspan.

As the other new interns, a mix of young men and women earnestly dressed in their nicest business attire, began filtering into the conference room on the fourth floor of the EEOB, I sat there nervously. This was my first professional experience outside the safe confines of the LGBTQ movement. While it was only a baby step into a world filled with progressive Democrats, I had quickly learned that such bona fides were no guarantee that a person would be comfortable with and supportive of trans people.

The thoughts that had become routine in my mind came rushing in. *What do these other interns think of me being here? What will they say?*

The coordinator of the intern program, a young staffer who would be our main point of contact for the next several months, entered the conference room and stood at the head of the table.

"Welcome to the White House, everyone!" She began to give us directions. We'd be escorted to our offices. There'd be a security briefing the next day.

Looking around at the other interns, I couldn't help but think that while many of our responsibilities overlapped, I held a unique position as a transgender person in that setting. I wanted to utilize my six months in the White House to put a human face on trans rights for the people whom I would be working with and for.

Even if you hold the right positions on paper, it is easy to deprioritize something that feels abstract. When our workplaces began including openly gay, lesbian, and bisexual people, it changed companies', governments', and people's priorities. Now there would be a trans woman walking the halls, joining them in meetings, and sharing coffee with them. It's impossible for our rights to remain abstract when a person is, quite literally, sitting across from you.

As I had realized throughout my coming-out experience, and as I would routinely reiterate, I'm an admittedly imperfect messenger for that role. My privilege and experiences limit my perspective. It's easy to express—and genuinely feel—empathy for a young, white, conventional-looking trans girl; it's another to maintain that empathy when your differences are compounded by race, gender expression, class, religion, or circumstance. Nevertheless, I'd made it into the White House and I hoped to utilize it to do some small good.

To do that, though, I first had to accomplish my day-to-day responsibilities and do them well. I was assigned to the office I was hoping for, Public Engagement, and with the staffer I had interviewed with, Gautam Raghavan, the LGBTQ liaison for the White House at the time. Gautam, an openly gay thirty-one-year-old man, had worked within the administration on the repeal of Don't Ask, Don't Tell, the military's ban on openly gay, lesbian, and bisexual troops, and moved over to the position within the White House about a year before. A passionate LGBTQ advocate, he had read my public coming-out note just two days before interviewing me for the internship and was clearly interested in expanding even further the administration's work on trans equality.

In addition to working with Gautam, I was also placed under a whip-smart twenty-six-year-old woman named Monique Dorsainvil, who, among other portfolios, managed all of the events for the Office of Public Engagement that included the president and first lady.

Helen had warned me that the hours in the Office of Public Engagement were severe. There were days when I had to be in at six a.m. and would not leave any earlier than nine p.m. But they also told me it would be well worth it.

The Office of Public Engagement was located toward the front of the EEOB, which helped spur its nickname, "The Front Door of the White House." The office, tasked with coordinating and communicating with various identity-based communities across the country, was filled with motivated and friendly young staffers, former organizers, and advocates. Many had been with the president since the election, some even earlier than that.

There was Darienne Rakestraw, who managed outreach to veterans. Darienne had previously served as the front desk receptionist in the West Wing, welcoming members of Congress, foreign heads of state, leading advocates, and celebrities for their meetings with President Obama. Her role led the president to nickname her ROTUS (Reception of the United States), a play on the nickname staffers use when referring to the president: POTUS.

There was Julia Chavez Rodriguez, who managed outreach to Latino communities. Julia was the granddaughter of the noted civil rights and workers' rights activist Cesar Chavez and a powerhouse advocate in her own right.

Nate Tamarin oversaw outreach to labor. Nate had been with the president since he was a little-known Illinois state senator running in a seven-way primary for the U.S. Senate. Nate would recount stories from the old days, like his first day working for then–state senator Barack Obama in 2003. They were placed last in the Chicago St. Patrick's Day Parade, forced to dodge poop from the horses that had marched ahead of them. They were so far back in the parade program, he told us, that the visibly inebriated spectators hurled and mocked this new candidate, disgustingly shouting crude comments and comparing Obama's name to Osama bin Laden.

Five years later, rising from complete obscurity, Barack Obama had ascended to the highest office in the world. *Change is possible*, I thought.

The Office of Public Engagement was headed at the time by Jon Carson, who had managed the field operation for the 2008 presidential campaign. Jon reported directly to Valerie Jarrett, senior adviser

and assistant to the president for public engagement and intergovern-
mental affairs.

No one in the White House was closer to the president and first
lady than Jarrett; their relationship dates back two decades to when
she hired Michelle Obama for a job in the Chicago mayor's office. Ms.
Jarrett, or VJ, as she was called throughout the office, would end up
sticking by the president's side through all eight years of the administration.

The office combined the excitement and breakneck pace of a campaign with the seriousness of cause of government work, and the
staff treated the interns like full partners in the effort to, as President
Obama often said, "build a more perfect union." And we all became
close, working late nights practically every day.

As an intern, my responsibilities did not include the stereotypi-
cal fetching of coffee and making copies. I worked with Gautam on
LGBTQ engagement and Monique on major events with the president, from meetings with progressive leaders to a welcome ceremony
for the returning U.S. Olympians and Paralympians. While the hours
were long, each day went by in the blink of any eye, filled with meetings, incredible events, and the occasional sighting of the president or
first lady.

There was a constant buzz and energy that permeated the halls
connecting the various offices. It became clear very quickly that the
Office of Public Engagement was a family atmosphere filled with
"true believers": people who not only believed in President Obama but
also the mission of the administration.

It was hard not to be inspired by the work. Each day we invited
in members of mostly marginalized communities so they could hear
a little bit about what the administration was doing to help and we
could hear from them about what more should be done. And it wasn't
just advocates living and working in D.C., but leaders from across the
country. Activists from South Carolina and Michigan, Kansas and
Alaska.

If you ever—even for a moment—forgot where you were, you were snapped out of your jaded spell by the awe-inspiring comments from people who may have never dreamed of coming to the People's House. There was a reason that the saying in the office was "You can't spell *hope* without *OPE*."

For the first few weeks, I had worked and engaged with my fellow interns with the presumption that they automatically knew I was transgender. I had lived the last four months figuring that everyone could tell, either because of how I looked or how I talked. But one afternoon, riding down the elevator with a fellow intern, Sonia, it became clear that not everyone realized my background.

Still I was wearing that long brown wig. As I scratched an itch, I commented, "I can't wait to get rid of this thing."

"What do you mean?" Sonia responded curiously.

"This wig. I can't wait to get rid of it," I said, figuring that it was clear what was on top of my head.

"I didn't realize you were wearing a wig," she exclaimed, genuinely surprised. She paused for a moment and considered her next question. "Can I ask why you're wearing a wig?"

"Because my hair is still too short for my liking," I responded.

She looked confused. I stared at her for a few more seconds, not getting the obvious.

"Wait," I hesitantly responded. "You know I'm transgender, right?"

"You are?" Her eyes widened. "No, I didn't! But I guess that explains some things!"

I had come out only four months before and was surprisingly jarred by the exchange with Sonia. A few months earlier, I had upended my life and jumped into a new world, operating under the assumption that my trans identity was self-evident. Every decision I made was influenced by that fact. And if strangers on the street didn't know, sure enough everyone with whom I had an extended conversation would come to the conclusion one way or another, I thought.

Somewhat dazed, I walked back to the office I shared with my boss, Monique, and a gregarious, tall New Yorker named Jarrod, who managed Jewish outreach for the White House. Next to Jarrod and Monique were two large desks, one for Gautam and another for our intern coordinator, Quinn.

It was a small room, made even smaller by our four and a half desks and the piles of papers scattered everywhere. Hovering just over my computer screen was a large print—a jumbo, as they are called in the White House—depicting President Obama eating an apple at a grocery store.

I sat down at my desk and turned toward Quinn and Gautam. "I just had a really surprising interaction with Sonia. She didn't realize I was trans."

A smile spread across Quinn's face. "Oh, yeah, Akshar"—another intern in our office—"didn't realize that, either. I was talking about your coming out and he had no idea."

My heart sank. Quinn had said nothing wrong, but for some reason this news hit me like a ton of bricks. And I didn't know why.

"Do you think the others know? Should I tell them?" I asked Gautam.

"I don't know if they do, but how are you feeling? You seem a bit . . . shaken," he responded in a soft, paternal voice.

On the one hand, I thought I would be happy that they didn't know. I'd wanted to blend in for months. But something just felt off.

I was confused and didn't fully understand my reaction. There had been several times, from the waitress on my date with Andy to strangers on the street, when I had been hurt by the fact that I figured someone could tell I was trans. There were few things I thought I had wanted more than to "pass," a term frequently used to describe when someone is not read as transgender.

I also hated myself for that reaction. There is nothing wrong with being trans. I knew that. But in a society filled with messages that to be read as trans is to be perceived as "ugly," it becomes hard not to internalize that observation. I shouldn't want to "pass," but I did. Or at least I thought I did.

There is no question that a trans person being able to blend in comes with a great deal of privilege. At the most base level, blending in becomes a source of physical security for many transgender people. If people cannot tell you are transgender, the risk of facing antitransgender violence or discrimination decreases dramatically. I recognize that the mere ability to feel uneasy about passing is a privilege in and of itself; nevertheless, I couldn't shake the odd feeling.

Sitting at home that night, it finally began to make more sense. Was I disappointed because, as someone said, I wasn't "being honest with people"? No. No one is entitled to any information about me or who I am. These folks were seeing me as a woman, which I am. They just didn't know that I was also transgender. Seeing me as a woman isn't a deception.

Was I disappointed because I was nervous how people would react when they did find out?

No. I knew, by now, that my colleagues would greet my news with support.

I realized that I was disappointed because I want people to know who I am because I'm *proud* of who I am.

I'm proud to be transgender.

Our identities matter. They help make us who we are and shape our outlook. Existing in them is a radical act, one that requires, in many instances, courage, hard work, and determination. I am a better person because of the experiences and insights that I've had because I'm transgender. I'm a more compassionate person than I was before I accepted that part of my identity.

I've joined a community of people who have made the empowering decision to live whole, complete lives. We have stood up to a society that tells us that we are wrong to live our lives to the fullest. It's a daring act of authenticity. There is no doubt that society places unfair and unjust barriers in front of transgender people, but that is a flaw in society, not a problem with being transgender.

Still, for many, being publicly out and proud is not an option, even for those who have transitioned. Too often we universalize the need for LGBTQ people to be out in order to move equality forward. This is an unfair burden to bear for an already marginalized community. Some of us may decide to be out—and there's no question that that is a good thing—but we shouldn't force anyone to live their gender or sexuality in a particular way, even if we feel that there may be long-term benefits for the movement.

Every person's life is their own. Their experience is too precious for others to require them to betray their own security or well-being to make a point. This is particularly true for transgender people, for whom being out about that identity may significantly inhibit their ability to be seen, totally, as their own gender. This is, no doubt, a direct result of a world that often denies our gender identity when people find out we are trans, and it can cause real pain that no one should have to go through.

I've been blessed with a community that does not see my woman-hood and "transness" as mutually exclusive. I won't lose my job or my friends. I'm less likely to face violence. These realities allow me to be public, and in my mind, those privileges call on me to utilize what-ever platform I have to try to open hearts and change minds. Being student body president allowed me to do that, and now, being at the White House gave me that opportunity with some of the most power-ful people in the country.

A week after the exchange with Sonia, I was sitting at my tiny desk working on a memo outlining all the outstanding policy goals of the transgender community, from inclusive health coverage to an executive order banning discrimination by companies that do busi-ness with the federal government, when the door opened. I swiveled around in my chair to see Michael Strautmanis.

Strautmanis, affectionately called "Straut" in the White House and well liked within OPE, is part of the original Chicago "Obamaworld." He first met Michelle Obama when he was a paralegal for her at Sid-ley Austin, the law firm where Michelle first met and fell in love with

Barack. Straut had moved to Washington when Obama was elected to the Senate, serving as his chief counsel. After serving in senior roles in the presidential transition, he joined the White House staff and, when I interned in 2012, was a deputy assistant to the president and senior counselor to Valerie Jarrett.

A few days before Straut walked into my office, I had run into him in the hallway. As I was making my way through the bright corridors of the EEOB, he motioned for me to walk with him to his next meeting. He was likely trying to get to know the different interns and asked me about my background. I told him where I was from, where I went to school, my different interests; I didn't mention my trans identity.

Now peeking into my office, he again motioned for me to join him in the hallway. I popped up from my desk and joined him in the hallway where we had talked three days before.

"I hope this isn't inappropriate," he started, "but I didn't realize you were transgender when we were talking last. Yesterday I was in a meeting with Valerie and trans issues came up. I mentioned that I didn't know any transgender people and there were none in the White House, when she stopped me and said, 'We have a transgender intern. You need to be more aware of your surroundings.'"

He continued, "I was really hoping we could maybe get lunch and you could tell me a little more about your story, if you're comfortable?"

I could tell that he was worried about making me feel tokenized, but I had told my bosses that I was more than willing to talk with anyone about trans rights. When I later mentioned the conversation to Monique and Gautam, they made clear that he had talked to them before approaching me.

"I would absolutely love that," I told Straut eagerly.

A week later, we met for our lunch. We sat down over sandwiches at a lunch shop located catty-corner to the White House complex. Over our meals, I recounted my journey. He occasionally interjected with questions but mostly listened.

After I finished telling him my story, Straut reflected on his own background as a Black man from Chicago. He then told me about the attitudes toward LGBTQ people in his neighborhood growing up: "We never talked about this when I was a kid." Though, looking back, he said there was someone who lived down the street from him when he was growing up who may have been transgender.

We sat for an hour, a significant amount of time for someone in a senior leadership position at the White House. I had the opportunity to humanize an issue—a group of people—for an old friend of the president and a senior staffer at the White House. No more could Straut say he didn't know anyone who was transgender.

At the time, the percentage of Americans who said they knew someone who was transgender was still in the single digits. As trans activist Faye Seidler quipped, more Americans said they had seen a ghost than knew a transgender person, according to some polls. For much of the first term of the president's administration, a similar percentage of White House staffers would likely have said the same thing. Increasingly, though, that was changing. Not just because of my presence but because, more and more, transgender people were coming to the White House for events and meetings. Increasingly that included a prominent trans health advocate, my friend Andy.

Since our date in August, just a few months earlier, I'd thought about Andy a lot. Almost every morning on my way to the White House, I'd listen to the song that he had played for me in his car on our first date. But our communication also grew infrequent. He'd text me to let me know he was thinking about me, to share a funny experience, or to see if maybe I would be free to have dinner with him. I was, unfortunately, running around so much—and working such late hours—that we managed to meet up only twice for dinner, and I rarely texted him back.

Nevertheless, he persisted. Time and again, he could have given up. He could have thought, *This isn't fair and this isn't worth it.* But he didn't. He was patient and gave me the space I needed, all the while,

I found out later, forwarding my admittedly infrequent texts to his friends and asking for their interpretation.

"What do you think this means?" he'd ask them. "Should I take this as a good sign?"

I worried about giving Andy the wrong impression. I wasn't sure if I was really ready for a relationship. The White House was consuming my time and I was still settling into my new life. *I don't know if I have room for someone else*, I thought.

In November, three months into my internship and just after the president's reelection, my boss Gautam was scheduled to have a meeting with LGBTQ activists to discuss priorities in the new term. I wasn't planning on attending Gautam's meeting, as I had to help my other boss, Monique, with a meeting that the president was hosting in the West Wing.

Across the alley from the EEOB, Monique and I walked through the double doors to the West Wing and down a narrow hallway to the Roosevelt Room, a large conference room across the hall from the Oval Office. A portrait of Theodore Roosevelt riding a horse hangs over a large fireplace at one end of the room. His Nobel Peace Prize hangs just to the left of the mantel and a large oak table fills the space. Surrounding the table are sixteen seats, including one that rises about two inches above the rest. That seat is reserved for the president.

Guests were about to arrive, so Monique and I hurriedly set up the room. I placed the president's coaster in its place and a placard that read "The President" at his seat, as if anyone would have dared to take his chair.

"Oh, we forgot a few name plates!" Monique nervously exclaimed. "Can you run back to our office and get them?"

Before she could finish the sentence, I was sprinting to our office. As I turned the corner, I noticed a group walking down the columned, marble hallway. They had their backs to me, but I noticed, in the center of the pack, what appeared to be a man about a foot shorter than the rest, dressed in a nicely fitted suit.

*That looks like Andy*, I thought to myself. *Wait. That is Andy*. I was afraid if I called to him I'd signal something I wasn't ready for. I still hadn't sorted everything out. Or so I thought.

*Don't say anything. He'll get the wrong impression.*

"Andy!" I yelled down the hall, almost uncontrollably.

Andy, startled by the outburst, turned around. He looked just as suave as he had when he got out of his car on our first date. When he realized that it was me who had called out to him, a smile crossed his face. He knew exactly what it meant.

And I knew what it meant, too. It seems simplistic, but standing in that hallway, I knew that I would eventually be with Andy, and I knew that this was what I wanted.

A few weeks later, when a friend of Andy's and I were scheduled to serve on a panel together back in Delaware, Andy enthusiastically volunteered to give up his entire weekend to come along on the thinly veiled pretense that his friend needed a ride, an otherwise cheap and easy trip on Amtrak.

Wanting to save both of them the cost of a hotel room and to spend more time with Andy, I invited them to stay with me at my parents' house. Although the house was about an hour away from the panel site, Andy quickly jumped at the offer. Even though he was technically the tag-along on the trip, Andy was an instant hit with my parents and my friends. He made a lasting impression on my mom when, as I slept in on Saturday morning, Andy made his way downstairs to our kitchen.

As my mom washed dishes, he sat down at our kitchen table and said with a familiarity that my mom's warmth instantly invites, "Sal, come on over. I'd like to get to know you." My mother sat down with him and talked about our family and our story, about their fears when I came out, but about how positive the trajectory had been. Then she asked Andy about his life.

Every relationship is the result of a series of events and coincidences that lead people to one another. For both Andy and me, our developing relationship was built on a unique, shared experience: the by-product of years of each of us fighting to be ourselves. While there were a number of different reasons I was falling for Andy, our shared identities as transgender people were at the center of those early interactions. And for both of us, it was a connection a lifetime in the making.

• • •

Andy's own journey had begun a few years before mine. He was born in 1986—four years before me—in the small town of Chippewa Falls, Wisconsin.

"That's where Leonardo DiCaprio's character in *Titanic* is from," I exclaimed, when he first told me the name of his hometown.

"Yeah, our town went wild when Jack said that in *Titanic*," he laughed. "One of the biggest things to happen to us."

Andy had a fairly privileged childhood, much like mine. If my neighborhood in Delaware was like *Leave It to Beaver*, Andy's Chippewa Falls was Mayberry. The tree-lined neighborhoods were filled with American flags hanging from the front porch of every other home. A main street with brick-front stores leads down to the Chippewa River. And with just over thirteen thousand residents, everyone knows one another.

Andy's family, the Crays, was almost like Chippewa Falls royalty. His grandfather Seymour Cray was considered "the father of the supercomputer," the precursor to our modern personal computers. In the computer industry, Seymour Cray, a brilliant but eccentric man, was the 1960s and '70s version of Bill Gates. Cray Research, which consistently produced the fastest and most advanced computers in the world under Seymour's leadership, was one of Chippewa Falls' largest employers for decades.

Seymour's first wife was Verene, a feisty minister's daughter who was so progressive that during the height of the Vietnam War she managed to get herself appointed to the Chippewa Falls military draft board just so she could ensure that only those who wanted to serve were drafted. Seymour and Verene had three children: Susan, Carolyn, and, Andy's father, Steven.

In the late 1970s, as a law student at the University of Wisconsin–Madison, Steven married an incoming law student, Ardis Audorf. And after graduating and starting their own separate careers as attorneys in Chippewa Falls, Steven and Ardis had two kids, Andy and Scott.

From a young age, Andy was clearly talented. He started talking early. He was athletic, playing baseball and basketball. He was artistic, learning multiple musical instruments, from the clarinet to drums, from the guitar to the trombone.

He was also a rule follower. Once, when asked what the worst thing he had ever done was, an eight-year-old Andy replied, "Sometimes, when my mom tells me to go to my room and think about what I've done, I don't think about it."

As with any transgender person born before the twenty-first century, when Andy was growing up, transgender identities were out of sight and out of mind for most. And while he asserted nearly from day one that he was a boy, his parents, like most at the time, just assumed he was a tomboy. For his fourth birthday, he was consumed with the concern that people would give him "girls' toys" for his birthday.

"What do I do if someone gives me a doll?" he asked his mom.

"Tell them 'thank you' and we'll return it later," she instructed him.

A few days later, Andy was given a Barbie by a family friend, Mitch.

"Thank you, we'll return it later," he announced.

In middle school, Andy's parents divorced. Steven went on to marry a woman he went to high school with. And Ardis married the father of one of Andy's best friends, the town dentist Richard Sweeney.

At about the same time that Andy's parents separated, and still clearly trying to find himself, Andy became an evangelical Christian, a not-uncommon phenomenon for LGBTQ people struggling with their identity. Despite neither of his parents being particularly religious, Andy became a dedicated member of a church in Chippewa Falls throughout high school.

After graduating as valedictorian from Chippewa Falls High School, Andy moved to Chicago to attend Northwestern University, first majoring in film and then, following in his parents' footsteps, law.

Andy's faith remained a significant part of his identity when he went to college, but he was increasingly struggling with his other identities. He took a big step when he started dating his first girl-friend, Heather, and when he started venturing out into queer circles.

It was at a queer sorority party on campus during the first semester of his freshman year that Andy met another first-year named Kelsey. In no time, the two became best friends. Both Andy and Kelsey identified as lesbians and evangelical Christians at the time. Together, they'd grapple with their mutual identities. They started an LGBTQ Bible study together. They'd explore gay life in Chicago's LGBTQ neighborhood, Boystown. Already into *Star Wars*, it was through Kelsey that Andy's interest became a joint obsession. Andy was R2-D2 to Kelsey's C-3PO.

Through sophomore year and the summer after, Andy began to read more and more online about trans identities. Like me, budding social media platforms like LiveJournal and Myspace opened up a window to people who were just like Andy. And when he returned to school for junior year, he and Kelsey met back up.

"I think that I'm a guy," Andy blurted out.

Kelsey looked up. "Me, too," he responded.

Andy's admission had given Kelsey the permission to open up about his gender identity, too: "I feel like we're brothers."

So they stepped out into the world and began their transitions together.

# CHAPTER 5

# The political is personal.

"Why doesn't Andy join us?" my dad piped in, clearly excited about his own idea.

In just a week, our family was scheduled to fly to Barbados for a family trip. My dad had rented a house on the southern Caribbean island with close friends and their family. Unfortunately, the other family backed out due to a work-related conflict.

Sitting around a table at a restaurant in downtown Wilmington, Delaware, my parents and I brainstormed people to join us and to help fill the house, which was now twice as large as what was needed.

"I'm serious. What about Andy?"

Bringing Andy on the family trip had crossed my mind. Both my parents had come to love him since that first visit to our house in Delaware a few months earlier. They were both as excited about my budding relationship with Andy as I was. Since finishing up my semester internship at the White House, Andy and I had been spending more and more time with each other. The kindness I saw on that first date proved to be as real as his brilliance. When he was working, we were texting or chatting over GChat. When he wasn't working and I wasn't in class finishing up my final semester of college, we were together.

I was spending an increasing number of nights at Andy's apartment, located in a large, art-deco building at the top of a hill in the center of Washington. His apartment was an eclectic mix of mature adult and immature kid, with his law books displayed on a shelf right next to the toy robots he had collected throughout his childhood. Andy's place felt like a home, filled with pictures, knickknacks, framed artwork, and toys for Andy's two black-and-white cats, Flapjack and Waffles. After four years of sparsely furnished and cold college student apartments, Andy's one-bedroom was a welcome and warm escape from campus.

We'd sit on his big, L-shaped brown couch and indulge in our favorite pastime: eating. Fortunately for both of us, Andy was an exceptional cook. On his nights, he'd orchestrate a delicious, elaborate meal with sides and restaurant-quality protein. Flavorful roasted chicken? Check. Perfectly cooked salmon? Check.

On my nights, I'd whip out store-bought taco mix or spaghetti. Ever the kind soul, Andy would eat those meals as if the greatest chef had made them. And each night was like a date night. We'd dim the lights, light some candles, and eat our delicious—or not-so-delicious—home-cooked dinners.

Even though Andy was working a traditional full-time job as an advocate at the Center for American Progress, he'd operate on my college-student schedule, staying up late with me to watch movies and, perhaps most commonly, enjoy our mutual addiction to terrible reality television. We'd talk into the early hours of the morning about events, policy, and the law, and explore issues of philosophy and morality.

He'd challenge me to be a better person. He'd encourage me to fight for equality in a way that respected every person's dignity, to abide by certain unbreakable "first principles." When a conversation about outing anti-equality politicians who are secretly LGBTQ themselves came up, he pushed back when I initially sided with the arguments that we should expose those politicians' hypocrisy.

"There are certain lines we should not cross," he told me. "Yes, hypocrisy is bad, but if exposing that hypocrisy requires us to commit an even greater evil, then we shouldn't do it. We should challenge people on their ideas. We won't bring others to our side by harming people, even hypocrites. It may feel satisfying, it may even be in pursuit of the good of revealing hypocrisy, but it violates a first principle."

I still pushed back. "But these people are harming so many others with their policies."

"What if you outed someone and they committed suicide because of it?" he shot back. "That's not an impossible outcome. Is revealing hypocrisy worth someone potentially losing their life? Are you willing to bear the responsibility for that outcome? Is that one person's hypocrisy really worth, potentially, their life?"

He was right.

Principles are worth something only if you stick by them even when they feel inconvenient. It's easy to rationalize and find seemingly altruistic reasons for betraying a moral imperative, but that's exactly when our principles are most important. We shouldn't try to build a world in which every person has individual agency over their own gender or sexual orientation by utilizing tactics that remove or undermine that right. If your ultimate goal isn't an unbreakable principle, then what is?

I was in awe of Andy. His insights repeatedly blew my mind. As someone still in college and four years Andy's junior, the more I got to know him, the more I was amazed that he was interested in me. But that was the thing about Andy; he'd routinely make clear that he felt the same way about my feelings for him.

We both felt lucky to be with each other, a feeling that only intensified as we discovered, slowly but surely, our shared, cringeworthy affinity for baby talk and nicknames.

At some point in his life, Andy had started calling his bed a "beanpod." And given the fact that neither of us were morning people, we began referring to each other as "beans stuck in the beanpod." Soon enough, he became "big bean" to my "little bean," partly a reflection of our age difference, but more so an ironic commentary on the pervasive gender stereotypes that told us that we should be insecure about the fact that I was taller than him.

By the time of our family trip to Barbados, Andy and I were inseparable, either physically together or constantly communicating. So when my dad suggested that I invite Andy, I jumped at the idea. I immediately stepped out of the restaurant and called him.

"Bean, I know this is ridiculous, but would you want to come with me and my family to Barbados in a week?"

"Uh, are you kidding me?!" he responded. I could tell he was giddy at the invite. Fortunately, Andy had flexibility when it came to getting off work for a week on such short notice. He also worked so hard that he was likely long overdue for a vacation. "Let me just rework some meetings, but I am so in."

His friends later told me that the moment he got off the phone with me, he went into hyperdrive, buying new clothes and bathing suits ahead of the last-minute trip with my family.

Together, we flew to Barbados a few days later. Andy, already close with my mom, seamlessly ingrained himself with my family. As two attorneys by training, my dad and Andy listened to the recordings of the Supreme Court's oral arguments on the Defense of Marriage Act and California's ban on same-sex marriage, Proposition 8, by the pool.

Andy and I routinely cooked breakfast for everyone, serving eggs, bacon, and toast on a beautiful patio table surrounded by a lush green yard and towering palm trees. We rented Jet Skis with my brother and skied the open ocean, me in the driver's seat and Andy holding on to me for dear life as I dangerously flew over small cresting waves. I could tell he was terrified.

On our second-to-last day in Barbados, Andy and I took the family rental car to the north shore of the island. The day before, my parents had visited the northern end of the island, a sparsely populated area with large cliffs overlooking the ocean, and recommended the sight.

The drive, they warned us, was an overwhelming forty-minute journey, first through a crowded marketplace with narrow streets and then along a winding road. To make matters more confusing, drivers in Barbados drive on the left side of the road but still use cars built for driving on the right side. It's like dropping an American-made car onto the streets of London.

Andy looked at me, frightened at the prospect.

"Uh, Bean, I don't know if I can drive. That sounds horrifying," he blurted out.

I smiled and hopped in the driver's seat, then guided our car through the narrow streets of Speightstown's busy marketplace. The tiny streets were packed; passersby surrounded our slowly moving car as traffic drove by in the opposite direction, with each car missing the passenger-side mirror by a mere inch or two.

"Oh my God! Oh my God! Oh my God! I'm going to hit something or someone!" I screamed the entire way.

Eventually, we made it through the town, completed the winding, forested second leg of the trip, and came to a dead end. We were pretty sure we had taken a wrong turn on our way to the main tourist spot along the cliffs, but after seeing the water through some bushes with the sun about to set, we decided to cut our losses and check it out.

We parked the car and Andy grabbed a bag from the backseat and followed me toward the water. I made my way through the bushes and, sure enough, found myself standing atop the towering cliffs lining the northern shore of the island, two hundred feet above the ocean.

The sun was setting to our left, filling the sky with bright orange and yellow hues and almost repainting the brown cliffs into a soft gold. The peacefulness of the scene, completely devoid of people, was interrupted only by the crash of the waves on the cliffs directly below.

As I turned around, I saw Andy setting down a blanket and pulling out food for a surprise picnic. Sitting on the blanket facing the setting sun, Andy and I took in the beauty of the scene.

"It's breathtaking," I said, looking out toward the ocean.

Andy didn't respond.

"Isn't it, Bean?" I turned toward him, but he was already looking at me. Our eyes met and he took a deep breath. "Can I say 'I love you'?"

It had been almost eight months since our first date and four months into our more serious relationship. We were spending nearly every day together, but we hadn't yet said "I love you."

"Yes, of course you can."

"I love you," he said with a warm smile.

"I love you, too," I responded, and kissed him.

I had known this moment was coming. As a society, we often get so consumed by the gender identity of transgender people that we forget that behind these national debates on trans rights, behind the newspaper stories and policy papers, are real people. Real people who love and laugh, hope and cry, fear and dream—just like everyone else.

When I came out, I never anticipated the possibility of falling in love with another transgender person. It wasn't that I thought about the potential and dismissed it; the possibility honestly never occurred to me. I grew up so isolated in my own trans identity that I always imagined my life as the only transgender person in my community—a permanent solitary existence. Not devoid of friends or family, just absent anyone else like me. And while two transgender people falling in love is not uncommon in the trans community, it's certainly the exception, at least in my experience.

Our shared identities had connected us, but our connection was so much deeper. We brought out the best in each other—a mutual undying belief that change is possible. If our interests didn't always overlap, they almost always complemented one another. And underlying everything was our drive to push equality forward.

When we returned from Barbados, I began slowly moving more and more of my clothes and personal items into Andy's apartment. My signed Obama campaign poster was placed just under his Hillary-decaled skateboard on the wall. Some of his toy robots had to make way for my Delaware knickknacks. We talked about our future together. I told him I eventually wanted to move back to Delaware, and we talked about how he would be able to continue to work in D.C. or find something in Philadelphia, just a thirty-minute drive from my hometown of Wilmington. At the time, I was also preparing to graduate from American University. And with graduation on the horizon, I started exploring moving home.

My love for Delaware is boundless. I'm known as the ultimate "statriot," a word my friends made up as a mix between "state" and "patriot." When anyone asks me where I'm from, I always respond, "The greatest state in the union, Delaware."

Washington was exciting, but the pace was exhausting. The slower life and the smallness of Delaware were always more attractive to me. It is a state of neighbors, and the closeness of its people allows for a civically engaged person to have an outsized opportunity to effect change. More than anything else, though, Delaware was my happy place. It was a short drive from D.C. and, at least for the time being, Andy. My family was there. My friends were there. Delaware, for me, has always been home.

But as I prepared to graduate, I was faced with a decision that no one should have to make. It's a decision that is all too common for LGBTQ people: the choice between living in a place we love or being safe and secure. Delaware law, which lacked nondiscrimination protections based on gender identity, wouldn't allow me and other transgender people to have both. When I returned to Delaware from school on the weekends, it was still legal to deny me service at a restaurant simply because I was transgender. If I moved back after college, I could still be denied a job—or fired from one—because of my gender identity.

Most transgender people in Delaware live with this threat of discrimination every day and don't have a choice in the matter, lacking the means to move or, understandably, unwilling to leave their family and connections. This everyday threat of discrimination was not a reality exclusive to Delaware. A majority of states, and even the federal government, still lack clear and explicit protections from discrimination for LGBTQ people. While an overwhelming majority of Americans presume that all forms of discrimination against LGBTQ people are permanently and clearly illegal, the reality is surprising and, sadly, far bleaker. And despite our historic progress, in most places in this country, LGBTQ people are still at risk of being fired from their jobs, denied housing, or kicked out of a restaurant or store simply because of who they are.

The promise that we will be judged on our merits at work and ensured equal access to basic necessities no matter our identity is a sacred covenant upheld and defended by our government. It is the foundation for any person to pursue the American Dream, and as I had learned as a little kid reading history books, each generation has been defined by whether or not they opened the doors of equality, opportunity, and prosperity for people long unseen and forgotten.

During the last century, our local, state, and federal governments have, often too slowly, sought to remove barriers and expand opportunity for communities once excluded. It's the fight that led suffragettes to picket the White House for the right to vote and, later, for women in the 1970s to expand educational opportunities through laws such as Title IX. It's the cause that propelled Dr. Martin Luther King Jr. and hundreds of thousands of Black Americans and allies to march on Washington, leading a movement that included the passage of the centerpiece of America's nondiscrimination laws: the Civil Rights Act of 1964. And it's the legacy that allowed a Republican president, George H. W. Bush, to stand on the south lawn of the White House to sign the Americans with Disabilities Act and call for those "shameful walls of exclusion [to] finally come tumbling down."

These protections exist through a series of sometimes complementary and other times overlapping city, state, and federal laws. The most famous of these statutes, the Civil Rights Act of 1964, banned certain forms of discrimination in employment, some public spaces, and federal funding.

While most of these laws typically include protections on the basis of characteristics such as race, religion, disability, national origin, and sex, most states and the federal government still do not explicitly include sexual orientation and gender identity in them.

Unlike in Delaware, I was protected when I was at college in Washington, D.C. The District of Columbia had passed clear protections from discrimination for transgender people a decade before. Delaware had passed a nondiscrimination bill for lesbian, gay, and bisexual people in 2009, making it the last state to pass protections for one part of the LGBTQ community while leaving other parts—transgender people—out. Since then, the larger movement has listened to trans voices and rightfully come to the conclusion that it is wrong to leave any part behind, particularly the identities and segments of the community most vulnerable to discrimination or violence.

I wanted nothing more than to go home to Delaware. The possibility of coming back to live, work, and potentially start a family with someone I loved had seemed like such a long shot. But in the past year everything—from the response of my family and community, to my time at the White House, to my budding relationship with an incredible partner—demonstrated that one of the biggest barriers to change was my own misguided belief that certain things were impossible. That something was too hard. That people weren't ready.

And so I resolved to help change Delaware law to make it inclusive of the needs of transgender people across the state. I joined the board of directors of Equality Delaware, a volunteer role. Equality Delaware, the state's primary LGBTQ advocacy organization, had started a few years earlier, and since its founding, Delaware had passed sexual orientation nondiscrimination protections in 2009 and laws permitting civil unions, a precursor to marriage equality, in 2011.

The group was led by two attorneys, Lisa Goodman and Mark Purpura. Mark, a tall, bearded openly gay man, had come out four years before and dove headfirst into LGBTQ advocacy.

Lisa, who sported short brown hair with a streak of gray, had been involved in advocacy for a bit longer and was a master at legislative strategy. Lisa is one half of a Delaware political power couple. Her wife, Drew, had been executive director of the Delaware chapter of the ACLU and would later go on to serve as Governor Jack Markell's chief of staff during the last year of his term.

With Delaware having passed sexual orientation nondiscrimination protections and laws permitting civil unions in 2009 and 2011, Equality Delaware now set out to close the circle and pass both marriage equality and gender identity protections in 2013. It was a lofty goal. Other states had attempted to do the same—to pass both a marriage equality bill and a nondiscrimination bill in the same year—but none had succeeded. In each instance, elected officials had come back to activists: *We're doing only one of these issues this year. Two is too many.*

"The same will happen to you" was the message from other state and national advocates. "They're going to push marriage because it's higher-profile and you'll end up with nothing."

"I won't let that happen," I told the older, more experienced activists who warned me.

Honestly, no one thought we would succeed, save maybe for Mark, Lisa, and me. The gender identity bill alone was an uphill battle, but doing it within a month of the marriage bill would be next to impossible. There was a reason it had never been done before. "Good luck with that" was the nearly universal dismissive reaction from political observers in and out of the state.

Despite my confident assertions, I was unsure if I could fulfill the promises I made to other transgender people that we'd pass the bill. I was twenty-two years old and new to LGBTQ advocacy. Any hope would rest on building relationships with legislators and my current one with the governor. And so I began to work with Equality Delaware and other transgender people to lay the foundation.

A few months earlier, during the summer of 2012, right after coming out publicly as transgender, I met up with Jack Markell. He was in Washington for a college tour with his son, Michael, when he texted me out of the blue.

"Hey, Sarah. Any chance you are free tomorrow to show Michael and me around American University's campus?"

While he had called me every two weeks after I first told him my news, this would be the first time we interacted in person since I transitioned. It was always nerve-racking "meeting" someone for the first time as me. Inevitably, there'd be some awkwardness, something I just had to force myself to break through.

I met Jack and Michael in the middle of the open green quad at the center of AU's campus. Jack greeted me with a huge hug and we began to make our way around campus, but as I tried to show him around, he kept interrupting my tour to ask me questions about gender and trans identities. I could tell Jack was taking me in, and knowing that Michael was unlikely to actually attend AU, I welcomed the opportunity to educate him.

"You still want to come back to Delaware, right?" Jack asked me, aware that I had always wanted to move back.

I thought about my answer for a second. "I do, but I'm honestly nervous to come home. I can't come back to a state that doesn't protect transgender people from discrimination."

I told him about the pervasive discrimination and the culture of violence that many, particularly trans women of color, fear every day due to the not-so-random toxic mix of transphobia, homophobia, misogyny, and racism in this country. Delaware needed to join the growing list of states—fourteen at the start of 2013—that protected trans people from discrimination in employment, housing, and public spaces.

Jack thought for a moment, then looked me in the eyes and said with a determined tone, "Okay. Let's change that."

If anyone could help push through legislation that would protect transgender rights, it was Jack.

That fall, while I interned at the White House, Jack had won re-election by a landslide of epic proportions, nearly 70 percent of the vote. A few months after the election, Jack publicly declared his support for marriage equality and made clear he would support an effort to legalize same-sex marriage in Delaware during that legislative session year.

While it wasn't news to me, I was thrilled by this public declaration, but the concern that the trans equality bill would be scrapped entirely in the effort to pass a marriage equality bill rushed back to the forefront of my mind. I wanted to pass each of the bills and Delaware's LGBTQ community deserved both; same-sex couples deserved and needed the right to marry, and transgender people, who didn't even have basic protections from day-to-day discrimination, desperately needed action.

One of our first steps was to schedule a more formal meeting with Jack and his staff to discuss strategy for both bills. The Human Rights Campaign, the nation's largest lesbian, gay, bisexual, transgender, and queer civil rights organization, was working closely with Equality Delaware to provide support in our historic undertaking, and a representative from the organization would join us for the meeting with the governor.

Ahead of the legislature's six-month session, we made our way to Jack's office in Wilmington. It had been four years since I was in the governor's office, located on the top floor of a large state office building downtown. After we waited for a few moments in a conference room, Jack and his chief of staff entered from a side door that led to his private office. I had been in that room many, many times while working for the governor, and I knew Jack like a family member. Still, I was nervous in a way that I hadn't anticipated. This was my first time on the outside, advocating in.

After exchanging pleasantries, we launched into the plans Equality Delaware and the Human Rights Campaign had for the coming legislative session. The Human Rights Campaign would be sending field staff to Delaware to help organize an issue-based campaign that was unprecedented for the state.

Sitting there, though, my palms were sweaty and my heart was racing. I knew Jack walked into the meeting supportive, but this was the time to see whether he was as committed as he seemed in that conversation on AU's campus the previous summer.

I was prepared and ready to interject whenever the conversation steered too exclusively into the marriage bill, but from the start it was clear that this wasn't necessary. Every time we talked about marriage, Jack would pipe up:

"And what about the nondiscrimination bill?"

"You're planning the same for the trans bill?"

"That will be the same for the gender identity bill, right?"

He was determined and was making it clear that both bills were a priority for him.

He closed the meeting with an unexpected declaration: "We need to pass the marriage bill, but we *really* need to pass the nondiscrimination bill." It was clear that Jack wasn't like other state leaders when it came to LGBTQ issues. Two bills weren't too many. I was relieved, but mostly proud of Jack.

While his commitment was integral to pushing the bill, he wasn't the only statewide elected official we hoped to gain support from. Since we anticipated that opponents of the gender identity bill would import talking points from the fight for trans rights in other states, we knew we needed help from an elected official with strong public safety credentials.

In other battles for trans rights, anti-equality activists and politicians had stoked unfounded fears that protecting transgender people from discrimination throughout daily life, including in restrooms, would allow sexual predators to dress up as women to harm or assault women and, particularly, young girls.

The argument was completely disingenuous. A person intent on committing a crime in a restroom is offered no cover from laws that merely protect transgender people from discrimination or harassment. More than a dozen states and more than a hundred cities had passed similar bills without any problems of that kind. These arguments were just recycled talking points from previous gay-rights fights.

"Protect our children," read the antigay signs in the 1970s and '80s. "Preserve parents' rights to protect their children from teachers who are immoral and who promote a perverted lifestyle." Just as these arguments preyed on people's stereotypes and ignorance about gay identities, so too do these new antitrans arguments. They feed on the lack of understanding of trans identities. They were wrong and false then and they are wrong and false now, but they were politically potent.

Delaware Attorney General Beau Biden, a smart, young, handsome elected official, had made protecting children from sexual assault a centerpiece of his time in office. The son of Delaware's longtime senator and U.S. vice president Joe Biden, Beau was a rising star in the national Democratic Party. He had skyrocketed to the nation's public consciousness with a heartfelt and compelling introduction of his dad at the 2008 Democratic National Convention and had served as a JAG officer in Iraq during his father's first term as vice president.

Like Jack, Beau was a former boss of mine. When I was sixteen years old, I had interned on Beau's first race, his successful 2006 campaign for attorney general. He won in a close contest against a longtime state prosecutor and was sworn in early the next year.

Beau and I hit it off on the 2006 campaign, and four years later, I returned to work for his reelection campaign during the summer of 2010. In that role, I occasionally revisited the old responsibilities I had with Jack, serving as a traveling aide and driver for Beau. While campaigning together up and down the state, we were often asked if I was Beau's kid because of our similar smiles and comfortable rapport.

I'd occasionally hold over Beau's head the fact that voters would think he was old enough to have a kid my age, but he was the type of boss who didn't mind a harmless ribbing. Beau was eminently down-to-earth and notably compassionate. Similar to Jack, he was the type of elected official who was exactly the same behind closed doors as he was out in public.

When I was coming out to close friends and family, I had wanted to come out to Beau personally, but given his national profile, I held off on reaching out, worried that I would burden him. Instead, Beau learned about my news through my public coming-out note. That evening, I got a call from him.

"Sarah," he started. I was struck by his seamless adoption of my new name. "It's Beau. I just saw your coming-out note."

He was driving with his wife, Hallie, and wanted to call to express his love and continued friendship. "I'm here with Hallie and we just want you to know that we love you, we stand with you, and you are still as much a part of the Biden family as ever. This doesn't change anything."

A few weeks after my meeting at the governor's office, I reached out to Beau to get together, catch up, and talk about the gender identity nondiscrimination bill. I told him we'd need his help to push back on the lies that would inevitably come from our opponents. I worried that bringing up the counterarguments to our bill might cause Beau to beg off, not wanting to get into the middle of a controversial fight. But he was unequivocal in his support and his willingness to help.

"Just let me know what you need," he assured me.

Two weeks later, I ran into Beau again at the vice president's official residence, the Naval Observatory, in Washington, D.C., at an event celebrating the second inauguration of President Obama and Beau's father. He informed me that one of his top deputies, the head of his Child Predator Unit, Patty Dailey Lewis, would be working with us to pass the gender identity bill. It might seem weird that the head of the child predator office would be running point for our trans equality bill, but Patty was perfect. She was a kind middle-aged woman who worked on defending children from sexual assault, and there was no one better positioned to push back against the myth that trans protections would embolden those wishing to sexually assault young girls in bathrooms.

After talking with Beau, I made my way across the tent to say hello to Vice President Biden and potentially grab a picture with him.

I hadn't spoken to the vice president since coming out, although I had seen him several times while interning at the White House. I walked up to him with my phone in hand, ready to ask for a picture. But before I could even say anything, he put both arms on my shoulders and looked me square in the eyes.

"Hey, kiddo. I just want you to know that Beau is so proud of you, Jill is so proud of you, and I'm so proud of you. I wanna know one thing, are ya happy?"

"I am," I responded, taken aback that he had even heard about my transition.

"That makes me so happy. Give me a hug!" He pulled me in for an enveloping embrace, a quintessential gesture for the gregarious vice president.

It was a powerful moment for me. As much as I had cherished that signed Joe Biden schedule growing up, this small interaction meant infinitely more to me. If meeting Joe Biden at eleven had assured me of my love of politics, his embrace at twenty-two helped confirm my belief that despite the cynicism that surrounds politics, there are still good and decent people in the arena. And with the support of both the Bidens and the Markells strongly behind us on the gender identity bill, I felt prepared for the fight to come in Delaware.

Unfortunately, support from statewide elected officials, even powerful ones such as Jack and Beau, could get us only so far. To pass the bill, we would need to convince a majority of legislators in both chambers—at least twenty-one members of the State House and eleven members of the State Senate—to vote in favor of the Gender Identity Nondiscrimination Act of 2013.

While the Democrats controlled both houses, Delaware's leading party had always been notoriously cautious. Conservative Democratic elected officials from the southern part of the state, although shrinking in numbers, had blocked social progress for decades. And even in 2013, the number of conservative Democrats and Republicans was still large enough that we would need to hold every progressive Dem-

ocrat in both chambers and gain at least one Republican in the State
Senate.

*Joe Biden was a giant to me growing up; he and his son
demonstrated such compassion after I came out.*

Our bill was not likely to come up for another few months, in May
or June of that year, as they always hold the most controversial bills
until near the end of session. But beginning in January, every day that
the legislature was in session and I was not in class, I would drive
to our state capitol in Dover, sometimes with Lisa and Mark from
Equality Delaware, often with my mom, and when he was able to get
out of work, my dad would join, too. While my parents were still getting used to my transition, they didn't hesitate when I asked them to
join me to lobby for the bill. As they had made clear, they supported
me and would stand by me no matter what.

Delaware's capitol, Legislative Hall, is a colonial redbrick building modeled after Independence Hall in Philadelphia, where the founders declared independence and signed the U.S. Constitution. It sits at the end of a large green in the heart of Dover's government district. By state-capitol standards, Legislative Hall is on the smaller side, which only adds to the bustling atmosphere of tourists, lobbyists, activists, and legislators who fill the halls each day the General Assembly meets.

While we worked to assemble a larger army of transgender people to advocate for the bill, I effectively camped out at Legislative Hall. One by one, I'd meet with lawmakers. We started with friendly legislators and worked our way out.

At first, I felt lost. I had been so used to advocating on behalf of others—candidates or a student body—that I didn't quite know how to explicitly advocate for myself. I wanted to talk about facts and statistics. I thought that if I could present the most cogent case, my arguments would win the day. Talking about myself felt self-indulgent.

I didn't know how to be personal in my approach, but I'd watch legislators react to my parents—many of them were moms and dads themselves and sympathized with my parents' fears. My mother would tell legislators through inevitable tears, "We were so scared when Sarah came out. All any parent wants is for their child to be happy, healthy, and fulfilled."

Watching her get through to them successfully, I felt like my voice didn't really matter. "I don't know, I just don't feel like I'm connecting," I expressed to my mom in the car ride back from Dover one day. "I feel like I'm useless."

But my voice did matter. It just turned out that I wasn't actually using it. What I was saying could have been offered by anyone. Making a cogent case wasn't my job; I needed to make a compelling case. I was ignoring the emotion that was at the heart of my own progressivism: empathy.

I had understood the importance of building empathy during my time at the White House, but the moment I went from subtly educating to blatantly advocating, I abruptly forgot that lesson. In part, I think I moved to what felt like colder and more distant arguments so that I could protect myself from feeling personally rejected if the bill failed. I knew that for many of these legislators, I was the face that came to their minds when the bill was discussed, and that reality would escalate in the months ahead.

How could I not take it personally, though? For all of us, the political is personal. And the truth is this: Sometimes vulnerability is the best, or only, path to justice. Those with power or privilege won't extend equality easily. Logic isn't enough. The legislators had to see that transgender people are *people*. They had to understand our fears. Our hopes. They had to see our families. They had to feel the humanity of the issue. And then, we hoped, they would no longer be able to look us in the eyes and deny us the equal protection of the laws they swore to uphold.

There had been a debate about which bill would come first, the marriage bill or the trans bill. I discussed the point extensively with Lisa, Mark, and the rest of the Equality Delaware board. I started to worry that the warnings of the older activists would come to fruition if we pushed the marriage bill first.

"Legislators will be exhausted after the marriage fight," I said to Lisa and Mark. "They won't have any energy left for the fight that they are less excited about."

Lisa is a "legislator whisperer" if there ever was one. "I actually think the legislators will be energized after the marriage fight," she said. "They will feel empowered after making history and they'll be fired up to do it again."

It was a risky gamble, but if accurate, it was likely the best bet to pass both. The fact of the matter remained that the trans-rights bill likely wouldn't have had the same impact of energizing legislators.

While we laid the foundation on the trans-rights bill by meeting with legislators and developing relationships, the marriage equality bill moved forward. On April 23, it passed the State House by a vote of twenty-three to eighteen, and three weeks later, the bill came to the Senate floor.

Activists had swarmed Legislative Hall in anticipation of its passing, and Governor Markell had promised to sign the bill immediately upon passage. I sat in the gallery to watch the final vote. Debate stretched on for hours in the Senate. At one point, an older conservative Democrat stood up in opposition to the marriage bill.

"And what's next?" the eighty-five-year-old senator cried in his deep southern accent. "We pass this bill today and we know they'll come back to us with that transgender bill!"

Eventually, after a long debate, the marriage equality bill passed by a vote of twelve to nine, and just two hours later, Jack stood behind a small desk on the landing of the grand staircase in the middle of Legislative Hall surrounded by hundreds of celebrating advocates.

"Tonight, with the signing of this law," he proclaimed, "we say to any Delawarean, regardless of sexual orientation: If you have committed yourself to somebody, and you've made that pledge to spend your life together in partnership, your love is equally valid and deserving and your family is now equal under the law."

He sat down at the desk with the seal of the state of Delaware on its front. Several pens sat before him as he signed each letter with a different one, handing the pens to Lisa, Mark, and several lawmakers as souvenirs. He put the last pen down and stood up with the bill in his hand, thrusting it into the air to thunderous applause and countless flashes of cameras.

I was exceptionally proud to have worked for Jack that day and moved by the history we were witnessing, but I could feel the butterflies in my stomach as we jubilantly walked out of Legislative Hall. The marriage bill had passed. Now eyes turned to the trans equality bill.

*Showtime.*

# CHAPTER 6

# "Please pass this bill."

DELAWARE TRANSGENDERS MAKE BID FOR EQUALITY read the front-page headline above the fold in the Sunday *News Journal*, Delaware's main paper. The grammatical error aside—transgender is an adjective, not a noun—the headline announced that the time for our bill had arrived. I could almost hear the disbelief and skepticism that had been expressed to me across the state: "Good luck with that."

We were going to need all the luck we could get. After the successful effort to pass the 2013 marriage bill, Equality Delaware's board of directors and its field team, assembled with support from the Human Rights Campaign, hunkered down for the next battle: passage of the Gender Identity Nondiscrimination Act of 2013.

Over the preceding weeks, we had secured our top goals for prime sponsors, the legislators who would lead the effort in the Senate and House on our bill. In the House, based on Lisa's recommendation, I met with Representative Bryon Short, a small-business owner respected by both sides of the chamber, and asked him to serve as the primary sponsor in the lower house of the General Assembly. He initially asked to think about it but quickly came back with an emphatic yes, possibly a by-product of a conversation with his progressive and fiercely politically active wife.

In the Senate, we had the two highest-ranking women in the chamber serve as our co-leads: Senators Margaret Rose Henry and Patty Blevins. Henry, then majority whip, is a progressive figure who could also personally speak to the evils of discrimination as an older Black woman who had been in politics for two decades. She would serve as the bill's "floor manager," helping to steer the legislation through committee and then lead the debate on our side when it came before the full Senate.

Blevins, the chamber's president pro tempore, the top figure in the majority caucus, is a warm but unassuming woman who, through her position, had control over the Senate's calendar. Both are incredibly smart and, as longtime legislators, understood the Senate better than anyone.

As we prepared for introduction of the trans equality bill, we worked to build momentum, meeting day in and day out with legislators while our field team knocked on doors and made calls. To begin to foster public support and demonstrate the backing of leading statewide elected officials, Governor Markell wrote a *Huffington Post* op-ed calling for passage in clear and personal terms: "Kindness, decency, and fairness are the values that Delawareans live by on a daily basis. They are the values I have encountered in towns and cities throughout Delaware. We look out for one another in this state of neighbors. Yet, for years, we have left one group of our friends, relatives, and colleagues behind. And it is past time to make things right."

Just ninety-six miles north to south, Delaware is larger than only Rhode Island among all of the United States. The "small-town feel" fosters a neighborly atmosphere in a state where everyone has, as the saying goes in Delaware, "dated, mated, or is related to" one another.

As a former business executive, Jack went on to straightforwardly outline the economic case for building a diverse and inclusive state, but then he got personal.

"While this law will benefit our state and our economy, it also goes to the core of who we are as a community. My young friend Sarah, who just graduated from college in Washington, D.C., and happens to be transgender, has told the first lady and me about her fear of returning to Delaware, the state she loves, without basic protections. There are countless more transgender Delawareans who live in fear of or face discrimination on a daily basis. As a lifelong Delawarean, I'm convinced this is not the Delaware I know and love."

Beau Biden, whose deputy, Patty Dailey Lewis, was scheduled to join us for the hearings and floor votes, filmed a short online video declaring his public support and dedicating his office to fight for passage of the nondiscrimination law. He talked about the need for equal protection under the law and protections from discrimination and violence based on gender identity or expression.

And like Jack, he closed by getting personal. Talking about our relationship, he said, "A young friend of mine, who is transgender, has spoken to me about her fear of living without basic legal protections. For her and for all of our transgender citizens, I want you to know this: I support providing protection from violence and discrimination based on gender identity and expression under Delaware law, and I will work with our General Assembly to provide such protections this year."

The messages helped to demonstrate that the gender identity bill was a mainstream position and communicated to inherently skittish legislators that they wouldn't have to stand alone, that these two popular statewide elected officials would stand with them. And reading and watching these two messages, I knew that Jack and Beau were also standing with me. They had already done so much for me, through their friendship and mentorship.

A year prior, as I prepared to come out, I worried that even our past friendships might hurt them politically. But now here they were, sticking their necks out for me and for so many people just like me across the state.

• • •

Lisa, Mark, and I had spent months meeting with dozens of legislators, reciting the same stories and statistics over and over again. We'd received strong messages of support from many of these state legislators, and we had our prime sponsors in place and ready to defend the bill on the floor. Our next step was an important one: a whip count. It seems simple enough on its face: You poll the legislators to see who is a yes, who is a no, and who remains undecided.

In reality, getting answers in a whip count is closer to herding cats. We had to track down the legislators to confirm how they planned to vote in whatever ways we could find them, which often meant stopping by their offices unannounced or waiting outside their offices to walk them to their next meeting. Some lawmakers are difficult to find, oftentimes intentionally, when they know you're not going to like their answer. Setting dignity aside, I was forced to stake them out, waiting outside a meeting or even outside a bathroom to get their attention when they least expected it.

While prime sponsors are the leads on the bill, cosponsors are like casual champions. They are a little more than just supporters, but they don't have the responsibility of overseeing the legislation through passage. In the Senate, we secured five cosponsors in addition to Senators Blevins and Henry, and fourteen in the House, including Representative Short. In both instances, we were three-quarters of the way to the minimum number of votes we needed for passage with just our sponsors and cosponsors, a very promising place to be.

But there are always votes beyond the sponsors and cosponsors. The whip count did more than give us a clearer picture of our bill's prospects—it also had the impact of forcing legislators to look us in the eye and commit one way or another on the bill. For all the negative stereotypes about politics, the integrity of a person's word is vital to gaining respect. Legislators understand this and genuinely try to stick to their verbal commitments.

According to our count, in the House, where a majority is twenty-one, we had twenty-four or twenty-five votes. Potentially more. In the

Senate, where we needed eleven votes to pass the bill, we had a firm ten votes, with several more unaccounted for. So we were down to needing one more vote to pass the bill. While the Democrats were in the majority, there were a few in the party who were clear nos, vestiges of an era of conservative Democrats that has slowly dwindled over time, leaving us with two choices to push us over the top: one moderate Democrat or one moderate Republican. We needed only one of them to vote our way.

After meeting with the moderate Democrat, it was clear we were unlikely to get his backing. He seemed personally distraught over the bill, wanting to support it but concerned he would be getting too far out ahead of his district. He "abhorred discrimination" but worried that both marriage equality and trans rights in one session would be too much for voters to handle.

He likely wouldn't vote *against* the bill, instead opting to formally abstain by "not voting." It's a symbolic difference, and it didn't help us get to where we needed to be. Symbolism doesn't change the need for eleven votes to gain a majority.

The other potential vote, Republican Cathy Cloutier, had voted in favor of marriage equality, civil unions, and sexual orientation non-discrimination protections and came from a solidly Democratic district. She managed to return after each election by building a strong relationship with organized labor and voting on the more progressive side of social issues as well. She is probably, to this day, one of the last "liberal Republicans" in any state legislature in the country.

While Lisa, Mark, and I, along with my parents, worked Legislative Hall, the field operation run by Equality Delaware and HRC had built an army of allies who were already emailing and calling legislators in support of the bill. While calls or emails may seem like a small gesture, lawmakers look closely at the number of constituents chiming in on a particular topic, and it can weigh heavily in their decision-making process.

Some legislative aides reported calls ten to one in favor of trans equality, a striking balance in our favor. The field team also collected support for the bill from more than two hundred small businesses from across the state, a key constituency for more moderate Democrats and Republicans. Other national groups, like the National LGBTQ Task Force and the National Center for Transgender Equality, helped us locate trans people throughout the state willing to share their stories and lobby their legislators.

These transgender Delawareans were the stories that highlighted the urgent need for the bill, that put a face and a name to the issue at hand. There was the older transgender woman in southern Delaware who was mocked and ostracized at the factory that she worked in. There was the transgender boy who was beaten up after the school forced him to use a girls' restroom. There was the transgender woman who was summarily fired from her job at a grocery store after she informed her boss that she was transgender.

And there was Matthew, a twenty-three-year-old trans man who had attended one of our trans community mobilization meetings. Matthew was just starting to transition, and he was slender, with short hair and small wire-rimmed glasses; he looked a few years younger than twenty-three. Out to some close friends, Matthew was still in the closet to his employer, his peers, and even his parents. I was instantly struck by his eloquence and warmth, and as we learned later, he lived in the district represented by Cathy Cloutier, the moderate Republican in the State Senate who we hoped would support our legislation.

One of the more common refrains we heard from legislators, both in support and in opposition, was that they did not have any transgender people in their districts. It was an absurd conclusion to draw; after all, there were forty-one House districts and twenty-one Senate districts. Delaware is small, but even conservative counts estimated that at least two thousand transgender people lived in our state of roughly nine hundred thousand people. Later studies would estimate the transgender population in Delaware to be closer to 4,500.

Matthew, however, was the only transgender person to step forward from Cloutier's district. Despite not being out to nearly anyone in his circle of family and friends, he was determined to help pass the bill for his own sake. Matthew felt that a law like the Gender Identity Nondiscrimination Act would give him the legal tools—and personal security—necessary to come out and to live authentically. When I asked if he'd be willing to meet with his senator, he quickly said yes, and with just a few days to the vote, we secured a meeting with her.

Matthew was fidgeting as we waited on a long couch in the Republican caucus's waiting room. His nerves were no doubt exacerbated by the fact that we were in the lion's den, the area of the building controlled by a party that opposed our basic rights and dignity. That opposed *us*.

Senator Cloutier came out to greet us, and we walked back to her office, a small corner room filled with a desk and two chairs. The sun illuminated the two large windows in her office, but instead of filling the space with light, the bright windows behind her made the rest of the room feel dark. I opened by introducing myself and Matthew as "transgender Delawareans."

"Hold on." Senator Cloutier stopped abruptly. "You are both transgender?"

She was clearly shocked at the declaration.

"Yes, ma'am, we are," I informed her, not wanting to have her focus too much on how we looked.

There is no question that opponents of our bill tried to paint transgender people into a caricature, but it's always a point I want to be careful in pushing back on. Transgender people shouldn't be treated with dignity because of how some of us look; we should be treated with dignity because we are human beings. The trans community is as diverse as any community. Some of us conform to traditional expressions of gender, while others transgress those boundaries in various ways, just like cisgender people. If our pursuit of equality is built on the ability of some of us to blend in, then we will leave many of the most marginalized behind.

I quickly pivoted the conversation to the reason for the meeting: getting to know a constituent of hers.

Matthew launched into his own story. "My family, my employers, and my peers are unaware that I am transgender, because, in all honesty, I am terrified to tell them," he explained. "I am terrified to tell my employers and peers because I know that right now there is no protection for me.

"I am a student with a two-year degree and a small résumé, and I am afraid to lose what few job opportunities I can find. Because of this, I have been delaying the medical and legal steps I need to feel safe and comfortable with myself, and struggle to hide my identity. It is a difficult and frightening position to live my life in, and often I feel absolutely alone."

Matthew began to tear up as he talked to the senator. "This bill . . . this bill would tell me, and people like me, that we are not alone."

He paused. "Can we count on your support, Senator?"

Matthew was still nervous. I could see his hands shaking as he talked, but he had clearly moved Senator Cloutier. With tears swelling in her eyes, she stood up from her desk chair, walked over to Matthew with open arms, and said, "Yes, Matthew. Yes, you can."

I felt a huge sense of relief. I was hopeful we could secure this senator's vote, but I wasn't entirely sure. With one individual and his story, we suddenly had enough votes to pass the Gender Identity Nondiscrimination Act through the Senate. Delaware would be one step closer to being safe for me to come home to, for Andy and me to start a life together there, and for all transgender people to live and thrive.

• • •

Throughout the lobbying, Andy and I did our best to see each other as much as possible. He'd come up to Delaware on the weekends and try to distract me as I'd count and recount the votes. The weekend before the all-important State Senate vote, when I called him nearly in tears, he left a work conference, jumped into his car, and drove straight to Wilmington to help calm my nerves. We'd watch movies and take walks around the beautiful tree-lined neighborhood I grew up in, each excursion broken up by a frantic rehashing of the vote totals.

*Maybe I'm missing something*, I'd nervously think. Obviously there was no new information and the numbers had not changed, but each time I'd recount I'd breathe a sigh of relief.

Just after two p.m. on a humid Thursday in June 2013, the State Senate, the upper house of Delaware's legislature, gaveled in. On most days, the gallery of seats above the Senate floor is empty. On that day, the seats were filled with transgender people and their loved ones anxiously waiting. Delaware is the only state in the union that allows members of the public to sit on the floor when the Senate is in session, and Senator Henry had reserved some spots for Mark, Lisa, my parents, and me just a few feet away from the senators on the Democratic side of the aisle.

It had already taken ten years for the sexual orientation nondiscrimination bill to pass through the State Senate in Delaware. But this was the first time a bill explicitly related to the transgender community had been brought before the state's legislature. *Please, God, don't let this take another ten years*, I routinely thought to myself.

Matt Denn, the candidate who nine years before had let my friends trail him with a video camera during his first race for insurance commissioner, was now lieutenant governor and, therefore, presided over the Senate. After a few minutes of technical business, he called on State Senator Margaret Rose Henry, the prime sponsor of the gender identity bill.

Senator Henry rose from her desk and addressed the presiding officer. "Mr. President, at this time I request that Senate Bill Ninety-seven be brought before the Senate for consideration." My heart swelled with pride when she started reading from remarks that I had helped draft for her: "I'm proud to stand as the prime sponsor of Senate Bill Ninety-seven, the Gender Identity Nondiscrimination Act of 2013. This bill would add basic protections on the basis of gender identity to their stated . . . to the state's . . . to the state's pre-existing . . ."

She paused after getting tripped up. "I'm sorry, I'm just a little nervous," she explained, clearing her throat. She was obviously feeling the weight and attention of the issue that now rested on her shoulders. The fact that a veteran legislator was so clearly nervous only amplified my butterflies.

Senator Henry continued: "This bill simply provides for the same protections already afforded to everyone on the basis of race, religion, ethnicity, and sexual orientation. It would bring Delaware law in line with the values and actions exhibited by Delawareans on a daily basis. It's time for the transgender boy who faces bullying in our schools every day to know that things will get better. Quite simply, it's time to treat everyone fairly," she said in closing. "At this time I'd like to call as a witness Sarah McBride."

The Delaware Senate sometimes welcomes individuals to testify when considering bills. They usually try to limit the testimony to a few people, but my parents and I would be speaking, in addition to Mark and Patty Dailey Lewis, Beau Biden's deputy in charge of the Child Predator Unit, who would be representing his office.

I nervously made my way up to the podium. Standing at the lectern, facing the senators, I looked past them—out over their desks and up to the balcony, where members of the transgender community patiently and anxiously watched.

I have to admit that I had mixed feelings about my central role in everything, but particularly in the Senate debate. On the one hand, privilege shields me from much of the worst discrimination faced by the transgender community; on the other hand, those same privileges allow me to shoulder the burden of public education with less risk to my safety, security, and economic well-being than would be imposed on others. Additionally, my existing personal relationships with these legislators made it even harder for them to say no to me and, therefore, the broader community. I felt a moral responsibility to use that privilege and those relationships to subvert the power of prejudice.

"Thank you, Senator," I began. I could feel the lump in my throat.

With the Democrats seated to my left and the Republicans to my right, I instinctually gravitated toward addressing the senators on the friendlier side of the aisle, so I had to consciously force myself to also look at the side readying to oppose the bill.

"My name is Sarah McBride and I'm a transgender Delawarean. It's an honor to speak to you today.

"The last time I spoke in this chamber was when I participated in the Youth in Government program four years ago," I said, referencing a Delaware high school program organized by the YMCA that brought students down to the capitol for a model legislative experience to debate and pass faux legislation. I had joined the program for my senior year of high school and loved every minute of it. We would take over Legislative Hall for a weekend, and at the end of the program, we'd write handwritten notes to the actual legislators whose desks we'd occupied. Standing at the lectern, I could see that many of the senators had the handwritten notes from that year's class displayed under the glass on their desks.

"I was one of those kids who left a note for a senator on their desk, and it spoke to my appreciation and respect for you and this Senate," I improvised, hoping that the anecdote would remind them that I, too, was an idealistic kid who looked up to the body I was now addressing. "I thought that the next time I would be here would be to work for one of you fine people. But life intervenes, and now I'm here for a different reason: to ask to simply be treated fairly."

I stood before the Senate and recounted my journey to self-acceptance, the fear of coming out, and my parents' evolution. When I got to a sentence about my dad, I began to tear up. "While it was hard for my parents at first, in time, my dad said that he didn't feel like he was losing a son, he felt like he was gaining a daughter."

My voice began to crack. My parents were sitting against the wall to my left and I tried to avoid looking at them, knowing that the sight of my mom and dad beginning to cry would likely make me unravel.

"While my experience when I'm with my family and friends has been positive, when I'm in Delaware, I live in constant fear that discrimination lurks around every corner. I have to build up so much courage to leave my house to walk down the street, to run an errand, or to go out to dinner with my family. Every day without protections, I am just one person's kindness and acceptance away from being discriminated against.

"The Gender Identity Nondiscrimination Act of 2013 would allow me to come home to my family without fear. For every young person struggling and simply in dire need of hope, and for every parent just like many of you who simply want their child to come home to their family, please . . . please pass this bill."

I exhaled. A few months before, displaying such vulnerability before that body seemed impossible, but through the last several months I had found my voice. I had realized that I could speak from a place of power if I spoke from a place of authenticity.

Having done my part, it was now my parents' turn. Holding each other's hands, my mom and dad stood beside each other at the lectern and my mother began to read her remarks. "Good afternoon. We are Sarah's parents, Sally and David McBride. We are here today to tell a story.

"We have three children. Sean, who is the oldest, has just finished up his medical residency at Harvard. He happens to be gay, but that is just a part of who he is. Our second child, Dan, is a prosecutor in the Delaware Attorney General's Office. He's straight, but that is just a part of who he is."

And then she got to me. She described my work on political campaigns, my time at American University, and then the Christmas Day I came out to them as transgender. When I came out, she recounted

how they were frightened my "future would be shattered by discrimination." She told the legislators what she had told me: "I don't want to
lose my baby."

But, she explained, she had come to the realization that I was not
only still her baby, but that I hadn't really changed. The wrapping
was just a little different.

"She's still my best friend and still a bright and compassionate
person who wants desperately to come back to Delaware. As you can
see, being transgender is only a part of who she is."

My mother, now crying, moved to the side, and my father stepped
up, looking sad and, almost, in pain.

"When Sarah first came out to us," he began, "one of the first
things I did was I went online to learn about what had just been told
to us. And I came to a publication.

"And it described the treatment of transgender people. It indicated
that forty-one percent of trans people attempt to commit suicide because of the prejudice and discrimination that they experience. You
can imagine how frightened I was that first day reading that. But I
also read that that percentage comes down dramatically when the

My parents and me in our family living room during the fight for trans rights in
Delaware. Our family had become the primary spokespeople for the Gender Identity
Nondiscrimination Act of 2013.

person is accepted by their family, and even more so when they are accepted by their community."

My dad talked about our family being embraced by everyone from our church to our governor. Those experiences, he said, "gave us the faith that people are genuinely caring and fair. And it has caused me to realize how much better this world would be if we cared for each other's children like we care for our own."

As I watched my parents plead with the State Senate for basic dignity, I was not overcome with pride, but instead guilt. I felt bad that they were forced to bare everything before our legislature and the media. I felt embarrassed that they had to come defend me, as though I had committed a crime and they had to attest to my character. I worried that they felt humiliated, like they were groveling for respect.

As I sat against the wall on the Senate floor, I began to cry. A photographer across the room zoomed in on my face and took a picture of me tearing up, an image that would be splashed across the front page of the newspaper the next day.

At the same time, Democratic state senator Karen Peterson looked over at me and got up from her desk. Karen was our state's only openly LGBTQ state legislator. While she and her spouse were well known in Delaware political circles, she had never discussed her sexual orientation or her relationship on the record until a few weeks before, when she came out publicly during the marriage equality debate.

"If my happiness somehow demeans or diminishes your marriage, you need to work on your marriage," she had said, declaring her sexual orientation on the floor of the Senate.

I had known Karen since my days working for Jack's 2008 campaign. She had endorsed Markell. Her spouse, Vikki, and I had taken to each other so much that I had started to call her my "campaign mom."

Other senators saw that I was crying, but Karen was the one who walked over to comfort me. And as my parents continued their testimony, she sat down next to me and held my hand. I think she knew exactly what was going through my mind. She knew the indignity of having to plead for your most basic rights. As another LGBTQ person, she never had to say that. Her presence and her actions were clear enough.

When you come out as an advocate to a legislative body, it's difficult to feel empathy or even sympathy from those you are lobbying. After trying to explain your basic humanity to people over and over and *over* again, it can make your own government feel entirely foreign to you. And when you look around and see no one like you in the legislature, that foreignness is compounded with a profound sense of loneliness. It's enough to dissuade even the most dedicated activist from believing that their government is capable of truly seeing them.

That one, subtle interaction with Karen was enough to demonstrate that my pain was acknowledged and, most of all, understood. I stopped crying. And ever since, that simple gesture has served as a constant reminder of the importance of diverse representation in elected office.

There's a saying that goes, "If you're not at the table, then you're on the menu." That helps to explain the substantive need for diverse representation, but Karen's action reflected its symbolic importance. A government cannot be "of the people, by the people, and for the people" if wide swaths of the people have no seat at the table, if large parts of the country feel like there is literally no one in their government who can understand what they are going through.

Fortunately, more and more out LGBTQ candidates are being elected to offices, from city council to the U.S. Senate. To this day, though, only one openly transgender person has been elected to and then served in a state legislature. And none have been elected to Congress. Yet.

As my parents wrapped up their remarks and Mark Purpura, a co-president of Equality Delaware, stepped up to the microphone, you could feel the empathy for my parents in the room. You could see it in the faces of the legislators, even the ones who were going to oppose the bill. In my parents they saw themselves. Unfortunately, empathy is not enough to win everyone over.

Now standing at the lectern, Mark outlined the legal history and purpose of the bill but spent the majority of his time rebutting the dreaded "bathroom predator" myth.

In the days leading up to debate in the General Assembly, the Delaware Family Policy Council, Delaware's chapter of a national anti-LGBTQ group designated by watchdogs as a "hate group," had released a dramatic online ad. The black-and-white commercial featured a bearded middle-aged man with sunglasses following a young girl into the bathroom at a park. The ad closed with the ominous text "Is this what you want for Delaware? Tell your Delaware legislators to vote NO on Senate Bill Ninety-seven today."

The ad would be laughable if it wasn't so offensive and, sadly, effective. The crux of the objection to our bill was that our nondiscrimination law would allow predators into women's bathrooms to prey on children. And in the absence of a stronger understanding of trans people and identities, fearmongering and scare tactics fill the void, embedding themselves as rational ideas in the public imagination.

Anti-equality activists had performed rhetorical acrobatics, saying it was not transgender people they were talking about, but someone "pretending to be transgender." The scenario—a completely unfounded one—allowed for a shield from accusations of bigotry, but in the public's mind, the nuance was lost. They just remember "transgender" and "predator."

Mark addressed this lie head-on. "That is just categorically false. There is no interpretation of this bill, legally, that would permit that conduct. That conduct is currently criminal and it would remain criminal after the passage of this bill."

The Republican leader in the State Senate, Gary Simpson, stood up, clearly prepared to be the defender of the myth. "I have been inundated over the last few days with emails that are just filling up my inbox," he launched, seeming incredulous that he had to deal with this issue. "And ninety-eight percent of those are women that are afraid that it will permit—or not stop—sexual predators from using those public accommodations."

Senator Simpson was referring to emails from supporters of the Delaware Family Policy Council. After the DFPC's executive director, Nicole Theis, and her supporters had come off as too venomous in the Senate Judiciary Committee hearing the week before, they decided to remain quiet during the full Senate debate and allow conservative legislators to carry their water.

Senator Simpson asked Mark, "How will this bill prevent that from happening? And show me in the bill language where that scenario will not be permitted."

"Well, I think the answer is, that language is in the criminal code," Mark calmly offered back. "The language that prohibits it is in the criminal code. And today if a predator goes into a bathroom and commits a crime, then that is prohibited. And this bill does not change that. This bill does not permit someone to pretend to be of a different gender identity and go into a bathroom and commit a crime."

Simpson shot back, "You're saying the bill does not allow it or does not promote it, but how does it stop it? You said that the bill doesn't allow someone to dress as a woman just to do that, but it doesn't stop it?"

Mark, again, patiently responded, explaining that the nondiscrimination law provides no cover to a person committing a crime. Delaware had passed protections based on sexual orientation a few years ago, but that law didn't allow or facilitate a man intent on harming a boy in a restroom to do so.

With the questions taking a nosedive into the bathroom conversation, Senator Henry interrupted by calling Beau Biden's deputy Patty Dailey Lewis to testify. Patty had testified in front of the legislature before, but never for something as high-profile.

"First, let me just say that the attorney general does support this bill and that the attorney general would never support any legislation that would put children at harm," she began.

After she reiterated some of the points Mark had just made,

Senator Simpson leapt back up and challenged her: "It seems logical that if we are telling people that they can go into the opposite-sex bathrooms, that it would be that sexual predators would do so."

"It does not permit sexual predators in—" she began responding, when Senator Simpson interrupted her.

"Well, certainly it doesn't permit sexual predators, but it allows people who are sexual predators to do it," he retorted, the first half of his sentence contradicting the second half of his sentence.

"No, it does not," Patty shot back. "A sexual predator, regardless of their excuse to be in any room, is not permitted to harm someone. And to take that argument a step further, we have people on the sex-offender registry—not transgender folks, but [nontransgender] folks—on the child-protection registry and the sex-offender registry today that are permitted to go into bathrooms. The same bathrooms with the kind of people they have offended against."

Her point highlighted the opportunism of these arguments. For all the talk of sexual predators accessing restrooms, these senators were holding transgender people's right to safely access a restroom to a higher standard than the current ability of actual, certified sex offenders to access restrooms.

Senator Simpson, increasingly argumentative, repeated various versions of the same question. Exasperated, he closed with, "Women don't want a man in their restroom! This bill allows it!"

"It allows a transgender person—" she began.

"Or a man wearing a wig and a skirt," Simpson interjected, interrupting her again.

Patty corrected him. "That's not a transgender person."

Simpson asked how she would prove that. Patty jumped at that question. "We're talking about the utilization of a restroom, which for most of us will take a mere two to four minutes. If a person goes in and does something that violates the criminal code, that's different than them needing to use a restroom that's there."

"But does it condone the possibility of a predator saying they are transgender?" Simpson retorted.

"If you were harassing someone," Patty tried to explain, "it wouldn't matter if a female was following the child into the bathroom or a male was doing it. It is not permitted."

Not understanding how the crime he was talking about would still be illegal, Simpson again retorted, "And then when you confront the person, that's his alibi. 'I perceive myself as a female.'"

Maintaining her composure, Patty tried again to reason with the senator. "But that 'alibi' isn't to the offense, it was to why you were in that room. If it was a female predator going into a female bathroom going after girls or a male predator going into a male bathroom to go after boys, the fact that they are going after a child in and of itself is the offense, it's not where they were doing it. A teacher who goes after a child in a school can't say, 'I'm a teacher so I'm allowed to be here.' It doesn't matter that you were allowed to be there."

The debate was going in circles, but by now Simpson, either realizing he was beating a dead horse or understanding the absurdity of his points, sat back down and another conservative senator, Colin Bonini, stood up.

Senator Bonini is an imposing figure and, while younger than most of his colleagues, is as conservative as they come. He is a contrarian through and through. Even when a vote is twenty strong in favor, he'll be the one dissenting voice.

Bonini rose from his desk in the back row and, with a raised voice, asked Patty the same questions the other senators had just asked. When she reiterated her responses, his voice raised even higher. "I have never been so offended by testimony. She's not answering truthfully!"

An audible gasp went through the chamber as Senator Bonini effectively accused Patty of perjury. Patty Dailey Lewis had spent twenty-eight years defending the interests of children against predators. She was a well-respected attorney, fair-minded and thoughtful.

A Democratic senator jumped up. "Mr. President," the senator said, addressing Matt Denn, the presiding officer, "that's an inappropriate comment."

Matt Denn responded from the dais, instructing Bonini to refrain from such language, a rare admonishment of a senator for disrespect-ful behavior.

I was fed up by this point. I wanted these senators to say these arguments to my face. I asked Mark and Lisa if I could speak again and they passed a note to Senator Henry: "Call Sarah up."

A minute later, I made my way back to the podium, now more angry than nervous. They had insulted Patty. They had figured out every possible way to insinuate that transgender women are men. They had painted basic protections for transgender people as a threat.

"You heard some of the questions raised today. Would you like to make a comment?" Senator Henry asked me open-endedly.

As Senator Henry spoke, I again looked up into the gallery at the faces of the transgender people and their families who had come to watch the debate. My heart ached that they had just spent an hour hearing a debate about their dignity and rights devolve into an argument about pedophiles and predators.

I thanked the senator for the opportunity to come back up, and in a tone probably a bit too heated, I called the arguments logical fallacies. "There are fourteen states and a hundred cities and counties that have public-accommodations laws that allow transgender people to utilize restrooms in accordance with their gender," I said forcefully. "And there has not been a single documented instance of a transgender person or a person claiming to be transgender going into a restroom or going into a locker room and doing anything that harms people or assaults people."

My train of thought was momentarily broken as I noticed Andy make his way into the back of the chamber. The Senate had started discussing our bill a bit earlier than anticipated, and because he was driving up from Washington, Andy had missed most of the debate. Like our first date and that day in the White House, I was immediately struck by how handsome he looked, how suave he seemed as he walked with his hand confidently stuffed in his suit pants' pocket to one of the open seats next to my parents with a proud smirk on his face.

I snapped back into the moment, invigorated by Andy's presence, and continued with my rebuttal. After a long, heated, explicit, and vivid debate, I was nervous that even a senator or two on the Democratic side had potentially been swayed, or at least made more hesitant to vote for our bill. I wanted to use an analogy that would make them fully understand just how absurd these points would be judged by history.

"These are the exact same arguments that have been utilized in every single battle for basic protections and human dignity. They were used to deny equal rights to gay people. It was wrong then, and it is wrong now."

Some might wonder why we put up such a defense over bathrooms on our side. Why not just exclude them from the bill to diminish the opposition? Those questions miss the point that bathrooms are just an excuse. If it were not bathrooms, our opponents would find something else to object to. And clearly they are willing to concoct any kind of scenario, no matter how absurd, to oppose our protections.

But even if the opposition was rooted entirely in "bathrooms," that doesn't change the fact that it is vital that these nondiscrimination protections include restrooms. As the gendered space most frequently accessed by every person, they are particularly dangerous for transgender people. Two years before our debate, an online video had surfaced of a violent attack against a transgender woman after she tried to use a women's restroom at a Baltimore area McDonald's. The woman was beaten so severely she appeared to suffer a seizure.

Unlike the dramatic bathroom scenarios imagined by our opponents, the video of the beating of that transgender woman was a real and vivid assault in a bathroom and representative of an all-too-common experience. One study found that 70 percent of transgender women in one community reported being verbally harassed, denied access, or physically assaulted in a public restroom. And because of that discrimination—and the fear of it—transgender people are often forced to avoid bathrooms altogether, sometimes causing medical issues because we are forced to hold it for so long.

But it's also important to remember that when we are talking about trans equality generally and nondiscrimination protections specifically, we're not just talking about bathrooms. The bill also impacted employment, housing, insurance, and all public spaces, not just restrooms. And with the exception of my initial testimony and my parents' testimony, the hour-long floor debate had revolved entirely around restrooms. I didn't want the senators to lose the forest for the trees, so I made sure to highlight some of the discrimination experienced outside of restrooms.

"Lisa, Mark, and I know someone who was hired for a job at a grocery store. They were given the job, put on the schedule. The moment the employer found out that they were transgender, they were fired.

"I know a young transgender woman who recently transitioned. She had patronized a restaurant for years, and the moment she came out and she went to that restaurant, they said to her, 'You can never come back here.'" I leaned into the microphone. "'Ever.' And there is no legal recourse for her in this state. Fourteen states have these laws and there is not one issue. And to suggest that it would happen in Delaware is disingenuous and not based in reality."

I headed back to my seat, still seething. I had exchanged tears for anger, and I was worried I had been too hostile.

"Was that too much?" I whispered to Mark.

"No, that's exactly what they needed," he assured me. "Plus, I think it's exactly what those kids in the balcony needed. They needed to see someone like you stand up to that bullshit."

The few Republicans who stood up again, including Senator Bonini, now offered far more muted opposition, focusing, instead of on bathrooms, on liability around discrimination claims. Their protests, harsh and forceful before, had turned almost sheepish, their tone resembling that of a recently admonished child.

The striking change in the tone of the debate underscored for me the centrality of trans voices in these efforts. When transgender people stand up, when our voices are heard, when we confront these myths about bathrooms head-on, we can make the politics of fear and division, of discrimination and misinformation, ineffective.

After roughly two hours, Senator Henry finally called for a vote. Lisa, Mark, and I sat with pens in our hands and a tally sheet with every senator's name and boxes for "yes," "no," "not voting," and "absent" next to each of them. We needed eleven votes to pass the bill, which means we needed to hold every senator who told us "yes" prior to the debate.

Denn instructed the clerk to call the roll. Senator by senator, the clerk called each name.

"Senator Blevins?"

"Yes."

We began checking the boxes on our tally sheet.

"Senator Bonini?"

"No."

Then one not voting. Another yes. Another no. Two more yeses. Another not voting. The roll call continued, the yeses and nos alternating with almost each name. Finally, it concluded. I squeezed my mom's hand and looked expectantly at Mark and Lisa.

"Mr. President," the clerk reported, "the roll call on Senate Bill Ninety-seven is eleven yes, seven no, two not voting, one absent."

We had done it.

"Having received its constitutionally required majority vote, Senate Bill Ninety-seven has passed the Senate," the lieutenant governor announced. As his gavel hit the dais, the gallery erupted in cheers.

My mom was crying as she embraced Senator Henry, thanking her for her leadership. Lisa hugged me and said, "Eleven votes. Not one vote to spare. You don't pass a bill when you can win in a landslide. You pass the bill when you have just enough votes."

But there was only one person I wanted to see. I looked around to find Andy. A crowd of people hugging and celebrating parted, allowing him to make his way through. I ran up to him and he gave me a big hug and kiss.

"I'm so proud of you, Bean. So proud of you."

Before I could respond, Lisa touched my shoulder from behind.

"I believe there are a few people hoping to speak with you," she said, as she gestured toward a group of reporters standing in the hallway outside the chamber.

I walked with Andy, past the senators and toward the media, catching a glimpse of the gallery. Seeing transgender people and their family members exchanging hugs and shedding a few tears made the two hours of insulting debate worth it.

Speaking into several microphones and tape recorders held up near my face, and with Andy proudly looking on from just a few feet away, I thanked the eleven senators who voted for our bill and declared, "Today, the Senate sent a powerful message to transgender Delawareans that the heart of this state is big enough to love them, too."

The vote result was a big step. It was no easy feat. But there wasn't much time for celebration. We were only halfway through the process, and while our whip count had us with enough votes to win in the State House, within minutes of our bill passing the Senate we started getting troubling reports.

Our vote count in the House was collapsing.

# CHAPTER 7

# One step closer to justice.

After an emotional and volatile win in the Senate, I didn't have time to enjoy our success before we had to begin gearing up for our fight in the State House, one that might be even harder.

After our opponents' loss in the Senate, they readied for a full-court press in the House. The Delaware Family Policy Council, having seen the power of families in our advocacy, blasted out an email to their lists calling on conservative women and their children to show up for the House committee hearing to oppose SB 97.

Before a bill comes to the floor of the full chamber, it must first make its way through a smaller committee hearing. Just a week after the Senate vote—seven excruciating, stressful days spent trying to firm up anxious, supportive legislators—the bill was heard in the State House Administrative Committee. The email from the DFPC worked. Dozens of mothers showed up to testify, in many cases dragging their kids along, too.

Emboldened by the stereotypes spoon-fed to them by the DFPC, the moms' testimony largely threw out the subtlety of the arguments we had heard from the Republican senators, who bent over backward to make clear that they weren't talking about transgender people but rather "individuals pretending to be transgender." The professed distinction between transgender people and "individuals pretending to be transgender" was disingenuous from the start, a dog whistle that lost its nuance with the larger public.

As I waited to testify, I stood behind a line of mothers who stepped up one by one, clutching their children tightly, as though they were in some sort of danger in Legislative Hall. Most of the women were middle-aged, some wearing T-shirts with trite antitrans slogans like "God made men and women" and "No men in women's restrooms," language the LGBTQ community would see in future nondiscrimination fights.

In their speeches, one woman referred to us as "freaks." Another as "sinners." But "predators" was, once again, the word of the day. Standing behind these women, I could feel the disdain they held for transgender people, or at least who they thought we were. It was palpable.

My palms were sweaty as I patiently waited my turn to speak. Intellectually, I knew that their prejudice—their hate—was a by-product of their ignorance. They had been exposed only to lies and distortions about who transgender people are, and not just from the head of the DFPC, who stood in front of me, but also from the media, popular culture, and too many pulpits.

As we waited in a line that led to the lectern in the center of the room, the head of the DFPC turned around and introduced herself to me. Her seemingly warm smile and respectful introduction belied the clear contempt she held for people like me, hatred so deep that it compelled her to spend her life opposing the rights of LGBTQ people.

She stepped up to the lectern first to deliver her remarks in op-position. I moved to her side, making sure that everyone could see my face as she delivered her hateful talking points. When she closed, it was my turn. I stepped up to the lectern and delivered the same remarks I had given in the Senate, an introduction of myself and my humanity.

And as I spoke—looking out at a sea of faces assembled to oppose my rights—I could see discomfort slowly cross the faces of many of the moms who had shown up to oppose our bill. It wasn't discomfort at being in the presence of a trans person. It was discomfort at the slow realization that the caricatures they had in their minds were unfounded. It was discomfort at the guilt they were clearly feeling as I outlined, in emotional terms, the simple fact that I am a human being. Their shame was visible.

Fortunately, the mobilization by the DFPC didn't stop the bill, at least at that point. The committee voted it through and to the full House by a vote of four to zero. Among those four was a moderate Republican woman from a suburb of Wilmington. I was surprised by her vote. My mother and I had met with her a few days prior, but despite her voting for sexual orientation nondiscrimination protections in 2009 and knowing my mother for years, we didn't anticipate that she would end up voting for our bill. Her comments in the meeting with my mother and me hinted as much. When she voted to move the bill out of committee and on to the full House, I was impressed. *Perhaps she's had a change of heart*, I thought.

As she packed up her papers from the dais, I walked up to her.

"Thank you for your vote, Representative."

"You're welcome, but I want you to know I won't be voting for the bill when it comes to floor," she replied.

"You know us. You know our family. Why can't we count on your support?"

She coolly informed me that "it's just too soon. You haven't done enough public education yet. The public isn't ready for this."

I tried to reason with her. "Representative, people are losing their jobs and their homes. Without these protections, transgender people don't feel safe stepping out publicly. It takes a huge risk to educate."

"It's just too soon."

"When you ask transgender people to allow a conversation to occur before you grant us equal rights, you are asking people to watch their one life pass by without dignity and respect," I said. "The question has been called, Representative. Either you vote for the protections or vote for discrimination. It is as simple as that."

"I voted for the gay rights bills," she offered in her defense.

"Then explain to me why you believe my brother should be protected but not me."

"I'm a good person," she said, almost pleading for forgiveness. She wanted me to absolve her of her guilt for voting no.

But I wouldn't give in. "Then show me that with your vote. Otherwise it's just words."

I walked away. Frankly, that representative was the least of my worries. The nerves among the Democratic ranks were fraying, particularly after witnessing the brigade of conservative women show up for the committee hearing. The calls and emails against the bill were starting to compete with the numbers on our side. Word was coming back to us that we were losing votes.

During the few excruciating days between the committee vote and the full House's vote, Mark, Lisa, and I met with our field team in the "war room" we had set up in a downtown Wilmington law firm to strategize and reach out to legislators on the fence. The usually calm and tranquil Lisa and Mark were clearly concerned about the vote count.

"She is very, very nervous," Lisa told me, referring to one legislator from downstate Delaware, the more conservative region of the state. If this legislator rescinded her support, we could anticipate that other, less progressive representatives in more conservative districts would flip, too. "I'm not sure if we can hold her. She was actually crying and told me, 'I gave Sarah my word.'"

I had met with that legislator during the whip count and she told me she was a firm yes, but that was before the anti-equality forces geared up for the fight and inundated her with calls and emails. Legislators are constantly required to balance their own beliefs with the positions of their constituents. On some issues, such as traffic patterns, it makes sense to exclusively represent the needs and interests of your district. But on other issues, legislators are elected to exercise their own judgment. That's why we elect our representatives instead of making every decision by referendum. What's right isn't always what's most popular. And when it came to what Andy called first principles—issues such as equal rights—there was just no excuse.

"Should I go meet with her?" I offered, thinking that if she was emotional about her commitment to me, then seeing me might reinforce her resolve.

Knowing the currency of "their word" among these legislators, Lisa said we should do the exact opposite. This was the moment that the whip count was built for.

"We don't want to give her a chance to go back on her word. If you meet with her, that gives her the opportunity to change her commitment. No," Lisa continued, "we need to make sure she feels the love and firm up her spine, but her standing commitment to you might be the one thing that keeps her on our side." So we had our field team work to increase the number of calls from our supporters in her district.

"If you see her, run the other way," Lisa remarked, only half-jokingly.

The other faction of votes we were slowly losing was from a group of older and middle-aged men in the Democratic caucus. Moderates one and all, these legislators were already uncomfortable with the issue at hand.

"I think we need to bring in the big guns," Lisa said, referring to the governor. We had held off on having Jack wade too deeply into the fight, reserving his political capital for a bind precisely like this one. I had served as our primary liaison to Jack, meeting with him routinely to update him on the vote proceedings and getting his advice on messaging and tactics.

I stepped out of the conference room and called him. "We need your help."

I traded calls with him all day, touching base each time he spoke with one of the shaky, moderate good ol' boys. A request from the governor carries a different weight than an ask from anyone else. Even for these legislators, being called directly by the governor wasn't a normal occurrence, and knowing that they would likely, eventually, need something from Jack made saying no all the more difficult.

"I don't know if I convinced him," he'd recount. "These guys are pretty conservative. Some of them are Democrats just because they grew up Democrats."

Nevertheless, the calls from the governor were intrinsically helpful, demonstrating that this was a priority for him. He usually didn't actively lobby on particular bills like this. We worked through the weekend on these legislators, trying to figure out any pressure points we could exert. But eventually we ran out of time.

•••

I woke up the day of the House vote, June 18, unsure that we had enough yeses to pass the bill. And just as my family and I prepared to leave for the forty-minute drive to Dover, I got a call from Mark.

"We're going to have to amend the bill," he told me. "There just aren't enough votes. Too many Democrats are scared over bathrooms."

*"Fuck."*

I started pacing around my family's living room as Andy waited on the couch next to my mom and my brother Sean, who had come down to be with us on what we had anticipated would be the final day. Even an acceptable amendment would mean we'd have to go back to the Senate to have it approve the new version of the bill. I worried that there wouldn't be the appetite to revisit what had been a contentious vote in the upper chamber.

"What's the amendment going to look like?" I asked.

"We're working on it now," Mark said, referring to the lawyers including himself meeting in a room at Legislative Hall to iron out

the language. "It would, one, clarify that gender identity 'may be demonstrated by consistent and uniform assertion of the identity or other
evidence that it is part of a person's core identity.' Two, it will allow
for 'reasonable accommodations' to be made in facilities like locker
rooms."

The first clause was in response to the continued argument that
a person might pretend to be transgender in order to enter a sex-
specific facility. It tried to reinforce what had been our messaging all
along, that trans identities are deeply held, not some "wake up in the
morning and decide to do it" kind of thing.

The language was left open-ended and vague so as not to require
presentation of evidence to, say, enter the restroom. It also contained
a key legal word: "may." "May," as opposed to "shall," makes the entire
sentence optional.

*Fine*, I begrudgingly thought.

The second clause was more of an actual compromise. While it
didn't impact restrooms, where there were already partitions, it did
allow for businesses with locker rooms to make accommodations
specifically for transgender people so long as we were still allowed
to utilize facilities consistent with our gender identity. For instance,
a curtain could be installed and they could request a transgender
woman change her clothes behind it within the women's locker room.

Transgender people are concerned for their privacy just like everyone else. Many of us are already petrified of being in a locker room,
and to the degree that we utilize them, we are in and out as quickly as
possible without drawing attention to ourselves. That a transgender
person could be separated from everyone else was stigmatizing.

The discomfort of others shouldn't be grounds for differential
treatment. And when you do that, when you single us out, it puts a
bull's-eye on our backs for harassment and bullying and reinforces
the prejudice that we are not really the gender we are.

The language in the amendment was discriminatory, but the choice
before me was between passing the rest of the bill with the language,

potentially having a worse amendment added, or passing no bill at all. And we needed to make a decision within the next two hours.

"Okay," I responded tentatively, thoroughly unsure of my decision to agree to the compromise amendment.

As Andy and I drove down to Dover, I had him review the language of the amendment. I needed a lawyer who was trans to take a look. I needed to know that it would work.

The amendment wasn't great, but he thought that the language might allow us to get around it in regulations, meaning that the wording was vague enough that we could interpret it after the fact in a way that left it relatively toothless, erasing as much negative impact as possible.

When we arrived at Legislative Hall, I walked into the House majority leader's office to see Mark, Lisa, and our prime sponsor, Bryon Short, huddled over a table. Everyone was dressed to the nines, wearing their "Sunday best" in anticipation of what they, too, hoped would be the final day of the battle, followed by a signing ceremony with the governor that evening. But now that we were going to have to go back to the Senate, it felt all for naught.

Mark walked toward me in a huff. "We have another problem."

A Democratic member, in his own misguided attempt to bridge the divide on the bill, had drafted his own amendment without consulting anyone. His potential amendment would make bathroom access determined by one's assigned sex at birth, meaning that if we ended up using restrooms at all, trans women would have to use the men's room and trans men would have to use the women's room.

"Are you fucking kidding me?" I screamed. My normally restrained use of the f-word was flowing freely that morning.

The amendment was about as discriminatory as you can get. It didn't exclude bathrooms from the protections; it effectively *banned* transgender people from restrooms consistent with our gender identity. It was similar to the policy that conservatives would pass in North Carolina three years later, but it was even worse because it wouldn't be limited to just government buildings like the future HB2. The proposed amendment would set discriminatory bathroom policies in every workplace and business impacted by the law.

The legislator in question wasn't a bigoted person, just ignorant on the topic. He was sincerely trying to help, but in his failure to consult with any of us and come in at the eleventh hour as a hero, he had drafted the worst amendment possible.

"We'll kill our own bill if this gets added, right?" I asked.

"We'll have to kill it," Mark confirmed.

The thought of losing the entire bill after coming so far was disheartening and incredibly frustrating, but permanently passing into law a ban on trans people in bathrooms consistent with our gender identity was poison. If transgender people can't access restrooms consistent with who we are, it becomes almost impossible to participate in public life. The other nondiscrimination protections wouldn't mean much if we couldn't leave our homes for more than two hours. And if we had the gall to use the restroom of our gender, the language would only embolden the already dangerous discrimination that transgender people face in those spaces.

"I think he'll pull the amendment if we can get to him," Mark said. "But if it gets filed"—referring to the process of formally submitting a bill or amendment to the House clerk—"it may become impossible to defeat the amendment. Republicans and moderate Democrats will jump on it, and they may have the votes to add it to the bill."

Simply put, if the bad amendment were made public, it would likely become an unstoppable force. We'd have to kill our own bill.

I raced to the representative's office to try to stop him. He wasn't there.

*Shit, he's filed the amendment,* I thought.

I ran down two flights of stairs to the basement room where legislators formally file bills and amendments with the nonpartisan clerk. I asked if they had seen the legislator in question.

"No."

*Thank God.*

As I ran back upstairs to his office, I came across my mom. Knowing the power of her presence, I told her to join me, and we both hurried to the legislator's office to camp outside. While we waited there, we filed our own amendment. Problematic as it may have been, it was one we could live with. Eventually, the representative I was waiting for arrived.

He's a jovial man, warm and friendly, supportive of the bill, but clearly failing to grasp the central controversy of the legislation.

"I heard about your amendment," I told him. I didn't want to seem argumentative, lest he get defensive. "And while I want to thank you for trying to help us out, we've drafted an amendment that we think will satisfy concerns."

A simple "thanks but no thanks."

"Oh, that's great," he said, completely unaware that he had almost destroyed our bill.

"So you won't be filing your amendment?" I hesitantly asked.

"I guess not! I was just trying to help. But if you all have a solution, that's great," he happily responded.

"Thank you! Thank you! We are so appreciative of your support for this bill." I jumped up to shake his hand. He was probably confused by my enthusiastic reaction, not knowing the heart attack he almost gave all of us. Now wasn't the time to pile onto him for his almost-fatal mistake.

I ran across Legislative Hall to meet Mark and Lisa outside the office of the leader of the Senate, Patty Blevins, one of the two women who sponsored our bill in that chamber. We sat in silence as we waited for her to get out of a meeting. We needed to inform her that there would be an amendment and that, should the bill make it through the House, it would have to come back to the Senate.

As supportive as Senator Blevins had been, we worried that her caucus would balk at the second vote and that political exhaustion would end up destroying our chances for getting the bill all the way to Jack's desk for his signature. The amendment was our only way to save the bill in the House, but it could end up destroying the bill anyway, if the Senate was feeling cowardly.

Finally, Blevins was ready to see us. Lisa explained that we were adding an amendment in the House and that we'd need to return to the Senate. We all held our breath as we waited for her to respond.

Blevins let out a frustrated exhale. We weren't sure whether she was frustrated that the House couldn't stand up to the bigotry of the bathroom arguments like the Senate had done or because the Senate would have to deal with the issue again.

Even though Lisa asked the question, Senator Blevins looked right at me.

"This is the most important bill we will vote on this year. If you can pass the bill through the House early enough today, we'll take it back up immediately tonight. If it passes the House too late today, we'll take it up first thing tomorrow." With that, she stood up from her desk and, continuing to look at me, said, "Don't worry. We won't let you down."

After three different fires that morning, all our ducks were in a row. We just needed enough Democrats to return to our side to give us a majority of twenty-one.

While the Democrats met upstairs, we waited patiently but nervously in the lobby. The House caucus meeting was dragging on and on. Minutes turned into hours. There were clearly disagreements.

I sat there and talked with Andy to pass the time, playing boring games like tic-tac-toe and hangman. I could hardly focus, my nerves overwhelming any other thoughts. As we played, I heard someone call my name.

"Sarah!"

I turned around to see an angry woman, maybe one of the moms who had showed up to the committee hearing the previous week.

"I just have one question for you. Have you had the surgery yet?"

"Um. I don't think that is any of your business," I replied, stunned.

To this day, it always amazes me when people think they are entitled to information about my body. I would never ask a stranger about their genitals. But I quickly got the sense that this woman didn't care if she was imposing, let alone offending me.

"Oh, I think it is my business," she insisted. "And if I ever see you in the women's bathroom with me, I'll chop it right off."

Still processing the initial rudeness, I almost didn't realize what the woman had just said to me: that she would assault me if she saw me in the restroom. Andy, who was still standing right next me, jumped in.

"Ma'am, that is completely out of line," he said, pulling me away from the situation and offering her the respect she was unwilling to offer us.

He walked me over to Lisa and Mark, and astounded and angry, I recounted the exchange to them.

"That woman threatened to violently assault you," Mark remarked, shocked at her comments. He suggested I report the woman to the Capitol Police.

I reluctantly decided to do it. I wanted a record of this woman's comments and threat of physical violence, but I was embarrassed and worried about the reaction I'd get from the officers. I didn't want to talk to them about my body, even if it was just in reference to the comments the woman had made. I was worried that they'd laugh at me.

Frankly, in the grand scheme of things, being laughed at by the police would have been a relatively tame encounter for a transgender person interacting with law enforcement. One survey found that among transgender people who had interacted with a police officer who thought or knew that they were transgender, 58 percent reported mistreatment. That might include officers unintentionally or intentionally disrespecting trans people's identities by calling them by the wrong pronoun. It could include profiling of trans women as sex workers, a presumed offense many people call "walking while trans."

For others, it could include violence, and for trans women of color, the risk of this treatment skyrockets.

These experiences led more than half of transgender people overall to say that they were uncomfortable asking the police for help. Even though my race, my social status, and the setting ensured that being laughed at was the most I had to worry about, I was still apprehensive.

But I stepped into the small office of the Capitol Police, right next to the metal detectors and X-ray machine at the entrance to the building. Word for word, I told the officers what had happened. I wasn't laughed at, but I didn't get the impression that the officers cared much for my report. They implied that the woman's threat was par for the course. They suggested that it was what I got for working publicly to pass a controversial bill.

*They're probably right*, I thought.

But as I walked over to the House chamber with Andy to wait in a part of the building away from the woman who'd threatened me, I realized the absurdity of that suggestion. No one should ever be threatened with violence for exercising their constitutional right to advocate to their elected representatives. I had come to terms with the physical risk of advocacy, but that doesn't mean I should have to tolerate it. The threat of violence shouldn't be part and parcel of advocating for your own dignity.

Was I surprised that someone threatened me? No. But the fact that it wasn't surprising should be an outrage. It further underscored the need for the bill and, in particular, for protections from discrimination and harassment in restrooms. It also brought front and center the risk of being the public face of a bill that came with the potential for retribution.

You can get lost in the fear that comes with that risk. It can consume you, but I just had to do my best to put it in the back of my mind. There was too much work to do and too many people for whom that fear was even more warranted.

Finally, at about three p.m., the caucus broke and we anxiously awaited any news on the preliminary vote they had taken in the meeting. A few minutes later, the speaker of the House entered through a side door of the chamber and caught my eye—he gave Mark, Lisa, and me a thumbs-up.

"We've got it," Lisa quietly but confidently affirmed.

*Thank God.*

We didn't want to celebrate too early; we still had the floor debate and then had to go back to the Senate. But with the speaker's confirmation, we could feel more than just cautiously optimistic.

When all the members had returned to the chamber, the House officially convened and took up our bill. Our prime sponsor, Bryon Short, the handsome small-business owner, did an excellent job answering questions on the legislation. He had perfectly retained all of the points we had laid out in a briefing book I put together the week before. Unlike in the Senate, we weren't going to spend time on our witnesses. We wanted to pass the bill as quickly as possible and, we hoped, to get it over to the Senate that same day.

Unfortunately, the Republicans weren't going to let us have it that easy. They knew that the longer they stalled, the less likely it would be that the Senate would take the bill up that night. And they knew that any delay would give the Delaware Family Policy Council a greater chance to destroy our slim majority in the Senate, however small their chance was.

After fielding the predictable questions—about bathrooms, locker rooms, liability, and other objections—Representative Short called up the compromise amendment. It passed with twenty-five votes, four more than a majority. It was a good sign, but it was still possible that several votes in favor of the amendment might not go with us on the overall bill.

After the amendment was officially added to the bill, one of the wavering Democrats, an older man named Earl Jaques, rose to ask a question. Jacques, pronounced "Jakes," looks like a television evangelist, with big 1980s glasses and slicked-back, thinning, jet-black hair. He hadn't historically been good on our issues.

"I just want to make clear, this amendment was meant to address the concerns some of us have raised regarding locker rooms?" he asked of Short, a softball question that would allow our sponsor to give him clear cover.

"Yes, sir," Representative Short responded, with a smile on his face demonstrating his appreciation for the easy question.

"I wasn't sure how I would vote on this bill," Jaques continued. "But last night I called my granddaughter. I told her we were considering this bill and I asked her if she had heard this word 'transgender.' She said, 'Of course, Grandpa. There's a transgender kid at my school.'

"And when I told her what the bill did, she was amazed that it wasn't already the law."

This was a refrain we heard several times in Legislative Hall. Legislators couldn't understand the issue, but when they spoke to their kids or grandkids, they understood that there was a clear side to be on.

A deeply religious man, Jaques closed: "And if Jesus can love the leper, then I can vote for this bill."

A faulty comparison to be sure, but given the circumstances, I'd most definitely take it. Jaques had made clear that his faith called him to the side of compassion, but his granddaughter had provided him with the answer.

Throughout the fight for equality, young people have been on the front lines of change. When President Obama endorsed marriage equality in 2012, he cited something very simple for his change of heart: conversations with his daughters. Earl Jaques's granddaughter had given him a glimpse into the future. That, coupled with his own faith and a little political cover, provided him with a clear path to yes.

Sensing the power of the moment and the permission that Jaques's comments gave to other Democrats to vote for the bill, Short called for a roll call. Out came our checklists and pens, ready to tally the votes. One by one, the clerk of the House called out the names of members of the State House.

My pen struck through the yes blocks next to each representative's name one at a time, but there was no need. We knew exactly who we needed by memory, having agonized over this list for weeks.

After forty-one names were called, the clerk read the results, "Twenty-four yeses, seventeen nos, zero representatives not voting, and zero absent."

Like in the Senate, the gallery exploded with cheers when the speaker gaveled the bill passed. We were on the brink of victory, but I felt like I couldn't exhale until the bill finally cleared its last hurdle and landed on Jack's desk. It still needed to go back over to the Senate for approval of the amended language.

While it was too late to go back to the Senate that night, Senator Blevins kept her word and brought the bill up for a vote first thing the next day. The delay by the Republicans in the House had meant that Andy wouldn't be able to be there for the final vote in the Senate, as he had been for every other vote, but I knew he was there in mind and spirit.

My parents and I sat in the same chairs we had occupied in the Senate two weeks prior. Mark, Lisa, and I all hoped that the debate would be short and we could pass the bill, as amended, without much debate. But when Senator Henry, again managing the bill on the Senate floor, tried to move things along rather quickly, the conservative Republicans, largely just out of spite, put a wrench in the operation. It was clear they were going to make us wait.

"The fact that this bill has come back before us is a sign that this should slow down," remarked one conservative senator. "The people aren't ready for this."

Karen Peterson, the openly gay senator who had held my hand while my parents testified the first time around, rose to speak. She was clearly annoyed that the Republicans were just delaying the inevitable and wasting everyone's time.

"Do you need Sarah to come back up so she can remind you of the discrimination faced by this community?" she asked rhetorically, basically saying, in so many words, "We can get Sarah back up here to lecture your asses again."

Senator Henry seized the moment and popped up from her chair. "Roll call, Mr. President."

For one final time, the clerk called the roll on SB 97. Confident that we still had our eleven votes, I looked up from my vote tally sheet and took in the moment. Each yes felt good—viscerally good—a needed affirmation for the trans people again gathered in the gallery. When each supportive legislator said "yes," each of us heard something far more personal and powerful. We heard, "I see you and I love you."

When we reached that eleventh vote, I let out a huge sigh of relief. *We did it. I can't believe it. We fucking did it.*

Almost no one thought we would succeed. Six months before, this bill seemed impossible to most. And people thought there was no way we could pass both marriage equality and trans protections. But over the last several months, hundreds of transgender people had written, called, and met with their elected representatives. Thousands of allies had spoken out. We had endured the indignity of the hate spewed at us throughout the process. And we had prevailed. Our voices had been heard. And our little state made history by taking one of the single largest leaps forward on equality of any state in one year.

Trans folks from across the state crammed into the governor's ceremonial office on the second floor of Legislative Hall with us to witness the official signing.

Jack walked in and gave me a big hug before taking his place at the lectern with the large seal of the state of Delaware on the front. I stood just behind him as he addressed the media and assembled crowd. "Today, we guarantee that our transgender relatives and neighbors can work hard, participate in our communities, and live their lives with dignity and safety."

As he continued to speak, he turned toward me. "I especially want to thank my friend Sarah McBride, an intelligent and talented Delawarean who happens to be transgender. Her tireless advocacy for passage of this legislation has made a real difference for all transgender people in Delaware."

He then closed his remarks and asked if I'd like to say something. I nodded and changed places with him.

"Today is a great day for Delaware and I could not be prouder to be a Delawarean. I'm grateful for the compassionate and courageous legislators who stood up for basic fairness for all people, for the governor and attorney general's support, and for the LGBT activists and allies whose tireless work made this day possible. After today's vote, transgender people now know that Delaware is a safe and welcoming state for everyone to live and work.

"Tomorrow, transgender Delawareans will wake up and finally know that the state they love loves them, too."

Announcing, "This is Senate Bill Ninety-seven," Jack began to sign the bill, declaring, "Now, with this signature, and effective immediately, it is, in fact, the law of Delaware."

The room burst into applause as Jack held up the newly enacted law. It had been less than a year since Jack and I met up on AU's campus and talked about the need for this bill. "Let's change that," he had said to me. And we did.

Five years after I stood behind him on the night he won the governor's office, I was now standing behind him as he signed the Gender Identity Nondiscrimination Act into law.

After his victory in 2008, standing beside him, I felt hope for the potential for change. Now, as he held up the newest law of the land, I felt a renewed sense of hope. But it was a stronger hope than I'd felt in 2008 with both Obama and Jack's elections.

It was a hope rooted in the progress that I had seen since coming out. And even though I had come out just a little more than a year before, and had been so frightened and so scared at the time, now I realized that I had never felt so hopeful. It was a hope displayed in the faces of the countless everyday LGBTQ Americans I helped welcome into the White House as guests of the president of the United States; of the openly gay Marine who proposed to his future husband in front of a Christmas tree just outside the Blue Room; of the transgender kids seen and affirmed by the nation's first Black president. It's the hope infused with the warmth of finding love with the type of person who made me want to be a better person in every single way. And it's a hope that was now etched into the law of my home state, the only one to enact both marriage and trans equality in the same year.

That night, my parents and I sat down for a celebratory dinner at a small neighborhood restaurant that we refer to as our "happy place."

"This was the hardest thing I've ever done in my life," my mom said. "But it's also the most fulfilling thing I've done in all my life."

"And we did it together, as a family," I toasted.

As our glasses clinked, I got a message from one of the transgender people who had helped us pass the bill. He was out with his family at a restaurant, too. "I'm out to dinner with my folks," it read. "And

*Jack holding up Delaware's newest law, the Gender Identity Nondiscrimination Act of 2013. Mark (right) and Representative Bryon Short applaud behind Jack. I had never felt more hopeful than I did at this moment.*

for the first time in my life, I feel like I belong here. This place finally feels like home."

When you've never felt like you really belonged somewhere, it's almost impossible to know what it will feel like to finally feel at home. As openly transgender people, we had taken the steps we needed to alleviate that constant feeling of homesickness when it came to our gender identity. But without social and legal equality, as tranquil as we may feel within our own identities, our souls still ache for a physical home, a place where we can feel welcomed, affirmed, loved, and seen. It's a desire at the center of our shared humanity as people and one that mirrors our own experiences transitioning.

And while no law will ever be a silver bullet, no bill can change every heart or open every mind, and no protection can stamp out every act of discrimination, these laws provide a foundation. That night, we were one step closer to justice.

# CHAPTER 8

# "Will you still love me?"

From coming out at the end of my term as student body president, to the experience at the White House, to the gender identity nondiscrimination bill in Delaware, it had been an eventful year. Honestly, I was exhausted. But as ready as I was to move back to Delaware and settle down, I also felt compelled to continue the fight.

In Delaware, I had seen the power of our voices to make change when they were matched with resources and institutional support. But throughout that effort, and particularly in the aftermath, I couldn't stop thinking about the people still denied the basic rights we finally had at home. Until every single LGBTQ person is protected by the law and treated with fairness, our fight isn't over.

A person's safety or dignity should not depend on their state or zip code. Equal means equal. But a majority of states still lacked the same basic yet critical protections from discrimination that we had just fought so hard for in Delaware. Arkansans and Texans and Virginians deserve these protections every bit as much as Delawareans and Californians and Minnesotans.

As has been the case in every effort for basic equality, there is only so much progress that can be achieved by going state by state. National laws, such as the Civil Rights Act and the Americans with

Disabilities Act, are necessary to ensure equal protection from discrimination regardless of whether you live in the most conservative rural county or the deepest blue city.

With the Delaware bill passed, I felt much more comfortable coming back to the state I love, but it was too soon. I didn't want to "get mine" and then go home, ignoring the widespread problems that remained. I wanted to help, in any small way that I could, to bring the change I worked on in Delaware to the nation. I knew that we could make strides at a national level, and I wanted to be a part of this important moment of change.

In D.C., there were hundreds of advocates spread across dozens of organizations doing just that at places like the Human Rights Campaign, the National Center for Transgender Equality, and the Center for American Progress. Andy, who was one of those advocates in D.C., was a big draw for me to stay in town. Throughout my work on the gender identity bill, we would spend weekends together, alternating between Delaware and D.C., where he was still working at the Center for American Progress on LGBTQ equality in health care. While we could have maintained a somewhat long-distance relationship—after all, Delaware and D.C. are only about two hours apart—both of us were ready to begin the next phase of our relationship under the same roof.

Delaware would always be there for Andy and me in the future, but for now we both wanted to be part of what was shaping up to be a historic moment in the movement for equality. With more and more states passing marriage equality bills, and the decision by the Supreme Court in June 2013 striking down the nationwide act that barred federal rights and benefits to legally married same-sex couples, the momentum on that issue was picking up steam.

Trans visibility was also increasing at a rapid rate. Laverne Cox burst into the mainstream consciousness with the premiere of *Orange Is the New Black* on Netflix. That year, 2013, was eventually dubbed the "transgender tipping point" by *Time* magazine. And D.C. felt like the center of it all.

I applied for a job on the same team as Andy at the Center for American Progress, the Washington-based think tank that has been called the "brain of the Democratic Party." CAP worked on every policy issue, from the social safety net to national security to immigration to LGBTQ equality. The offices are located two blocks from the White House and the four floors of roughly two hundred employees were filled with both past and future Obama administration and White House staffers.

Always a conscientious employee, Andy notified HR of his relationship with one of the applicants. They didn't see it as a problem; he wasn't a part of the hiring process and wouldn't be managing the role I was applying for. And after an interview with the incoming director of the LGBT Research and Communications Project, I was hired for my first full-time job as an advocate.

The team I would be working with was small, only about seven employees. I was the most junior, but given my experience in Delaware, my focus would be on our work advocating for LGBTQ nondiscrimination protections. The federal effort at the time centered on a bill known as the Employment Nondiscrimination Act, which everyone called ENDA. In Delaware, and in most of the states that had passed nondiscrimination protections, advocates had pushed for comprehensive laws that would protect LGBTQ people throughout life, from the workplace to housing and public spaces. But for the previous two decades, what was once a comprehensive civil rights bill had been whittled down to just protections in the workplace, the area of life with the most public support for passage of a law.

The theory was that because employment protections were the centerpiece of nondiscrimination laws, we'd focus on achieving those protections and then build out other protections incrementally, one bill at a time. First employment, then schools or housing, and then, down the road, public accommodations, which would include the dreaded discussion on bathrooms.

The approach had its drawbacks. First, access to a job does not begin and end with the application process; it also includes access to shelter, goods and services, and a quality education. For LGBTQ people to be able to live and thrive without fear of discrimination, it's not enough to be protected from nine a.m. to five p.m.

The strategy also presented a practical dilemma. Yes, employment protections are arguably the most important area of life, but if we pass the most popular part of our agenda by itself, the more controversial parts that we leave for later become even harder to pass. I wasn't inspired by this approach, but it was the strategy I was joining, and I was just one junior member of one team in one of a handful of organizations working on these issues. And in the end, I was thrilled to be able to continue to work on something that I was passionate about at one of the nation's leading advocacy organizations.

As I prepared for my first day at CAP, Andy and I moved into a new apartment together. Our new place was in the same building as his old apartment, but in making the decision and signing the lease together, it truly felt like *our* home. I had fallen in love with the apartment because of its gorgeous views of a park across the street. The large windows in our living room looked out over stately trees that parted in the middle to reveal a long grassy stretch frequently filled with picnickers and, on Sunday, a drum circle.

When I told friends that I would be going to work with Andy, several questioned, "Don't you think it will be hard to work with your boyfriend?" We'd now be living together, commuting together, and at CAP, our desks would be only about twenty feet apart. For some, it would be a recipe for disaster.

Both of us loved every minute of it.

Some of our colleagues didn't even know we were dating. We kept it as professional as possible at work, relegating our more coupley talk to Gmail and Facebook messages. Between calls with coalition partners and researching and writing on issues of equality, Andy would message me his traditional greeting of "Hellllllllew! Is a bean there?"

We did a pretty good job of keeping our professional lives separate from our home lives, focusing, as we always had, on cooking together and watching mindless reality shows to unplug at the end of the day. Other days, though, we would vent to each other about something outrageous or hilarious that had happened. After all, our jobs were a big part of our identities, and our work was inherently personal for both of us.

We squabbled and bickered, as any couple would, but the fights were always mild and quickly resolved. We were happy together and each inspired by our work. We capped each week with Andy's signature sangria on our rooftop and views of the Washington Monument and Jefferson Memorial.

It was a pretty good life.

Throughout the summer and early fall of 2013, as two young transgender people falling in love and fighting for the community we love, it seemed like we had a world of possibility and potential before us. I was twenty-three years old and I felt more fulfilled and happier than I'd ever imagined. But that all changed when Andy went in for a doctor's appointment in September.

Back in March, while we were on vacation in Barbados, Andy had started to complain about a sore on his tongue. Months went by, but the sore remained. By August, I was getting a little annoyed with him. The pain was beginning to sour his mood and I was agitated by the mood swings.

"Go see a doctor. You need to do something," I said, probably not fully grasping the pain he was in.

Eventually, I joined him at a small surgery center in suburban Washington for a short outpatient procedure to get rid of the sore. We had assumed that it was just a benign growth on his tongue, uncomfortable but easy to fix. It never occurred to us that the situation would be more than just a nuisance. Even after the doctor stopped the procedure early, saying that the growth was a bit larger than he'd anticipated, we were still completely unfazed.

"Young invincibles" is what they call people like Andy and me. The thought of illness for young people like us is so abstract that many don't even bother to purchase health insurance. While we were insured through our employer, the obvious never occurred to us. In retrospect, our obliviousness feels absurd.

A week after the aborted outpatient procedure, Andy went in for a follow-up that quickly crushed any feeling of invincibility. I was home in Delaware visiting my parents and we didn't expect it to be anything but a simple follow-up. Driving back to D.C. on my way to work, I got a call from Andy.

"Are you in a place to talk?" he asked me, his voice a bit shaky.

"I'm pulling into the garage at the office right now, but what's up?" I nervously asked.

"Um, just call me back when you aren't driving," he replied.

If the thought of serious illness had been nonexistent before, it all came rushing into my head at once. I immediately knew where this was headed.

"No, no, what's going on?" I pushed.

He paused for a moment and cleared his throat. "I have cancer . . ."

*I have cancer.* Three life-changing words you never want to hear.

He sounded completely defeated. Still driving down into the lower levels of my office's garage, I could barely say anything before my cell reception started to go. I got out of my car and ran upstairs to my boss.

When I reached her office, I was out of breath. My knees were weak and I felt like I was going to throw up. I told her I needed to leave. I was hesitant to share Andy's information, particularly since my boss was also his boss and I felt like it was his place to share that information, but I also needed to explain why I had to leave.

"Andy, uh . . . Andy, uhh . . ." It felt surreal to say the words myself. "Andy just found out that he has cancer."

I felt like my world was upside down. I felt like I was propelling forward without any idea of where and how Andy and I would land.

"Go!" my boss responded, immediately understanding my need to be by Andy's side.

I raced back to our apartment. It felt oddly still and calm as I burst in; the juxtaposition of my racing and cluttered mind and the deafening silence of the apartment was jarring. I walked through our small front hall and found Andy sitting on our couch, deep in thought, staring straight ahead. I ran over to him and gave him a big hug, interrupting an almost trancelike look on his face. He told me that the doctors had explained that the tests of the cells from the growth had come back and that it was malignant oral cancer—specifically, tongue cancer. They weren't entirely sure how much there was, but it was possible it had spread to the throat and the lymph nodes in the neck.

I think for anyone, when they hear that they or a loved one has been diagnosed with cancer, their minds almost immediately jump to the ultimate fear: death. I know mine did, and I'm sure Andy's went there as well. But we didn't talk about that possibility, at least not yet. Still, a dark conversation we had just a few weeks before was at the front of my mind as I tried to comfort Andy. Driving around doing errands, we had started talking about our biggest fears, and both of us had expressed just how scared of death we were.

"No, you don't understand, Bean," he told me as I drove us to Target. "The degree that I'm scared of death is unique. Some people are resigned to fate, but I'm not. I think about death a lot, more than most people."

Sitting on the couch in our apartment a few weeks later, he didn't have to remind me of that conversation or verbalize that fear. It was self-evident.

As Andy called his parents and stepparents in Wisconsin to tell them the frightening news, I stepped out of the apartment and called my parents.

"Oh my God," my mom exclaimed, and began crying. "Call Sean," she said. My older brother had recently begun working as a radiation oncologist at Memorial Sloan Kettering in New York City, one of the nation's premier cancer hospitals. Of all the focuses Sean could have decided on, he happened to be specializing in head and neck cancer: the very kind of cancer Andy had just been diagnosed with.

Pacing outside our apartment building's back door and under a bright, flickering orange fluorescent light, I peppered Sean with a million questions—some heavy, others more superficial.

"Uh, will Andy lose his hair?"

"Probably not."

While he couldn't provide me with too many specifics because he hadn't seen Andy's records, he told me that the likeliest path forward would be surgery, followed by radiation and chemotherapy. He described the surgery, a likely significant dissection of Andy's tongue, which would require a graft from his arm to rebuild the removed part.

"Is he going to be able to talk after that?!"

"Most likely, but it depends on how far the cancer has spread and exactly where it is in the tongue."

*Most likely,* I thought. *Jesus Christ.*

I was scared to ask *the* question that was at the front of my mind. I was afraid of the answer. All of my questions danced around the central issue. I couldn't ask, "Is he going to die?"

What if I ended up knowing more about Andy's future than he did? What if the prognosis wasn't good? My role now was to be the moral support for Andy as he underwent treatment. And I knew that if I appeared pessimistic in the least, he would be able to sense it.

"I don't know what to do, Sean!" I felt completely overwhelmed, a feeling that I'm sure paled in comparison to the fear that was consuming Andy.

"Have Andy's records sent to me. I'll take a look and I'll see if I can get him into Johns Hopkins," he reassured me, referring to the major hospital in Baltimore that, like Memorial Sloan Kettering in New York, was known as a leader in cancer treatment.

The next few days were oddly normal as we began to scout out treatment options. Andy and I went in to work. We cooked and watched our shows. But throughout everything, the cloud of cancer hovered, both of us bracing for an impending storm.

Sean managed to get us into Hopkins. As we drove the thirty minutes up to Baltimore for our consultation before surgery, we knew how lucky we were to have access to the resources and skills that would no doubt aid Andy's chances at a successful treatment.

"This is already so scary. I can't imagine having to do this without Sean's help and guidance," Andy told me.

Just like with my coming out two years before, Sean had rushed into the situation as a reassuring voice of support. Now he was help- ing to shepherd my boyfriend through what already seemed to be very serious cancer. Almost no one has an ally like Sean to help them get the best possible care available; many do not even have access to health insurance, something that took the cost of Andy's treatment down from well over a hundred thousand dollars to a few copays.

Fortunately, by the time of our appointment, we were feeling opti- mistic that with aggressive and competent treatment, Andy's cancer was curable. I had finally mustered up the courage to ask Sean, who by now had seen Andy's records, what his chance of survival was.

"Eighty to eighty-five percent," he cautiously offered.

I felt good about our odds.

Through our work, Andy and I were keenly aware of the discrimi- nation and mistreatment that transgender people often face in medi- cal settings. In one survey, 70 percent of transgender people reported experiencing some form of discrimination in a health-care setting, including health-care professionals refusing to touch patients. Not every health professional knew we were trans, but some figured it out, and others needed to be told.

We were also cognizant of Johns Hopkins's deeply troubled his- tory with trans people. Once a leader on gender-affirming treatment, in the 1970s and '80s the psychiatric department had come under the control of a right-wing extremist, Dr. Paul McHugh, who, while hav- ing no expertise in gender or sexuality research, harbored strong negative feelings toward LGBTQ, and particularly trans, identities. He would not only close down Hopkins's work on transition-related care, he would also go out of his way to advocate *against* the rights and dignity of trans people, calling us "caricatures" and "mad."

While McHugh, now much older, was no longer the head of the department, he was still teaching at the institution and a towering figure in its work. What if our providers had been acolytes of Paul McHugh's? What, if anything, might that mean for Andy's treatment?

So while stressing and worrying about all the typical things patients and their loved ones must deal with when facing such a serious diagnosis and invasive surgery, with each new doctor, and later with each new nurse, we wondered, *What do they think of transgender people? Will they treat us differently if or when they find out?*

As burdensome as these worries were, we decided that the risk was certainly not large enough to give up on the generally superior care that Andy would likely receive at Hopkins. After all, even without the Hopkins history, every interaction at any hospital would carry with it at least some of the fear we felt as we walked into the waiting area for our appointment.

After an hour's wait, we were finally taken back to meet with Andy's lead doctor, a surgeon and the chair of Hopkins's head and neck department. As he began talking, he immediately put our nerves at ease. Like Sean, he was a confident and reassuring figure.

He informed us that Andy would undergo the extensive surgery we had already learned about. The left half of his upper tongue would have to be removed and replaced with skin from his forearm. The cancer had, thankfully, not spread to his throat, but it had spread to some lymph nodes. The surgeon would have to remove a decent number of lymph nodes from Andy's neck, although the total number would be up in the air until they were actually in surgery.

"Will I be able to speak?" Andy asked, concerned with the ramifications that not being able to talk would have on his career prospects as an advocate.

"You may have a small impediment, but I think you will regain approximately ninety percent of your current speech abilities," the doctor told us.

Again, 90 percent was better than the alternative.

The surgeon also informed us that the neck surgery would make Andy's neck cave in a bit, and it would appear skinnier than it did now. And there would be a large rectangular wound, and later scar, on his forearm. Both of us were less concerned with the cosmetic outcomes than we were with the questions about his speech and, of course, his life.

"We can get you in for surgery in about two weeks. We don't want to wait much longer," the surgeon told us.

Andy took a deep breath. "Okay."

Over the next several days, Andy began to prepare for his extended absence from work. After surgery, he would be out of work for his recovery and then, again, for the six weeks of extensive daily radiation and weekly chemotherapy infusions.

He didn't like the idea of missing so much work. He didn't want to be left focusing solely on his cancer. He wanted, needed, distractions. So in the lead-up to surgery, I tried to give them to him. We went out to dinner most nights, knowing that he would be relegated to Ensure and milkshakes for a while after surgery and would have to relearn how to eat with his "new tongue."

Just a week before surgery, we went out for our last big date before our lives would be consumed with treatment. Sean and I had been asked to speak at the Human Rights Campaign's National Dinner, a three-thousand-person gala for the LGBTQ civil rights group that had helped us pass our gender identity bill in Delaware. The organization was excited for our family to be able to talk about the good work HRC had done on behalf of trans rights in Delaware. And the image of an out trans woman and her openly gay brother onstage together provided the perfect metaphor for the larger movement for LGBTQ equality: gay and trans people standing as one family.

Sean and his husband, Blake, came down from New York. I invited my ex-girlfriend Jaimie, the one who, in breaking up with me, had initiated the chain reaction that led to my coming out, as well as one of my best friends since childhood, Read. And, of course, Andy.

Andy and me at the Human Rights Campaign's National Dinner. Andy put on a brave face as he prepared for major surgery to remove his tumor.

It was a big deal for us to be asked to speak at the dinner. It was the biggest LGBTQ equality event in the country and it would be my first time on a national stage of that kind. I had attended the dinner the year before with White House staffers during my internship but had only dreamed that one day I would be able to stand onstage at the Washington Convention Center.

Even though I knew Andy wanted distractions, I still worried that the dinner would be too much. I feared that I was being selfish.

"Are you sure you are okay doing this?" I asked him. "I can cancel."

"No. This can be our last hurrah before, ya know . . . everything," he responded.

Maybe he genuinely wanted to go. He certainly wanted to get out of the apartment. But I also got the feeling that he didn't want to come between this opportunity and me. He was always so supportive of my goals.

"Plus, it's a great opportunity for me to wear a bow tie," he added with a wink.

Sure enough, that Saturday night, he sported a dapper tux and a bright green bow tie. We were led to our table, near the front of a room that stretched at least two football fields across. I was seated between Andy and a personal inspiration of mine, civil rights legend Julian Bond. Bond had been a leader of the Student Non-Violent Coordinating Committee with John Lewis during Selma and later helped found the Southern Poverty Law Center, the nation's leading hate watchdog group. He was speaking that evening as well.

Attorney General Eric Holder, a staunch defender of LGBTQ rights in the Obama administration, opened the evening. Chad Griffin, HRC's president, gave a rousing speech. And finally, it was time for Sean and me to go onstage. I was excited but could feel the butterflies building.

The crowd was fired up from a mix of our movement's success and the evening's remarks, along with some help from alcohol. We waited backstage as Chad finished up his remarks and the "voice of God" came over the loudspeaker.

"Please welcome Sarah and Sean McBride."

Music started playing and we walked out onto the stage. As I stepped up to the lectern, I could hear the song behind the applause. Purely by chance, it was "Safe and Sound," the same song Andy had played for me in the car on our first date.

I had never addressed such a large audience. The general assembly in Delaware paled in comparison. My legs were shaking from nerves. I began my speech, consciously trying to speak slowly and clearly as I recounted my experience coming out at AU and the love and support my family had given me. I talked about our fight for legislation in Delaware and the historic year we had just experienced, with both marriage equality and gender identity nondiscrimination protections passing.

I could hardly see anyone in the audience. It looked like I was speaking to a sea of black except for the occasional light that reflected off glasses, jewelry, or some of the shinier clothing. And just to my right, a few tables back, my eye caught Andy's green bow tie.

The tone of my speech was triumphant. I talked about how excited I was for the future. I spoke about how fortunate I felt. But in reality, in that moment, I didn't feel any of those things. And I knew Andy didn't, either.

The words rang hollow for me that evening. I wasn't excited. I wasn't feeling particularly fortunate. I worried that my positive tone on the stage would make Andy feel even more alone in his struggle and sadness. And I couldn't shake the feeling that this might be the last night of its kind for the two of us.

When I returned to our table, Andy greeted me with a kiss. He squeezed my hand and said, "You were so fantastic. I'm so proud of you, Bean."

His eyes were warm, but I could see the anxiety lurking behind them. For both of us, the end of that speech marked the beginning of a new chapter, one neither of us were fully prepared for. We were focused on the first step, surgery, but we knew that would be only the beginning of a grueling several months at best.

Ten days later, at five a.m. in a dark hotel room in Baltimore's inner harbor, we woke for Andy's surgery. Or, more accurately, I woke up. Andy hadn't slept a wink the night before, and as I rolled over to say good morning, I saw him sitting up and staring blankly into the darkness.

"What if I can't talk anymore?" he asked. Clearly, he'd been crying. "Will you still love me?"

"Of course, my love," I told Andy in the darkness. "But it really doesn't sound like that will happen."

I was hopeful it wouldn't come to that, but the possibility had been on my mind. Our boss at the Center for American Progress and I had already started discussing the possibility. "If it comes to it, we'll all learn ASL," she had suggested, referring to American Sign Language. "We probably should, anyway."

We met my mom; Andy's mom, Ardis, and stepdad, Richard; and his aunt Carolyn in our hotel lobby and made our way to the surgery center at the Hopkins hospital campus. For the whole drive, Andy never stopped holding my hand. His palms were sweaty and his grasp tightened as we got closer to surgery. By six-thirty a.m. we were all sitting around Andy's bed in the surgery prep center. Carolyn and I exchanged jokes with Andy, who seemed to be in surprisingly good spirits. Soon enough, the jokes ended when the surgeon entered and approached Andy's bed.

He asked Andy how he was feeling, then swiftly changed course to share some developments.

"Based on scans from yesterday, it looks like the cancer has spread to parts of the other half of your tongue. So we are going to have to remove more than we anticipated."

Andy's eyes widened at the news. "Does that change the prognosis for my speech?"

"I'm afraid it may. We won't know for sure until we are in surgery, but it's difficult to say"—no pun intended, I'm sure—"what your speech will be like at this point."

Andy looked at me with tears welling in his eyes, clearly shaken at the sudden realization that these few moments might be his last with the ability to speak. But there was no time to digest the news. Almost immediately, he was wheeled into what would be a ten-hour surgery. The surgeon had just dropped a bomb on us. As we watched the back of Andy's bed turn the corner, we knew we couldn't do anything to calm him.

The next ten hours felt like an eternity. I tried to do some work. I texted his friends and posted updates on his Facebook page per his instructions, but it was nearly impossible to focus on anything as we waited in a bright semiprivate alcove in the larger waiting room. I knew Andy was in skilled hands, but my heart was in my throat the whole time.

Halfway through, the surgeon came out to give us an update. He was confident they had gotten all of the cancer in the removal of the tongue and lymph nodes. He was now turning Andy over to his colleague, a reconstructive surgeon, to take skin from the arm and rebuild the tongue.

Another four hours went by. Ardis played on her iPad. Richard slept in his chair. Carolyn and my mom chatted. I could only send the occasional email as my eyes kept wandering to check the time and I wondered when we'd get the next update. Finally, the reconstructive surgeon came in and informed us that the surgery was complete.

"How does it look, Doctor? What do you think about his speech?"

Ardis, Richard, Carolyn, and my mom looked up anxiously.

"I think he'll regain, functionally, his ability to speak, just with an impediment."

*Thank God.*

This was the first moment when the potential news felt more positive than negative. Despite my concern that everything that could go wrong would go wrong, the news about Andy's speech was a welcome alternative to my sneaking pessimism.

They wheeled Andy into a room in the intensive care unit and the five of us were taken up to see him. Anyone who has ever visited a loved one in the hospital knows the feeling in the pit in your stomach as you prepare to see someone after an accident, illness, or surgery. I wasn't quite sure what to expect, but I was anxious to see him.

He was just waking up from the anesthesia as we entered his room in the ICU. The lower half of his head and his new tongue were significantly swollen. He had staples up the side of his neck and a large bandage over his left arm. He was hooked up to a million machines and tubes, including a feeding tube through his nose and a tracheostomy tube that went up his windpipe and exited through his lower neck, allowing him to breathe as his still-swollen, rebuilt tongue blocked the airway in his mouth.

"You look great, Bean," I told him with a smile. "They say they got all the cancer, and the doctor says that you should get pretty much all of your speech back."

He couldn't change the expression on his face, but he managed to lift up his right hand and give me a thumbs-up.

We had made it this far. The recovery would clearly be long and intensive, with the torture of not really being able to communicate through his swollen tongue exacerbating his frustrations. But there was certainly a light at the end of the tunnel.

Hopkins would keep him for about a week, first in the ICU and then, later, in a private room in a more general recovery wing. We got him a whiteboard so that he could communicate with us, and he had me send pictures of him with messages of love and thanks to a few friends and family, including Sean. He didn't want anyone to worry.

Over the next seven days, with the help of a stream of dedicated nurses, Andy's physical activity increased as his tongue decreased in size and he attempted a little labored speech. Some days I'd sit by his side doing work: Over the previous month, the Employment Nondiscrimination Act had begun to move through a committee in the U.S. Senate and had made its way to the Senate floor.

As he watched daytime television, I'd sit by his bedside on my laptop, crafting memos and research papers for senators debating many of the same issues we had just forged through in Delaware. ENDA had never passed the U.S. Senate, and while the prospects for passing the House were slim—very slim—we hoped we could at least push the bill through the upper chamber of Congress, building momentum for eventual passage down the road.

A few days after surgery, Andy's family returned to Wisconsin, but in their place came friends and colleagues making pilgrimages to Andy's hospital room to hang out, something that made the days bearable for him. The extended stay meant a nearly constant rotation of nurses. And with each new nurse, the fears that surfaced during that first visit to Hopkins came back. Every time a new nurse would walk into his room, Andy would glance at me with a simple look that said: "Can you tell them?"

For practical reasons, it was helpful for them to know that he was transgender. In the split second after I told them, I'd study their facial expressions for even the subtlest sign of discomfort. Discomfort can, even subconsciously, lead to mistreatment. Fortunately, every nurse was a consummate professional, and while we were nervous each time, they all offered no suggestion that they had a problem with who we were.

A week after surgery, I got the call that both Andy and I had been hoping for: He would be discharged, probably that afternoon. I left work, which I had returned to the day before, and hurried up to Baltimore to meet Andy in his room in the general recovery wing at Johns Hopkins. He would be released from the hospital in stable condition but still with the feeding tube, the large, shallow wound on his arm, and the tracheostomy tube. The tube had to be cleaned with an ominous gray suction machine every few hours to ensure air could pass through and he could breathe.

Afternoon came and went, and we still waited to be discharged. The hospital eventually told us that the supplies for Andy's home care were not yet available. Yet they were ready to discharge him, so a nurse gathered up as many supplies as possible onto a cart and wheeled it into Andy's room.

"This should hold you over until the rest of the supplies arrive and are shipped to your apartment," he told us.

Andy and I both looked in terror at the cart, overflowing with clear plastic bags and containers filled with replacement tubes, food bags, wound dressings, and more. The nurse, clearly overworked and trying to do his best for us in an unfortunate situation, quickly ran me through the steps to clean Andy's tracheostomy tube, dress his wound, and change his food.

By now it was dark outside. Andy was giddy with the prospect of getting out of the hospital. I felt woefully unprepared but knew how badly he wanted to get home. And admittedly, I did, too. So I packed his bag and helped him dress.

In total, Andy had four tubes coming out of his upper body: the feeding and trach tubes, plus two drainage sacks coming out of his neck and collar, which presented a challenge in getting him fully dressed. After a few tries to get his arms through the sleeves, I draped his button-down shirt over his back, clipped one button closed, and attached the drainage sacks onto the shirt with pins. He looked disheveled, but it would do.

Pushing the cart of supplies down the hallway, I looked back at Andy, who was a pace behind me, and noticed a small amount of light red blood coming from his mouth. I panicked, ran and got the nurse, and brought him over to Andy.

"Don't worry," the nurse reassured us. "A little bit of blood is normal. Only be concerned if the blood coming out of his mouth is thick and dark."

We both exhaled and made our way slowly down to the waiting car. I drove excessively slow on Interstate 95, like a brand-new parent with her baby in the car. Eventually, we pulled up to our apartment, where we found one of Andy's best friends, Wesley, waiting for us. He helped us carry the supplies to our apartment, which Andy greeted as though he had been gone for years. He was finally home and ready to begin his recovery on his own terms.

Except now the constant light-red blood had turned into dark, thick blood, softly gushing from his mouth.

*Fuck.*

I called the resident-on-call at the hospital, who could, understandably, provide little guidance based on my description. I then called Sean, who recommended, as a precaution, that I take Andy to the emergency room.

Wesley and I hurriedly helped Andy back down to our car, and I drove the short distance to George Washington University Hospital, a central D.C. hospital known as the primary emergency location for the president. We were home from Johns Hopkins less than fifteen minutes and now already on our way to another hospital.

As we pulled up to the entrance, Andy was covered in blood, still partly shirtless, and overwhelmed with tubes. The guard at the driveway was clearly shocked by the sight of Andy and urgently told us, "LEAVE THE CAR. GO STRAIGHT THROUGH."

We waded through the crowd in the waiting room, hundreds of patients and family members staring at this young man and wondering, *What the hell happened to this kid?* His weakness was evident in his walk. It was more shuffling his weight from his left to right foot and back again, lifting each foot about an inch off the ground and forward slightly as he waddled through the crowd. A nurse who saw Andy's condition pushed a wheelchair behind him just in time for Andy to collapse into it. Still conscious but very weak, Andy was ushered past the waiting room and sent straight into the emergency room.

A cancer patient being treated by an emergency room doctor is like a criminal defendant being represented by a corporate attorney. The cancer patient's experience and needs are so far outside of the ER doctor's wheelhouse that urgent care and oncology might as well be two different professions. Each of the young emergency room doctors, working the night shift, had a deer-in-the-headlights look as they saw Andy.

Since hospitals do not share records, we explained every aspect of Andy's recent medical history to the doctors to provide them with all potentially relevant information. Andy's tongue was so swollen, and half of it so new, that I mostly spoke for him. Several hours went by as the doctors monitored his condition. Eventually, the bleeding stopped and they were able to determine that his new tongue was just so swollen that his teeth had lacerated it, causing the bleeding.

By now it was one a.m., and Andy's tracheostomy tube hadn't been cleaned since the early evening—significantly more time than Hopkins told me was okay. We asked for help. The doctors and nurses looked around but could not find any suction equipment, which was strange, considering we were in a hospital. His breathing still seemed okay, and, eventually, at three-thirty a.m., Andy was discharged and we returned to our apartment, where we went straight to the bathroom to try to suction his tracheostomy tube. I unpacked the equipment as he sat down on the edge of the toilet.

The suction machine looked like something out of the late 1980s. It was a dark gray plastic machine with a small motor and a clear plastic container. Coming out of the container was a long translucent tube that was meant to be stuck down the pipe coming out of the makeshift hole in Andy's neck. I tried to push it down, but it wouldn't go.

I tried again. Nothing.

I finally pushed it in a little, but the suction tube wouldn't go very deep. I was clearly doing something wrong, but I couldn't remember all of the instructions. It had been a stressful whirlwind of a week, and I had been awake for nearly twenty-four hours. I was just out of college, and it felt like this entire person's life was in my hands. No nurses. No doctors. And it was becoming slightly harder for him to breathe.

I kept worrying he would stop breathing entirely. That he would die on me right then and there in our bathroom. *What if he stops breathing because of me?* I thought. He was clearly scared and beginning to get worried.

And then I lost it. My vision became tunneled, like it had when I'd first found out about his cancer, and I was pulled into a panic attack. I was so excited to have him home, but it was now hitting me just how hard this was going to be. I leaned back against the wall in our bathroom, fell to the floor, began to cry.

"I can't do this! I can't do this!"

I had tried to be strong for Andy, and I knew his plight was much worse than mine, but it had become too much. The stress of the last twenty-four hours, of the last week since his surgery, and of the last few weeks since his diagnosis was too much. I didn't know what to do.

In his desire to be independent and in control, he had expressed a desire to not ask his parents or family to help take care of him. Initially, I hoped to honor that wish. Maybe I could have, but during this crisis, my fears and stress took over.

"I need help, Andy. I can't do this on my own," I said still sobbing.

Sitting on the edge of the toilet, covered in blood, Andy looked at me with tears in his own eyes and just calmly said, as clearly as possible, given the state of his tongue, "It's going to be okay, my Bean. I'll do whatever we need."

We sat in silence for a little while as I caught my breath. We messed around with the suction equipment and his tube a little bit more and eventually figured out, through trial and error, the proper way to keep his windpipe clear.

I helped Andy to the bed, where we had placed six or seven pillows so he could sleep sitting up. I walked into the living room and fell asleep on the couch. By now it was four-forty-five a.m.

I slept, fitfully, for a few hours. Every so often, I woke up just long enough to listen to make sure Andy was still breathing.

I figured Andy had gone to sleep, too. In reality, he was up writing a note. Just as the sun came up, he took out a pen and three pieces of orange, brown, and tan construction paper and began writing a letter he never actually gave to me. I found it several years later.

"My darling," it started. "Yesterday was so hard. God, if every day were like that, who would want to do it?! But, all days won't be like this." He went into the logistics of how we'd make it all work, from the help of friends and family to bathing. "I can also have help from whoever to wash my hair and then I can clean my little tush," he wrote about washing himself. He talked about radiation treatment and his food intake. And then he closed with:

> Probably your biggest burden now is emotional. And that is living. . . . But most days will be good ones.
> This is my way of saying that I know this is horrible and has been a

*disruption. But we will have more normal days and I believe this will*
*not need to strain you too far beyond my emotional support needs.*

 *I can't repay what you already gave me in kindness, support, worry,*
*hope, strength, or love. But I will try with every bit of me to reply*
*with love, generosity, kind gestures, and support.*

 *This is, has been, and will be hard. But we will thrive by calling*
*in our forces and not just being a two-player version of our lives*
*for 2013 through 2014. Please don't give up. Please don't think you*
*aren't already always giving yourself to others (especially me)—*
*because you are succeeding! And we will come out of this stronger,*
*happier, and more in love than ever. I really believe that. I adore you*
*with every one of my nonsquamous cells.*

—*Andy Bean*

The note was his plea for me to stay with him.

I had never thought, for an instant, of leaving his side while he went through this. When I said, "I can't do this! I can't do this!" I had meant "I need help." But he had heard "This relationship is too much for me."

So on his first night home from the hospital, sitting up in our bed at sunrise, in pain and still scared, Andy worried that his best friend, girlfriend, and caregiver was about to leave. I shiver at the added fear I must have caused him. Yet he responded with patience, love, and understanding. That was Andy.

# CHAPTER 9

# "It hasn't taken away my voice."

Our apartment was now littered with medical equipment. Bandages and ointments spread across the kitchen table. Cans of liquid food for his feeding tube. Suction equipment for his tracheostomy tube. And without a home nurse, Andy's recovery was a full-time job for both of us.

*I don't know how parents, let alone single parents, do it,* I routinely thought to myself.

Because of the relative newness of both our relationship and my job at CAP, I didn't qualify for family leave. As flexible as they were, I still had to go to work most days. Fortunately, our family and friends came through in a big way. Andy's aunt Carolyn, a nurse by trade, flew back to D.C. for a few days to lend a hand. My mom came down from Delaware one weekend. And the community of friends that Andy had amassed over the previous few years took turns staying at our apartment with him while I went in to the office.

Many of our chosen family in D.C. were gay or trans themselves, and their support exemplified why we so often refer to LGBTQ people as the "LGBTQ community." It was a structure of mutual support and care that became a hallmark of "the community" during the 1980s and '90s, the height of the AIDS epidemic.

Ignored by their government, often rejected by their families, in the closet at work, and faced with a rapidly spreading deadly disease, LGBTQ people had stepped up for one another to provide support and care while, in many cases, multiple friends within the same chosen family passed away from complications due to AIDS. We were seeing just a glimpse of that rainbow of support that helped so many in the community get through such a tragic time.

Even with the help, I shudder to think what would have happened had we worked for an employer that did not offer employees like Andy paid medical leave and had not been so flexible with my own schedule. Most Americans are not afforded similar benefits, and they may not have the network of friends able to step in, either. An illness should never mean the loss of an income, even temporarily, but in many cases it does.

The days after surgery were a blur of anxiety. I'd wake up several times each night to listen for Andy's breathing.

"I worry something will get stuck in his trach tube and he'll stop breathing," I told my mom after a particularly fitful night of sleep.

Every two hours, Andy needed a certain cocktail of medications and his tube suctioned. We'd change and dress his arm wound. I'd help him dress and bathe.

"Can you wash my tush?" he'd sheepishly ask me while sitting in the tub, laboriously saying each word with his now-shrinking but still-swollen tongue. I could tell he felt bad that at twenty-seven years old he was asking his twenty-three-year-old girlfriend to bathe him. I think he worried that it infantilized him and removed the romance from our relationship.

But honestly, his strength and humor through it all only made me fall in love with him even more. We were going through life-and-death battles most couples our age never imagine, but it brought us closer, binding us together in unique ways. It felt like we had been together for decades. And the experience aged both of us.

Our spirits lifted each passing day as he regained his strength and made progress toward feeling like his old self. A week after coming home, his feeding tube and tracheostomy tube came out. Three days after that, he gained the strength and dexterity to finally put a shirt on himself. Jubilant, he posted on Facebook:

> I really didn't want my next few months to be too much of this, but it will be. Sorry y'all. I just put on a shirt for the first time since surgery, after feeling so embarrassed about being unable to dress properly for Dr's appointments and a visit to the ER. I am so incredibly happy I cried and scared Sarah. Oops!

Our eyes were always focused on the next step of recovery, and for someone as autonomous as Andy, each step toward independence felt like reaching the highest mountaintop. But we also made sure to marvel at the smallest victories. For instance, Andy was incredibly proud of himself when, on medication that made him drowsy, he managed to stay awake at the movie theater on our first date night since surgery.

Or the time we went out to our favorite neighborhood restaurant for his first solid-food meal with his "new tongue." Always in the mood for breakfast food, he conquered a plate of eggs, bacon, hash browns, and, his favorite, pancakes. I'll never forget the smile on his face when he finished. The simplest pleasures became moments of personal triumph, but more than anything else he was just excited to be gaining his independence back.

I can't help but wonder what role his trans identity played in his disdain for feeling dependent. I know I personally hate to ask for help, in part because I want to prove to society that I can be strong and independent. And while dependency is not a sign of weakness in the least—in fact, it can be a sign of strength—I've talked to other trans folks who avoid asking for help for that very reason: the fear that asking for or needing help will reinforce the prejudices and negative stereotypes many people have about those of us who are trans. I know I find myself overcompensating to show society that anything they can do I can do, too.

Andy, it seemed, was doing it at home as the patient. And as the caregiver, I was doing it at work, diving into my job to prove that I could do it all. Fortunately, there was a brief break in treatment before Andy would begin radiation and chemotherapy, giving him a bit of a respite, physically and emotionally. The break also happened to occur at the same time as the Employment Nondiscrimination Act reached the U.S. Senate floor. ENDA had failed by one vote in the mid-1990s, back when Ted Kennedy was the prime sponsor. Since then, Kennedy had passed away and handed the torch to a progressive senator from Oregon, Jeff Merkley.

Even though it was already an incremental, piecemeal bill— focusing only on employment—it was watered down even further with an overly broad religious exemption that would provide religiously affiliated nonprofits (which, in many cases, provide lifesaving services to the public) with a special license to discriminate.

It was an exemption not afforded to those same nonprofits for discrimination based on race, sex, or national origin. Even if you are affiliated with a religious institution, when you go into the public marketplace, even as a nonprofit, you shouldn't be able to discriminate. A nurse at a Catholic hospital shouldn't fear being fired from her job because she marries her wife. A custodian at a religiously affiliated senior center shouldn't lose his job because he comes out as transgender.

Due to changing attitudes and the political makeup of the Senate, 2013 was the first year in decades that ENDA had any chance of passing. CAP, the Human Rights Campaign, the National Center for Transgender Equality, and other organizations led the charge with the public, while Merkley masterfully shepherded the bill through the archaic rules of the Senate. The bill was dead on arrival in the Republican-controlled House, but passage through the Senate would help build momentum and demonstrate the bipartisan support for LGBTQ-inclusive nondiscrimination protections. It would be a symbolic victory, reflecting the often-glacial pace of progress in Congress.

While the Democrats controlled the Senate, a supermajority of sixty votes was necessary for passage, meaning we needed at least five Republican votes to reach the sixty-vote threshold. Still, when the Senate passed the watered-down ENDA by a vote of sixty-four to thirty-two, the bipartisan result reflected a sea change in popular opinion, particularly on trans rights. Six years earlier, gender identity had been stripped from ENDA in the then-Democratically-controlled House of Representatives. It was an offensive decision, throwing trans people under the bus through a compromise that singled out a class of people—trans people—for continued discrimination. Compromise is often necessary, but entire marginalized identities are not expendable chess pieces.

The fact that an inclusive ENDA had now just passed the U.S. Senate without any consideration for removing gender identity demonstrated the increasing political voices of trans people, the firming up of our allies in and out of Congress, and the public's growing embrace of our rights. It also helped that organizations such as the Human Rights Campaign, which had made the mistake of continuing to support ENDA in 2007 after gender identity was stripped out, had made clear that they would never support a noninclusive bill again and stood firmly with the trans community. Their commitment, much like I saw in Delaware on our gender identity bill, was absolute.

I joined with my colleagues around a flat-screen TV mounted on the wall at the office to watch the vote. And as the votes ticked up on C-SPAN and the gavel slammed on the Senate dais during the final vote on ENDA, I was proud and excited for the advancement. It was the first time either chamber of Congress had passed workplace protections for transgender people, and over the preceding weeks, my colleagues and I had been working overtime to make it happen, drafting memos and talking points and making visits to Capitol Hill to assuage nervous Democrats and even more anxious Republicans.

The vote was a long time coming and a lot of work. But the "victory" paled in comparison to the feeling of pride and hope that I had felt after Delaware's Gender Identity Nondiscrimination Act was signed. Since the Delaware bill actually became law, it had a tangible impact and real protections that would help people. That the symbolic victory in the Senate on ENDA came on such a watered-down piece of legislation only added to the feeling of an empty victory.

Still, in this work you have to acknowledge the advancements, no matter how small. As quickly as we need change to come, the race is a marathon, not a sprint. And as we celebrated in our downtown office, my mind was also on Andy, wishing he could be in the office with us, watching the historic moment.

That night, as we prepared for bed, Andy and I sat down and talked about ENDA.

"We win when we ask for what we need rather than what we think we can get," I vented to him, feeling emboldened by the win but un-inspired by just how limited it was. "People can tell when you aren't advocating from a place of authenticity. We need to excite people, get them behind something big."

"And we need protections in all areas of life, not just employment," Andy added, alluding to his work on nondiscrimination protections in health care.

We both hoped that someday the national movement would shift toward a bigger strategy, that we'd find our courage on the issue of discrimination and demand full federal equality. That night, we talked of a bill that didn't just include employment, but also shelter and public spaces, schools and hospitals: protections in all areas of life in all parts of the country. Little did we know that similar conversations were happening in other places around town as well.

It felt good to talk about something beyond cancer. With his treatment moving along, I could see Andy itching to get back in the ring, but we were still only halfway through his treatment. And while we tried to always look ahead with positivity, the darkness of cancer always loomed in the background. Everything felt drenched in it and the air always felt heavy with it. We never talked about the elephant in the room. "Death" was a word we still never uttered. But I imagine it was on his mind as much as it was on mine.

The brief interlude between surgery and the grueling schedule of radiation and chemotherapy was the calm in the eye of a hurricane that would come back in full force in just a few weeks. And when it returned, it did so with a vengeance.

After a few weeks, the radiation on his mouth and neck started to cause so much pain that it hurt him just to breathe.

"It feels like I'm being stabbed in the throat," he told me.

It seemed like the progress we had enjoyed was backsliding. He lost, again, the ability to eat solid foods. But through it all, we were determined to live as normal a life as possible. And with the holidays approaching, we were intent on celebrating as best we could.

We returned to Delaware together to spend Thanksgiving with my family. A week later, his mom and stepdad came out to spend some time with him during his daily radiation treatments. Andy and I both loved Christmas, so his mom and stepdad took us to Target to buy a fake tree and ornaments. We purchased *A* and *S* ornaments and decorations that reflected our favorite shows and jokes. Finally, the medical equipment was largely gone, replaced now with holiday decorations. Donning Santa hats, we danced around the apartment and filled it with ornaments.

When Andy's dad and brother were set to fly to D.C. to spend Christmas with him, I asked Andy if it would be all right if I went back to Delaware to spend Christmas Day with my parents.

"I want you to stay with me," he said, almost pleadingly.

I had always spent Christmas with my family. With his dad coming to town, I thought it might be a good opportunity for me to recharge a bit. But I could tell he was hurt that I wanted to go home.

"Please stay, Bean," he pleaded.

We went back and forth a few times. I wanted to be with my parents; he wanted me to be with him. Each of us was beginning to grow frustrated with the other.

"I need a break," I blurted out, regretting almost instantly the choice of words and emotions. I had avoided expressing any exhaustion to Andy, not wanting to make him feel like a burden. I had always tried to honor the "grief circle," always complaining outward, never inward. But I felt that I needed to rest in order to better care for him.

He glared at me. I could see the anger and indignation brewing under the surface. "You need a break? You need a break?! What about my break?! THIS IS MY LIFE," he shot back, bursting into tears. "THERE IS NO BREAK FOR ME!"

It was a release of all his pent-up frustration and exhaustion, emotions that I needed to let him vent. He needed the release and certainly deserved it. Almost immediately, though, he relented.

"I'm sorry, Bean. I'm sorry. You should go," he told me.

"You never need to apologize," I told him. Part of me wanted to meet his reversal with a complete reversal of my own, committing not to leave at all. But his dad was coming to town. This would be my one opportunity to get some rest.

I said I was sorry for what I had just said and how I had said it. "How about I just go for two days? I'll go up on Christmas Eve and come back the day after Christmas. How does that sound?"

• • •

The trip back to Delaware for Christmas was helpful, but it wasn't the escape I thought it might be. My mind was always on Andy. I constantly checked in, texting him every few hours. The Christmas two years ago when I had come out to my parents felt like a world away. And after my family opened presents, I looked at my phone and saw a text from Andy.

"I can't talk. I've lost my voice. I'm scared," it read. Since surgery, he had mostly recovered all of his speech. A slight impediment remained, like he had a few cotton swabs in his mouth. But it had largely returned.

"It hurts to talk?" I texted, realizing I couldn't call him to get more information.

"When I open my mouth to talk, nothing comes out," he replied.

I called Sean, who told me that it was a possible side effect of the treatment, but that it generally comes back.

"Generally?"

There was always the small risk that the radiation would permanently damage the vocal cords. *Merry Christmas, Andy,* I thought.

The next day, I met him in Baltimore, halfway between Delaware and Washington. Andy's voice had mostly returned when we met outside the hospital where he was getting his radiation treatments. Over the next few weeks, as we rang in the 2014 New Year, his voice would go in and out. Each time he'd lose his voice, he simultaneously hoped and worried, for different reasons, that it would be the last time. Fortunately, it always came back, and eventually for good.

And as we entered 2014, for the first time in a while, the news for Andy was *all* good.

Early in January I went with him and his mother to Hopkins for what would ideally be his last radiation and chemotherapy session. On most days, Andy had gone by himself, but he had company for the final few weeks, as his dad and, later, his mom were in town. Since I had to work, I had gone to only his first several sessions.

Walking into the waiting room now, six weeks after the start of treatment, Andy was greeted like the most popular kid in school.

"Hey, Andy!" one patient called out.

"Andy, how are you doing?" asked a nurse as she walked by.

"Andy, my man!" an older man yelled.

He had clearly made an impression on the other patients and nurses. His charm, wit, and charisma were infectious even in a cancer treatment center.

As he went in for his final radiation appointment, Andy's mom and I waited with other patients and their families in the waiting room. The average age in there had to be seventy. Looking around, it was clear that at twenty-seven, Andy was by far the youngest patient getting treatment. That is, until I heard the voice of a young woman from around the corner.

"Alex, it's time to go!" the woman yelled, not unkindly.

A little boy, no older than five years old, walked around the corner in a hospital gown and grabbed her hand. The little boy was smiling and laughing as he made his way toward a door that read CAUTION: HIGH RADIATION.

Any feelings of self-pity washed away. My eyes filled with tears. I sat there watching the grace of both this little boy and his mom. I knew how important insurance had been to potentially saving Andy's life. I assumed the boy in front of me likely had insurance, too. And watching the door close behind him as he walked into the radiation center, I couldn't help but wonder how anyone in this country could believe that someone, let alone a child, doesn't inherently deserve treatment for a disease that would otherwise end his life. How could anyone think that children with cancer deserve to live only if their parents are financially secure?

My train of thought was interrupted when a nurse came out smiling. "He's finished," she informed us.

Andy's mom and I waited by the exit until Andy emerged, clearly relieved, with a big smile on his face, knowing that the treatment was now in the past. Next to the exit was a small bell with a mallet attached to the wall. It was reserved for patients finishing their (it's hoped) final treatment, a celebratory routine that exists in cancer clinics across the country.

"Ring it," the nurse suggested.

Andy picked up the mallet and gave the bell a light tap.

*Ding.*

"Come on, hit it!" I said.

He tried one more time.

*DING.*

Everyone in the waiting room erupted in applause. You could feel the love and energy in the room. All of the patients and their loved ones were going through a similar experience. The mutual support was genuine, and you could tell they were all happy for him. Andy smiled again and bowed.

"Ah thank you! Ah thank you," he joked through his hoarse, soft voice.

He was ecstatic to be done with treatment. He was ready to move on. *We* were ready to move on.

Even before treatment ended, he had started working again, beginning at home, and then, more and more, in the office. Before his medical leave, he had been working with local and national advocates in D.C. to push the Washington mayor to issue guidance on transgender inclusion in health care, policies that he envisioned would be the most comprehensive in the nation. As a transgender person, he understood just how necessary it was for transgender people to be able to access all the care we may need, including transition-related care. It was the issue at the heart of his advocacy of health-care access for LGBTQ people.

One of the most common forms of discrimination faced by transgender people are blanket bans in health insurance plans that forbid the coverage of any treatment related to a gender transition. Most people think that if a trans person transitions medically, whether through hormone treatment or surgeries, they are utilizing care that is only ever accessed by trans people. That couldn't be further from the truth.

Practically every single medical procedure someone might utilize to transition is also offered for other reasons. The hormone treatment transgender people may utilize is also offered to people with hormone imbalances or to women after menopause. The different reconstructive surgeries some transgender people seek are also offered to others for various reasons, including, for example, a person with a damaged vaginal canal after childbirth or a mastectomy for someone with breast cancer.

In each instance, insurance covers every one of those treatments and more. But despite the fact that every major medical organization deems transition-related care to be medically necessary, insurance plans across the country often ban any coverage of this care for transgender people experiencing gender dysphoria, the diagnosis that refers to the mental anguish caused by having one's gender identity not seen and acknowledged by society.

To put it simply, a service is being provided to everyone but trans people. That is a textbook example of discrimination. And it's pervasive.

As a lawyer and policy expert at the Center for American Progress, Andy had led the charge nationally to remove the discriminatory bans. It was his legal reasoning that had become the nationwide model, and so far, almost ten states had forbidden insurance exclusions for coverage of transition-related care.

Throughout the last few weeks of treatment, even as his voice went in and out and it sometimes hurt to breathe, he had worked with a handful of advocates on D.C.'s new policies.

"It would be the gold standard," Andy had told me of the new insurance guidelines.

And now, a few months after concluding his cancer treatment, he stood with other activists as the mayor of Washington, D.C., announced the new rules to the press. Standing before cameras in a formal wood-paneled room, Mayor Vincent Gray announced, "Today, the District takes a major step towards leveling the playing field for individuals diagnosed with gender dysphoria. These residents should not have to pay exorbitant out-of-pocket expenses for medically necessary treatment."

Andy was thrilled. The policies that he had worked on in other states were typically announced with a press release, not a public ceremony. Used to working exclusively behind the scenes, Andy was empowered by the public celebration of the policies he had dedicated his short, but eventful, professional career to advocating for.

He returned to our apartment from the ceremony fired up like I had never seen him. He was recharged and ready to fight.

"I feel like I have a story to share," he told me. "I understand firsthand the need for people to be able to access health care that is both lifesaving and life affirming. I want to do more public advocacy."

It took a lot for the chronically humble Andy to fully grasp that he had something to say that was worthy of being heard. And it took losing the ability to talk temporarily—and facing the risk of losing the ability to talk permanently—for him to fully comprehend the power of his voice.

With the 2014 deadline to enroll in health care under the Affordable Care Act approaching, Andy began his public advocacy by writing an op-ed in *The Advocate*, one of the larger publications within the LGBTQ community, urging LGBTQ young adults to sign up for health insurance.

"I was once invincible. Or so I thought," he opened.

"Like many young people, I was convinced that worries about my health were a world away. That is, until my whole world came crashing down around me last September."

He talked about his diagnosis and the grueling treatment regimen. And though his treatment had ended in January, he wrote that "even now my body is still aching and tired.

"So it might not seem like I'm very lucky—but I'm certainly fortunate," he explained, always looking on the bright side. "That's because my employer has offered me high-quality health insurance that kept a bad situation from spinning out of control. Had my employer not provided me this coverage, I may have made the same potentially deadly mistake too many young people make: I would have chosen not to get health insurance. . . .

"Without health insurance, I would not have been able to afford treatment . . . without bankrupting myself and probably my parents," he continued. "Without health insurance, I may not have even gone to the doctor who diagnosed my cancer, and I could be living in ignorance about the fast-spreading disease that was inside of me."

Andy went on to bring in the big picture. Despite the stereotype that the LGBTQ community is made up almost entirely of wealthy gay men, Andy explained that most LGBTQ people are not as fortunate as he is. One in three LGBTQ people making four times the poverty level or less had no health insurance. Nearly two-thirds of people in our age bracket, eighteen to thirty-four years old, had delayed health-care decisions because they could not afford the costs of health insurance or care.

The ACA, which Andy admitted was not perfect, provided critical support for LGBTQ people. In addition to the subsidies that help lower-income Americans purchase coverage, the law also provides critical protections from discrimination in health care.

"Our LGBT community is resilient and strong, and particularly for those of us who are young and have our entire lives in front of us, it may feel like we are invincible. I've learned the hard way that I'm not. Cancer has taken a lot from me physically and emotionally," he confided. "But it hasn't taken away my voice, and it hasn't taken away my hope."

No, it had not. Even in the face of significant cancer, he remained as hopeful as ever. His attitude personified what Barack Obama called "the audacity of hope." And even in the face of losing his speech—even when he literally could no longer talk—Andy's voice was helping to expand access to health care and improve lives. I know because I was one of the many people who benefited from Andy's advocacy.

After coming out to my parents in 2012, I began taking hormones in consultation with an endocrinologist. And in March 2014, just as Andy regained his strength, I underwent surgery myself.

For me, just like the steps I had taken earlier in my transition, surgery was a step I knew was necessary to bring me peace. Surgery isn't what makes transgender people the gender we are, but it can affirm us in that identity and further alleviate that pain I had felt so strongly throughout my life.

Sometimes vaguely called "bottom surgery," but more formally called gender affirmation surgery, I had been anticipating the step for two years and had to schedule it a year out. The doctor I chose, a trans woman herself, is one of the world's leading surgeons when it comes to transitioning and one of only a handful within the United States who focus on it.

I don't usually talk about this aspect of my life publicly. Too often transgender people are reduced to our body parts, a phenomenon that dehumanizes us and simplifies our identities. I have been asked in the media and by total strangers intimate details about my body. Some of the questions came from people who were misguided and curious, while other people, like the angry woman in Delaware who threatened me, asked from a place of hate.

Regardless of my own comfort with the topic, the fact that strangers feel entitled to know about this aspect of my life and body, when they would never dream of asking a cisgender person the same questions, is just another indignity imposed on transgender people.

While I haven't—and won't in the future—talk about my body parts publicly, it wouldn't be fair to talk about my role as a caregiver for Andy without talking about his role as a caregiver for me. And it wouldn't do his work justice if I didn't make clear that, because of Andy, I have been able to access transition-related care, care that I needed to live and thrive as myself.

Driving up to the hospital in rural Pennsylvania where my surgery was to take place, my parents were a nervous wreck. My dad, in particular, was on edge like I had never seen him, fiddling his thumbs, tapping his feet, and clearly lost in thought. Now completely used to hospitals, Andy and I, on the other hand, were cool and calm.

While any surgery is major and gender affirmation surgery is not some short outpatient procedure, my four-hour operation paled in comparison to the ten hours Andy's took. My planned three-day stay in the hospital was less than half of Andy's seven-day stay. And after the fear of Andy's diagnosis and concern about losing his ability to talk, the hope I felt going into my surgery was cause for celebration.

As I sat in my hospital gown while we waited for my name to be called, the small butterflies were overpowered by an overwhelming sense of relief. I had thought about postponing my surgery given everything that had just happened to Andy, but factors had aligned—his recovery, his return to work, and his strength—to allow for me to take the final step in my own transition.

I had been hoping for this day for as long as I could remember, and it had arrived. I knew recovery would take a few weeks, but soon enough, I would finally feel whole.

"Sarah," the nurse called, signaling for me to follow her to the elevator.

A few hours later, when I woke up from the general anesthesia, I looked at my still-nervous parents and exclaimed, "See, all is good. No big deal. I feel great." High on morphine, I spent most of the day reassuring my parents about how fine I felt. In retrospect, of course I felt fine—I was pretty high. But as the effects of the morphine dissipated, the nurse gave me a Vicodin that didn't sit well with me. Andy was staying the night on a pull-out sofa in my hospital room, and at about midnight, a wave of nausea came over me.

"I'm really nauseous," I said.

"What?" Andy asked, as he got up and walked to my bedside.

"I'm . . . I'm . . . I'm really . . ."

*Uh-oh.*

I projectile-vomited all over Andy.

"Oh, God," I started to say, mortified at the disgusting scene, "I am so sorry."

Wiping my vomit off his face, Andy smirked and said, "Oh, Bean . . . what's a little vomit?"

I could tell he was almost happy it had happened, that it wasn't him in the hospital bed vomiting on me.

"Thank you, Bean," I said.

"For what?" he asked.

"For creating a world where I can do this," I told him.

He smiled and squeezed my hand.

Just knowing my surgery was successful helped me feel better. The homesickness that I'd been carrying around for so long was gone. And as was the case when I first started transitioning, the absence of a negative was more noticeable than any presence of a positive. I just felt at home. I felt complete, and most important, I felt like me. I didn't feel the pain.

In the conversation about trans identities and health-care needs, we are too prone to intellectualize, turning to abstract, theoretical discussion. Too many outside the community seek to find contradictions in our identities in an effort to undermine their validity.

I have been asked: Why would you need to change your body if you say gender is removed from anatomy?

Acknowledging that the two concepts are distinct does not preclude them from ever interacting. And no one would expect cisgender people to defend their individual feelings about their own body parts.

At the end of the day, it is difficult for anyone to explain a feeling. Pain is such a visceral emotion. So basic, so nonintellectual, that there are few ways to describe it but for the term itself. How do you describe, for instance, the sensation of a burn but as a burn?

Sometimes we feel like we have to make every part of our story incredibly emotional in order to fit a cliché people have about the trans experience. I'm not going to do that. Gender affirmation surgery can be a major milestone for many trans folks, but as important as it was for me, it didn't feel like a dramatic turning point. Perhaps that's because it was nestled in between all of Andy treatments, but also because my personal relationship with my surgery is a lot like many other people's relationship with any necessary surgery they need to alleviate a chronic issue. It was pain relieving and I was certainly lucky to be able to access the care I needed, but the proverbial choirs did not sing in its aftermath.

Some transgender people say that we never stop transitioning. I suppose that in many ways that's true, but I knew that the most significant steps in my transition were now in the past, along with my surgery. I was living the life I had always dreamed of, I felt seen, and now I felt comfortable and complete. And that's what mattered.

In the following weeks, Andy and my parents helped care for me, as I was largely relegated to bed. They brought me meals. They helped me to the bathroom. And most of all, they distracted me with conversation and endless episodes of *30 Rock*.

I could tell that Andy was relieved that the attention was off of him, if only for a little while. My recovery was relatively quick and easy—three to four weeks total—and as spring approached, my mind shifted to Andy's upcoming doctor's appointment, where he would get the results of his first follow-up scans since treatment.

I wasn't mobile by the time of the appointment in early April, so I couldn't go with him, but I kept my phone by my side, anxiously waiting for his call. Eventually it came and I nervously picked up. In the few moments before he said anything, I could barely catch my breath.

"Hellllllew," he opened, clearly excited. "They said I'm cancer-free!"

I jumped out of bed, started screaming and dancing. "Ouch! Ouch!" It was probably a bit too soon after my own surgery for that.

"How do you feel, Bean?" I asked.

He thought about it for a second.

"Free," he responded.

*Free*. Finally free. Finally, we hoped, cancer was in the past. Finally, we hoped, we could return to our work and be done with hospitals.

That June, we attended our first White House LGBT Pride Reception as a couple, two years after I had unknowingly run into Andy at the same event. As awe-inspiring as the 2012 reception was, this one was even better.

It was more celebratory, as the rate of change for LGBTQ people felt like it was accelerating. Trans rights were coming further and further to the forefront. A week earlier, President Obama had announced that he would sign an executive order banning discrimination based on sexual orientation and gender identity within federal contracts, an antidiscrimination rule that would impact one in five American workers.

The order was the single largest expansion of workplace protections for LGBTQ people in our nation's history. The president had promised to sign such an order for years, but his delay was frustrating advocates. Finally, after mounting pressure from organizations such as CAP and HRC, the administration finally announced that the time had come.

But more than anything else, the event felt different because, by 2014, I had gotten to know the community that now gathered throughout those two floors of the White House. It wasn't just national leaders; it was advocates and activists from across the country. It was a group of my friends.

I was there as myself, on the other end of my transition, with a cancer-free Andy, as well as Sean and Blake, who'd managed to get a last-minute invitation. I was surrounded by family, both blood and chosen.

When I came across Valerie Jarrett, the senior adviser who oversaw the office in which I had interned two years before, she greeted me with a warm embrace and a simple message: "Welcome home." And with everyone there, that's what it felt like. My heart was about as full as it had ever been.

The president was in a playful mood as he addressed the crowd in the East Room, with Michelle by his side. Talking about the White House's outgoing pastry chef, an openly gay man, the president joked, "We call Bill the 'Crustmaster' because of his pies . . . I don't know what he does, whether he puts crack in them or . . ."

The audience burst into laughter. Michelle interjected, probably knowing the absurd outrage at the joke that would come on Fox News later that night. "No, he doesn't! There's no crack in our pies," she protested.

She gave him a jokingly stern look, but he shrugged at her admonishment.

"I'm just saying that when we first came to the White House, the first year my cholesterol shot up. And the doctor was like, 'What happened? You had, like, this really low cholesterol.' And I thought, *It's the pie. It's the pie.* So we had to establish a really firm rule about no pie during the week."

The audience was in hysterics at the banter between the president and the first lady. The warmth continued as he recounted the progress we had seen over the previous year, from expanding marriage equality to unprecedented visibility for trans people.

"Perhaps most importantly, Mitch and Cam got married," Obama said, referring to the same-sex couple on the TV show *Modern Family*, "which caused Michelle and the girls to cry. That was big."

Michelle nodded and reiterated the president's point. "That *was* big," she mouthed.

But the president also knew the topic was deadly serious. He outlined the continued work ahead: the need for marriage equality in all fifty states, the lack of nationwide workplace protections, the violence faced by the community, and the continued epidemic of AIDS.

"This year, we mark the forty-fifth anniversary of Stonewall," he proclaimed, referring to the riot against police violence that had launched the modern LGBTQ movement. "And this tremendous progress we've made as a society is thanks to those of you who fought the good fight, and to Americans across the country who marched and came out and organized to secure the rights of others."

The president closed by articulating a view of America that frames our greatness not as the product of a bygone era, but rather from our ongoing journey toward a deeper understanding of freedom.

"That's how we continue our nation's march towards justice and equality," he told us. "That's how we build a more perfect union—a country where no matter what you look like, where you come from, what your last name is, who you love, you've got a chance to make it if you try. You all have shown what can happen when people of goodwill organize and stand up for what's right. And we've got to make sure that that's not applied just in one place, in one circumstance, in one time. That's part of the journey that makes America the greatest country on earth."

The evening was a celebration of love in every way. Love between same-sex couples. Love of LGBTQ identities. And for Andy and me, love between two transgender people. Walking through the White House holding Andy's hand, I looked around and realized that this was everything I thought I had given up when I came out. I had found a person I love and was doing what I love.

*How lucky am I?*

With everything settled, we now looked to a nearly endless horizon of experiences before us. We talked about our future, about getting married and spending our lives together. We talked about our goals in the coming years in our work. And as the weeks passed, Andy talked more and more about our upcoming trip, my first, to his hometown of Chippewa Falls, Wisconsin. We would be going for his favorite event, the biannual family reunion known as Volefest, a gathering of about forty of his relatives on his dad's side named after his maternal grandmother's maiden name, Vole.

Since near the beginning of our relationship, Andy had made clear just how much he wanted me to visit his hometown and to go to Volefest with him. He had never brought a girlfriend to one before, and the fact that I was coming was a big deal for him. I could tell it was something he had dreamed of since childhood.

Andy was giddy as we landed at the small Chippewa Valley airport just outside Eau Claire, Wisconsin. It was late July and we both welcomed the escape from the humid summer weather of D.C. Andy's mom and stepdad picked us up and drove us back to their house, a two-story home filled with family photos, knickknacks from their travels, and plastic versions of Andy's mom's favorite animals, flamingos. Lots and lots of flamingos.

"Time for a tour," Andy exclaimed.

He showed me his childhood bedroom and the basement, where he and his stepbrothers hosted parties in high school. We hopped in the car for a drive through the small town of Chippewa Falls. We drove around the public schools Andy had gone to growing up and the parking lots where he had band practice. We stopped for ice cream at his favorite ice-cream parlor.

The main road, Bridge Street, ran down the center of town and included small shops and the courthouse where Andy's dad, Steven, served as an elected county judge. After a few blocks of small offices and stores, the main drag passed over the Chippewa River just west of a dam that created the large man-made Lake Wissota. The pride for his hometown was evident at each stop.

"That's the island where my dad does fireworks for the town's Fourth of July," he told me, pointing to a small hill in the middle of the lake. "Isn't it great?!"

The family reunion took place that Saturday at Andy's late grand-father's house on the lake. I was nervous when I walked the long dirt path toward the split-level 1970s-era home. But the forty or so family members assembled in the backyard by the grill could not have been nicer. While the cousins, aunts, uncles, grandparents, and extended family came from all over, almost all were Chippewa Falls natives and exuded the term that I had already heard a few times since arriving, "Wisconsin nice."

Everyone wore T-shirts specially made for the reunion, with "Volefest 2014" on the front and a number on the back corresponding to your order of entering the family. Andy's grandmother Verene, a short older woman who looks and sounds like Betty White, was, of course, number 1. My T-shirt didn't yet have a number, but I was assured it would for the next reunion in two years.

"You just have to come back," I was told with a wink by a cousin.

It was the ultimate wholesome family reunion. We played different games crafted over the years by family members. We ate a bunch of pizza. And at the end of the day, with drinks in everyone's hands, we watched the sunset over Lake Wissota.

I was exhausted by the end of the day, but I had loved seeing Andy in his element surrounded by so many loved ones. It was clear he had waited for that day for a while. But throughout the trip, I started to worry that something might be seriously wrong.

A couple days before we left for Wisconsin, Andy had developed a cough. I wouldn't have thought anything of it, but it had followed two weeks of increasing back pain. Andy didn't think it was a big deal, but I had been on the lookout for signs of lung trouble since his diagnosis. A few months earlier, during Andy's chemotherapy treatment, I had asked Sean about the worst-case scenario for Andy's kind of cancer.

"What happens if it spreads further?"

"The likeliest place would be the lungs."

"What's the prognosis for something like that?"

"Well, if it spreads there . . . it would be terminal."

"How long?"

"Twelve to eighteen months."

I never told Andy about that conversation. He knew that lung cancer was always a possibility, but he didn't know that it would come with a terminal diagnosis. And I didn't want to burden him with that information.

Throughout the trip to Wisconsin, the cough continued, increasing with each day. By the time we were driving back to his mom's house from the reunion, it was incessant. But so was his smile.

Driving along the edge of Lake Wissota, I could easily see myself spending the rest of my life with Andy, but I also couldn't shake the feeling that our world was about to be turned upside down once again.

# CHAPTER 10

# "Amazing grace."

"If it turns out to be terminal, would you marry me?"

I don't think it's possible for a sentence to contain more tragedy and more love in it: eleven words that encompass the highest of highs and the lowest of lows. Sitting on our big overstuffed couch, just below a framed cartoon that almost cruelly read "Game Over," Andy asked me to be his wife.

Two days earlier, just after our trip to Wisconsin, Andy had gone to his primary-care doctor to get his cough checked out. X-rays had come back showing something in or around his lungs.

"What, uh, what does that mean?" I asked the doctor, not wanting to say the word "cancer."

"I'm going to have you go to the hospital up the street for more detailed scans, but he may have pneumonia and it's just some fluid around the lungs," he reassured us.

*Thank God.* I had convinced myself that the news would be more serious, and sitting in our doctor's office with Andy, I desperately wanted his guess to be right.

We immediately hopped in an Uber and rode up to Sibley, a small hospital in a sleepy neighborhood in northwest Washington. It was just a few blocks from American University, and I knew Sibley only as the place that my peers were taken to when they had too much to drink at a college party. I never imagined that it would be the scene of some of the most pivotal moments in my life.

"At least we DVR'd *Big Brother* tonight," I jokingly told Andy, wanting to act—no, wanting to pretend—like everything was normal. But even with the doctor's guess and our hope that everything was all right, my gut knew different.

After Andy finished his scans, we awaited the results in an alcove in the ER. An hour went by. Then two. Patients came in and out of the neighboring spaces. Every so often, I'd walk out into the center of the ER to ask a passing doctor or nurse how much longer things would take.

"Just a moment," said one, an hour into the stay.

"I believe the results should be coming soon," said another at the two-hour mark.

As day passed into night, a nurse finally came by to get Andy some water and check on us.

"How are you doing?" she asked.

"I'm okay," he answered, his voice a bit shaky. "But I'm a cancer survivor, so I'm just a little nervous."

"Oh, I'm sure everything will be fine. I believe the doctor should be in here shortly," she responded warmly, while pulling Andy's chart up on the computer. As she clicked on different pages, scrolling through, she talked with us about the weather. Then she got to one page and I saw her body language change. She stood upright and the small talk ceased. She abruptly, but calmly, excused herself.

"Let me go check on the doctor," she said with a smile that masked something darker.

Andy didn't notice the change in tone, but I did. I got up from my chair and walked over to the still-open computer screen. I pretended to look around the windowsill, not wanting Andy to ask what I was reading. But there it was. In the middle of a long paragraph filled with otherwise indecipherable medical terms was the news I feared.

"Masses have been found in both lungs," it read.

I tried to hide any surprise on my face as I turned around and looked at Andy, who was reading on his phone. I took him in for the split second before he looked up. He smiled at me and I managed to smile back.

*Oh my God, he's going to die,* I thought to myself, recalling the hypothetical scenario Sean had laid out to me months before.

Just then, a doctor pushed aside the curtain with two younger doctors by his side and calmly delivered the bad news. It looked like Andy's cancer was back and that it had spread to his lungs, something that tests would confirm in the coming days.

He didn't say anything about the prognosis and Andy didn't ask. The conversation was focused purely on the next steps. They'd admit Andy to the hospital for the night for monitoring and to drain some of the fluid that had begun filling the cavity around his lungs, fluid that was a result of the tumors. As Andy talked with his nurses about the logistics of being admitted, I stepped out to call his mother, Ardis.

"Andy's cancer is, um, back. It's spread to his lungs. He's being admitted to Sibley," I told her, trying not to scare them beyond what I imagined they would inherently feel.

"Do you think we should come out?" she asked. She was sensitive to Andy's wishes on the matter, and I think instinctively understood that the family flying out might spook him.

"I think it would be a good idea for you to come out," I said. I didn't know how much time Andy was going to have, but I wanted to make sure his family got as much time with him as possible. I also knew we were going to need help.

Time started to slow as the gravity of the situation began creeping up on me. It was like I was gradually getting the wind knocked out of me. With every passing second, the reality—that Andy was going to die—began to truly hit me. But it was still premature for me to tell her or Andy just how serious the situation was, that his cancer was almost definitely terminal. It was too soon, and it wasn't my place. I wasn't a medical professional, and I worried, particularly for Andy, that he would resent the person who delivered the news. I didn't want him to hate me, and the information wouldn't change the steps his doctors were giving him.

Still, I felt guilty. I wasn't sure I was doing the right thing. In moments like these, I've learned it's always hard to know for certain what's right and what's wrong.

"I love you," I told his mom as she hung up to tell her husband and call others in the family. I had never said "I love you" to his parents before, but I felt it and I knew they were going to need all the love they could get in the coming days and weeks. Nothing is more difficult than losing a child.

Then I stepped into a dark, single-stall restroom just off the center of the ER to call my own parents. As I waited for my mother to pick up the phone, I looked at myself in the mirror. Seeing my reflection made everything feel so much more real.

*This is real life. This is happening.*

When I heard my mother's voice, I burst into tears.

"Mom? His cancer is back. He's . . . he's . . . he's going to die!" I cried into the phone. I started hyperventilating. I could barely stand. Leaning against the sink in the dark restroom, I cried like I had never cried before. The type of crying that could burst a blood vessel. I was inconsolable.

But I needed to let it all out on the call because I had to return to Andy's side and be calm and present. I explained to both of my parents what we'd just learned and what I already knew: He had probably a year left.

"He doesn't know and I can't tell him. I need you! Please come down! I need you!"

My mom was, understandably, also hysterical at the shocking news, and my dad was concerned with her driving down to D.C. in her distraught state.

"Can she come tomorrow?" he asked, going into the calm, logical attorney mode that had helped us work through intense conversations before. I wasn't able to match his calm. I was a mess. I fell to the floor of the still-dark restroom.

"No! I need my mom! I need my mom! I need my mom! Please!"

Hearing the fear in my voice, my dad relented, and my mom bought a train ticket down for that night. With my mom on her way, I stepped out of the bathroom, cleared my eyes, and sat for a few moments to catch my breath. I walked back into Andy's room, where the nurse was helping him into a wheelchair for the trip up a few floors to his hospital room. He grabbed my hand and I walked beside him as he was wheeled up.

"I just can't believe I have to go through all this again. I'm exhausted and I thought I was done," he said. "But if I beat it once, I'll do it again."

My heart broke, but I just let him talk. I didn't know what to say. I didn't want to lie to him, but I also didn't want to add to his burden. He would find out in due course. I decided that my job was to provide positivity and reinforce his hope. My role was to love, not to be the realist. And after all, there are always those people who get a terminal diagnosis and end up defying the odds. Andy could be one of those survivors. Right?

It was just two days later, as Andy prepared to go with his mom to an appointment with his doctors at Johns Hopkins, that he asked me to marry him.

I had a feeling the question might come as he began to grapple with the possibility that the recurrence of the cancer was far more serious than his first go-round had been. And as the initial shock of the news wore off and he began to think about what came next, it was clear the thought of death was again on his mind. But it wasn't until his proposal that he acknowledged the realization to me.

I worried about every word I said to him, particularly in those first days after the diagnosis. I worried that if I said yes instantly to his proposal, he would interpret that as a sign that I had already given up. But obviously, I wasn't going to say no, either.

"Let's see what your doctors say before we start talking about that."

We didn't have to wait long. A few hours after Andy and his mother left for the doctor's appointment, I picked up my phone to a text from him: "They said it's terminal."

I didn't think, I just called immediately. It wasn't a surprise, but that didn't diminish the shock. Even though I'd had three days to prepare for this moment, I didn't know what to say. I told him that I was sorry. I told him that I wasn't going anywhere, that I'd be right there with him every step of the way.

"And to the question you asked before you left," I said, "the answer is obviously, certainly, without question, yes."

I waited anxiously with my mom for Andy and his mom to get back to our apartment. When he walked into our living room, he appeared completely deflated. He fell into the couch and just sat there, his eyes a blank stare.

I sat down beside him and held his hand. "What did the doctors say about next steps?" I asked hesitantly.

"That I have probably ten months to a year with treatment. That I . . . um . . . will start chemo, but that it will be to prolong my life, not save . . ." He trailed off.

It was practically exactly what Sean had said all those months before. Staring at the ground, Andy's eyes were filled with tears, the kind that just rest on your eyes, ready, at any moment, to burst onto your cheeks.

How do you console someone who knows that they are going to die? I couldn't tell him that it would get better. I couldn't tell him that he'd beat it. But I also wanted to be careful not to remove his last bit of optimism that would inevitably give him the strength to put one foot in front of the other, pursue the treatment, and grapple with the stages of acceptance and grief. I realized that I just needed to listen to him and love him.

Over the next few days, the shock subsided into crying. Lots and lots of crying. He was scared out of his mind, perpetually locked into a look of terror, the literal "fear of death" buried underneath his beautiful blue eyes.

"I'm so scared not to exist anymore," he'd scream through the tears, his voice still muffled and impeded from the surgery almost a year before. His cries and deep breaths merged into depressing gasps. "I'm so scared, Bean. I'm so scared."

And it wasn't just the fear of death. He also spent those days crying about what he wouldn't be able to do for other people: the friends he'd leave behind, the work that would remain unfinished, and the pain that he wouldn't be able to help alleviate for others, including me.

"I'm sorry I won't be able to be there for you, Bean," he told me, scrunched up on our couch in the T-shirt and shorts he'd been wearing the last few days. "I'm so sad that I won't be around to tell you that I love you, to tell you how beautiful you are, and to tell you how proud of you I am."

I tried to stay strong in front of Andy, but I couldn't hold it in. I couldn't bury the emotions anymore. I felt so bad for him. And here he was, facing death, apologizing that he wouldn't be able to be there for *me*.

Every passing day felt both precious and torturous. We were forced to appreciate every hour, no matter how excruciating or cruel they felt.

On August 9, ten days after the initial diagnosis, we celebrated my twenty-fourth birthday. We ordered pizza, another one of Andy's favorites. My parents and Andy's mom and stepdad were in town, as were Andy's stepbrother, his wife, and their three-year-old daughter, Addison. Addy, a giggly, cherub-faced little girl, was the apple of her uncle Andy's eye. He adored her, and as she played with her toys on the floor of our apartment, he tried to muster up his clearly decreasing emotional and physical strength to join her.

I hadn't been away from Andy for longer than a few minutes since he had learned that the cancer was terminal. We had both effectively given up going to work, a situation more than tolerated by our flexible and generous coworkers. So, with Andy surrounded by family during my birthday "party," I asked my parents to join me on the roof of my building for a few minutes.

"Is everything okay?" Andy asked, after I told him my parents and I were going to go up for a bit.

"Yes, yes, of course. I just want to get some fresh air," I assured him. I could see in his eyes that he knew we were going to go upstairs to talk about him. It was obvious. What else would we be talking about?

I had to let loose, though. I needed to vent to someone. Over the last week, Andy and I had effectively been confined to our one-bedroom apartment, the two of us largely alone with the creeping darkness of death hanging over us at all times.

Sitting on the roof of my building with Washington, D.C., spread out in front of my parents and me, I hesitated to speak at first. I was worried what I was about to say would be selfish. But I needed to process my emotions with someone, and I knew my parents wouldn't judge me for feeling sorry for myself.

"I really do always look on the bright side," I told them, almost pleading for absolution for what I was about to say. "I try to always understand that someone has it far worse. I try to find the silver linings in any of the challenges I face. I try to remind myself that negative experiences build strength and character, but aren't I already a good enough person?! Didn't being trans do that? Wasn't Andy's cancer enough? What other life lessons do I need?! Why is this happening to me?! Why is this happening to *him*?! Why is this happening to *us*?!"

I was trying to rationalize the irrational. I shook my head and looked down, suddenly ashamed. "Every day, I wake up and it feels like a nightmare," I confessed. "And I want this nightmare to end, but I also know what that means. The end is Andy dying, and I hate myself for feeling that."

"I find myself feeling the same way," my mom confided, sharing the burden of those feelings with me.

"It's okay," my dad said. "It's okay. This isn't easy. Sarah, you have had more life in the last few years than many people have in decades. And you and Andy have gone through more than most couples in a lifetime."

I needed permission to be human. I needed to be told that it was okay to be selfish, to feel sorry for myself. No one had to tell me Andy's plight was far worse than mine—that much was self-evident—but I did need to know that I could acknowledge and wrestle with my own emotions through it all. I just needed to hear "It's okay to feel like this."

Soon after we returned from the roof, Addison and her parents got ready to leave for the airport. They packed up her ladybug backpack and walked her over to her uncle Andy and me to say goodbye.

"Can you say goodbye to Sarah, Addy?" her mom prompted.

"Bye, Sarah," she repeated in the hushed tone of a three-year-old still learning to speak.

"Can you say goodbye to Uncle Andy, Addy?" her mom added.

"Bye, Andy," Addy whispered as they hugged.

As Addy disappeared out the door, Andy looked at me with tears filling his eyes.

"What if that's the last time I see Addison?" he asked, overcome with the visual of the world that would continue on without him, these cruel realizations occasionally hitting him. "She's too young. She's going to grow up. She won't remember me! She won't have any memories of me!"

The simple moments of life that had felt like such triumphs in his initial recovery, and that we held so dear in the months following, now took on a morbid darkness as he struggled with the knowledge that every experience could be the last of its kind for him. That the world he knew would go on without him. That a normalcy would return for everyone but him.

Between the tears, we talked about the coming months. We talked about traveling with friends. He told me that he wanted to continue doing the work that he had been doing for so long: trying to expand health-care access for LGBTQ people. He began researching cutting-edge technologies and clinical trials that might offer some small, last bit of hope for living.

And we talked about our wedding. With the ten- to twelve-month timeline the doctors had given Andy, we tentatively planned for a fall ceremony. Both of us had always wanted a wedding as the seasons changed, and a young coworker of ours volunteered her parents' farm in Charlottesville, Virginia, for free.

Daydreaming about it was our escape—a sunset wedding with the Blue Ridge Mountains as the backdrop, a crisp autumn evening reception under a big white tent right next to our friend's farmhouse. We both knew it would be emotionally difficult, but the idea of ensuring a big life event—a bucket-list item—for both of us, together, was a helpful distraction.

But then, on August 14, two weeks after the initial diagnosis and exactly two years to the day after Andy sent me that first Facebook message introducing himself, a doctor delivered news that threw ice-cold water on our plans.

"You might not make it to treatment," he said, referring to the chemotherapy that the doctors hoped would extend Andy's life for as long as possible.

Those were the first words I heard as I walked into Andy's hospital room. He had been admitted back into Sibley three days earlier, after his cough returned with a vengeance and his strength and energy had left him almost entirely bedridden. Since being admitted, his need for oxygen—initially a low dose through small nasal tubes—had increased dramatically.

"So you think I may only have two weeks?" Andy asked, his face completely white.

"Yes," the doctor answered. He paused. I wasn't quite sure where he was going next. There was silence. He seemed to be deep in concentration. I figured he was contemplating the next thing to say, since this couldn't be a more serious conversation.

Then he said, "Hold on, there is a fly. Let me kill it."

He slowly lifted his hands up in the air. Andy and I watched, our mouths still ajar. The silence continued, broken only by a loud clap. The body of the fly fell to the floor. "Hold on, let me pick it up." And he slowly bent over, lifted the fly's body, and threw it in the trash.

I wanted to scream at him, but I was too stunned by both the news and his appalling apathy toward Andy's emotions.

After several seconds, which felt like an hour, Andy broke the silence. "Nice job."

Finally, the doctor returned to the conversation at hand. One of Andy's lungs was failing at a rapid rate. "You need to decide whether you want to go on a respirator. Just know, given your condition, that if you go on a respirator, you will likely never be able to be taken off of it. And to put you on a respirator, you will have to be sedated. And given your condition, you would likely never wake up."

*Oh my God.*

For a few seconds it seemed like I might have to say goodbye to Andy right then and there. Forever. It sounded like the best-case scenario was that Andy would continue to physically live, but that the rest of whatever life he had left would be spent in a permanent, medically induced coma.

Moments later, another doctor came in and apologized. She had overhydrated Andy after thinking his heart was racing from dehydration. The fly-doctor seemed surprised and slightly relieved. The cardiologist prescribed some medications and reduced Andy's fluid intake. Soon enough, Andy's lung rebounded. By that afternoon, he was better than he had been since being admitted to Sibley three days prior.

The doctors left the room, seemingly impressed with their solution. But we were scared—and, more than anything else, confused.

He was better than he had been three days before, but still incredibly weak and requiring constant oxygen. Did Andy have two weeks left or was all of this a temporary problem that was easily fixed?

"Two weeks, Bean? I'm not ready for this *A Walk to Remember* shit," Andy remarked. He sounded more frustrated and exasperated than frightened.

We barraged every nurse and subsequent doctor who entered our room with questions, but no one could provide us with a clear answer.

"I don't have a good answer," one young doctor told us, "but I will say that you don't look like someone with two weeks left."

It wasn't a ringing endorsement, but it was something to hang our hope on. Within a day or two, the consensus was that Andy had largely stabilized and that the hospital had done everything they could to remedy the situation, and the decision was made to discharge him the next day.

"Finally," Andy said, his spirits lifted. He'd be discharged with a perpetual oxygen tank and he was still exceptionally weak, but he was coming home. He hated being in the hospital.

That night, Andy's mom pulled me aside in the hospital waiting room. "Sarah, dear. Have you thought about moving the wedding up?"

I could tell it was more of a recommendation than a question. I had thought about asking Andy the same thing, but I knew how he would interpret the suggestion. He'd see it as a sign that he didn't have much time left. The fact that his mother brought it up reinforced that it was probably the right thing to do. And while he had somewhat stabilized, things were still moving much faster than any of the doctors had predicted two and a half weeks earlier, when Andy first asked me to marry him. He might not have had the less than two weeks that the fly-doctor had coldly suggested, but he certainly didn't seem like he had anywhere close to a year.

The morning of Andy's discharge, I sat down on his hospital bed to broach the subject.

"Bean, what do you think about maybe moving up the wedding?"

"Are you giving up?" he immediately asked.

"No, no, no. I just think it's clear that your chemotherapy will likely take more out of you than we thought, so maybe it's best to do it before you start treatment."

He smiled in relief. I wasn't being entirely forthcoming, but what good would the truth do?

"I think that's a good idea," he said, putting his hand on my face and leaning in for a kiss.

Once we were finally situated back at our apartment, we invited our friend and colleague, Bishop Gene Robinson, over. In his mid-sixties, the bishop was a comforting figure, with gray hair and small, circular spectacles. Bishop Gene, as we all called him at the Center for American Progress, had been thrust into the spotlight when he became the first openly LGBTQ person to become a bishop in any major Christian denomination. His election in 2003 to serve as head of the Episcopal Diocese of New Hampshire set off a frenzy, causing a worldwide schism within the Anglican Church.

When he was installed as bishop, the threats on his life were so significant and credible that he had to wear a bulletproof vest under his religious robes. Now retired from his day-to-day role in the church, Bishop Gene served as a senior fellow at CAP, working closely with the LGBTQ team, including Andy and me.

Since we first started to plan the wedding, Bishop Gene had been our dream officiate. He had become a good friend to us, and the fact that he was part of the LGBTQ community put us at ease. We recognized that as two transgender people our love seemed unorthodox to some, and we knew he would preside judgment-free.

Bishop Gene didn't realize just how poorly Andy was doing when he first arrived at our apartment. As he walked into our living room, he looked around and took in his surroundings. He studied the knick-knacks and the small toy robots that I had found so adorable when I first visited Andy at the beginning of our relationship. Two years later, those items were now joined by my decorations, framed pictures of the two of us from throughout our relationship, and lots and lots of medical equipment.

Andy was sitting on the couch with his back to the wandering Bishop Gene, looking out our large apartment windows. The sight of a thin, clear tube stretching from Andy's nose across the floor to a large black oxygen generator made the bishop do a double take.

"Andy and I have decided to get married and we would love for you to preside," I jumped in, trying to distract from Bishop Gene's surprise at Andy's diminished physical condition.

Clearly overcome with emotion at the request and the sight of Andy, Bishop Gene cleared his throat. "Ahem . . . I would be honored," he replied. Just looking at Andy, he understood the urgency of the request and that any wedding would have to happen soon.

"We're thinking about this coming Sunday on the rooftop of our building," I told him.

"Not only would I be honored to officiate, but I would love to help organize everything," he said. "I have a small budget for these types of things and I'd like to help pay for it, if you are comfortable."

We hadn't really considered buying anything for the wedding. Given that we were now talking about a ceremony in five days' time, we figured it would be very simple. No flowers. No food. No decorations.

But Bishop Gene and, as it turned out, our friends had other plans. His generous offer stunned us. I looked at Andy and saw tears streaming down his face once again. For once they were happy tears.

"That is so thoughtful of you," Andy responded, wiping his eyes. "Thank you. Thank you."

My brother Sean, who had watched too many people, including young people, pass away from cancer, had told me that I should take stock in the beautiful acts of kindness that I'd begin to see. "Amazing grace," Sean called it. "You will bear witness to acts of amazing grace."

Bishop Gene's offer was just one example of the grace that was filling our lives in what increasingly appeared to be Andy's waning days. With nothing more than a color preference, Bishop Gene and an army of family and friends began organizing our wedding.

But as the wedding preparations continued, so, too, did the decline in Andy's health. He was sleeping more and more. He was relegated, almost exclusively, to a recliner that his stepdad had purchased for him while he was in the hospital. Going to the bathroom required the help of three friends.

"One, two, three . . ." we'd count, as we'd lift Andy from the recliner to the wheelchair, in which he'd then be rolled to our bathroom just twenty feet away.

He stopped being able to swallow his dozens of pills, so I'd crush them up and put them in his ice cream, about the only thing he could eat. But it soon became nearly impossible to eat even that, taking four hours to eat six spoonfuls. Almost immediately it would be time for the next meal-medicine mix.

A home nurse stopped by for fifteen minutes every few days to check his vitals and his strength, but that was it. Andy's friends, parents, and I were left to handle his care. And I became the taskmaster, a role Andy grew increasingly frustrated with as our conversations began consisting almost entirely of me nagging him to eat food.

He was scheduled to start treatment the Tuesday after our wedding, and he knew that he had to have some degree of strength to undergo the chemo. Otherwise, the doctors informed us, the treatment would do more harm than good: It would kill him.

"If you aren't healthy enough to be home, you won't be strong enough to undergo chemo," Andy's oncologist told us over the phone one day.

Andy was determined to make it to treatment, but if he didn't eat, none of that would happen.

Sitting with a bowl of soft food in front of him, hours would go by with Andy taking only a few bites.

"Andy, I need you to eat," I'd remind him.

He'd take another scoop and then sit staring at his food for another twenty minutes.

"If you don't eat, I'm going to have to take you to the hospital," I'd plead with him.

"Please don't do that," he'd cry.

"I don't know what else do to, Bean, you need to eat! You need to take your medicine!"

We'd repeat this routine over and over again, each meal taking so long that it would bleed into the next. A mostly full bowl was perpetually in front of him.

When Andy wasn't attempting to put his all into eating ice cream, he'd obsessively check his vitals with a fingertip clip that he asked us to buy for him. The small device that attached to his pointer finger measured his pulse and oxygenation level.

For people with cancer in their lungs, the oxygenation level is a key measurement. It indicates the amount of oxygen making it into the bloodstream. Measured on a scale of one to one hundred, healthy levels are in the high nineties. Fatal levels are in the sixties or seventies, but anything under ninety-five was problematic. We were told a person would likely lose consciousness somewhere in the eighties.

Each day, he watched as his oxygenation levels fluctuated between ninety-five and the low nineties. Sometimes it'd drop into the eighties and we'd have to turn up the amount of oxygen coming from the generator. Each increase would give him a little more energy, but as we approached the maximum output for the home machine, each increase also brought him closer to needing to go back to the hospital.

Our only respite from the now-constant struggle to keep him oxygenated, hydrated, and nourished was the wedding. Even with our friends handling most of the logistics, there were still small decisions for us to make. One was the song that would play after we exchanged our vows.

"Give me a thumbs-up when we get to one you want," I told him, knowing that talking was becoming too tiresome.

One by one, I played different songs as Andy drifted in and out of sleep. No thumbs-up. But then I got to the song he had played for me in the car on our first date, the one that I had listened to every day on my way to work at the White House, the one that had played when Sean and I spoke at the Human Rights Campaign's National Dinner just before Andy's first surgery.

When "Safe and Sound" started playing, Andy's eyes opened a little. He looked at me, managed a small smirk, and lifted up his thumb.

And then there were the vows. The next night, as a few of Andy's friends hosted a "bachelor party" in our living room for him, I hid in our bedroom and reviewed the draft Bishop Gene had sent us of the Episcopal church's wedding ceremony.

Andy's friends were determined to give him the full wedding experience. Completely relegated to his chair, they brought some small bachelor-party decorations and played music videos on our TV. I heard a burst of laughter come from the living room as Andy's fingertip oxygenation and pulse reader recorded an increase in his heart rate as a Beyoncé music video played on our TV.

"Someone's excited," a friend yelled, with Andy almost completely motionless in his recliner.

As Andy's friends "partied" in the living room, I edited the ceremony. Line by line, I went through it with a pen. The wedding would be hard enough emotionally. So I removed any mention of "death" and replaced it with "forever and ever." I wanted Andy to know that we'd be married long after he died.

Given his condition, I reduced the amount of lines we had to speak to three sentences:

"I do."

"That is my solemn vow."

And "Please accept this ring as a symbol of my abiding love."

I also knew it would be challenging for him to remember those lines, so I wrote them out, with their cues, on a half-sheet of paper.

The next morning, as I walked out of our bedroom, the early light filled our southern-facing living room. The space was strangely peaceful. By now, Andy was sleeping straight through much of the day.

"Beanie . . . Beanie . . ." I whispered to wake him up. "Can I read you our vows?"

He nodded a few times as he attempted to sit up a little. I tried reading the entire service to him for his approval, but he fell asleep pretty quickly. So when he re-awoke, I read just what was on the cheat sheet, including the line right before he was to say "I do." His cue was when Bishop Gene said, "Will you honor and love her forever and ever?"

After he said it was okay and began drifting off to sleep, I started walking back to our bedroom but stopped when I heard him mumbling. Thinking he needed something, I turned around, walked over to his chair, and leaned in. I couldn't quite hear, so I leaned farther in.

"Forever and ever," he whispered, now completely asleep. "Forever and ever, forever and ever . . ."

*Sweet dreams, my bean*, I thought. *Sweet dreams*.

...

I woke up the morning of Sunday, August 24, to a crisp, cloudless blue sky: Today was our wedding day. Andy's energy and spirits had marginally improved. His oxygen thirst had stopped increasing, stabilizing at a high but manageable level. He was even eating a little bit.

As I helped him eat some breakfast ice cream, our friends started arriving with decorations. Bouquets and tablecloths sat next to his medical equipment, filling all the remaining space. By four o'clock, I was in our neighbor's apartment getting ready. A few days earlier, I had gone out with two of my closest friends to a bridal shop just across the river in the colonial town of Alexandria, Virginia. After we explained the situation to the store owner, they agreed to fast-track alterations to any dress I picked and to have it to us in time for the Sunday wedding.

The first dress I tried on was absolutely perfect. The white lace floor-length dress with a V-shaped neckline that spread to off-the-shoulder sleeves needed very few alterations. Its low back led to a short train that spread out behind me. Now, standing in the calm of my neighbor's apartment, taking in the dress hanging on the closet door, the moment finally sank in: *I'm getting married.*

The thought was interrupted by three loud knocks.

*KNOCK. KNOCK. KNOCK.*

I opened the door to see one of Andy's best friends, Wes, out of breath and clearly shaken.

"Andy just had an episode. He started to collapse and go unconscious when he was moving from the recliner to his wheelchair. He is awake and his vitals are okay right now, but we called the police and the EMTs are on the way."

With my hair still up, I stormed into the apartment to find Andy in his recliner with Sean and our friends encircling him. I broke through and asked if he was okay.

He looked up at me, clearly feeling guilty that he had collapsed just before the wedding. "I'm sorry, are you mad at me?"

I felt guilty that Andy would even worry about that.

"Of course not, Beanie. Of course I'm not mad at you."

As the faint sirens approached, Sean leaned in and asked Andy a few questions to ensure he hadn't had a stroke.

"What's your name?"

"Andrew Cray."

"Who is the president?"

"Barack Obama."

"What day is it?"

His answer was a few days off, but he correctly identified it as "my wedding day."

The EMTs eventually came into our apartment and made their way through the wedding decorations and medical equipment to Andy's chair. They performed an EKG as they consulted with my brother, who had introduced himself as a doctor and informed them of Andy's health situation. As they talked, Andy interrupted them.

"I'm not going to the hospital," he declared, knowing what that would mean for our wedding and his chances at treatment.

The EMTs talked it over among themselves and with Sean, and with Andy's vitals normal, they agreed to his request. As they left, I asked Andy if he wanted to move the wedding to the apartment or cancel it altogether. He shook his head firmly.

"No. This is happening."

Sure enough, he rallied. With the help of three people, Andy was able to get into his blue button-up shirt and gray dress pants. Andy's friends were concerned that his bow tie might be too tight around his neck, so they scrapped tying it, instead draping it around his collar like James Bond's at the end of a long night. And with his oxygen tank in tow, he was wheeled up onto the roof of our building.

As Andy's wheelchair approached the crowd of fifty friends and relatives—most of whom had no idea that, just an hour before, EMTs had been ready to take him to the hospital—the guests started to applaud. A smirk crossed Andy's face, much of it covered by large, dark Ray-Bans. He lifted his fist in triumph. It was clear to everyone, including Andy, that it was a miracle that he'd made it up to that roof.

The wedding was filled with our families and the friends who had helped Andy through his first and now second round of cancer. At the front were our parents and siblings, and Andy's aunts and uncles. Two of our best friends—Kelsey, who had come out and transitioned alongside Andy in college, and Helen, my friend since middle school who had first helped me along my own journey to coming out—were prepared to read from scripture and a poem.

"Are you ready?" I asked my dad.

He stuck out his arm, ready to walk me down the aisle. I looped my arm through his and we made our way out to the roof.

In the weeks and months after I first came out, I worried that my parents would never truly see me as me. That they'd always love me as who they used to think I was, instead of who I am. But walking out on that roof with my dad, I knew they loved me as their daughter. I knew they loved me as Sarah. And in many ways, Andy's love for me helped them get there. Seeing someone love me as the woman I am provided my parents a path to do the same.

As I approached the crowd, I began to see the wedding that Bishop Gene and our friends had planned in less than a week. And it was perfect. The bouquets included some of my favorite flowers, purple orchids and blue hydrangeas. There were tables covered in purple tablecloths filled with food and desserts, including a small wedding cake topped with two robots holding hands.

*Amazing grace*, I thought.

I had always dreamed of a day like this: a beautiful wedding with a beautiful dress, marrying a wonderful person who loved me as me. I didn't anticipate it so soon. I certainly never anticipated it under these circumstances. But it was happening. Andy and I were both fulfilling a dream, however bittersweet the circumstances.

Passing through the crowd, we turned to walk down the short makeshift aisle, which led to a beautiful open white-topped tent about ten feet wide, reminding me of a chuppah. Flowers and ferns filled the inside. At the center sat Andy in his wheelchair, and beside him was Bishop Gene, smiling in his white, red, and gold wedding vestments. Behind them, the magnificent view of Washington, D.C.—the trees in the park just beside our building that gave way to views of the Capitol, the Washington Monument, and in the distance, the Jefferson Memorial.

My dad kissed my cheek and joined my mother in the row of chairs that circled the white tent. I stepped in front of Andy, who, shrunken in his wheelchair and with sunglasses on, almost looked like he was sleeping.

He clearly wasn't. He looked up at me, managed a smile, and mouthed the word "beautiful."

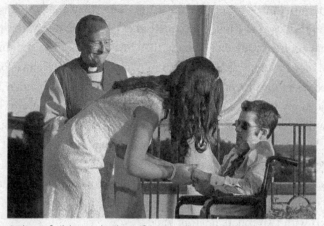

*Andy was frail, but on that beautiful August day, with Bishop Gene presiding, we made it up to our rooftop to marry each other.*

My mom always said that it was clear that Andy loved me from the first time he saw me at the White House Pride Reception two years before. I don't know about that, but what I do know is that Andy and I were committed to each other for life long before our wedding day that August. The ceremony merely formalized, before our family and by the state, what was already a reality between us. The vows we were about to take represented our transformational, transcending love. We had been through so much together already, having come into each other's lives at just the right time. He had helped walk me into my own authentic life and trans identity. And now I was there to help walk him to his death. Standing there, I knew that nothing in my life would ever be more important than what I was about to do.

"Andy and Sarah," Bishop Gene began, "you come before God to make public your commitment to one another and to ask God's blessing."

He turned to Andy, who tilted his head ever so slightly up to me as Bishop Gene continued. "Andy, do you freely and unreservedly offer yourself to Sarah? Do you commit yourself to love her with all of your heart? Say 'I do.'"

"I. DO," Andy responded breathlessly, the energy and difficulty of the sentence clear.

Bishop Gene asked the same of me.

"I do," I said directly to Andy.

The wind swept through the assembled crowd, rustling the flowers and carrying with it the sniffles of our friends and family.

"Sarah, in the name of God, do you give yourself to Andy? Will you support and care for him, enduring all things, carrying all things? Will you hold and cherish him in times of plenty and in times of want? Will you honor and love him forever and ever? Is this your solemn vow?"

"That is my solemn vow," I responded.

"Andy," he continued, "in the name of God, do you give yourself to Sarah? Will you support and care for her, enduring all things, carrying all things? Will you hold and cherish her in times of plenty and in times of want? Will you honor and love her forever and ever? Is this your solemn vow?"

"Th . . ." Andy paused. He couldn't say the full sentence. "Yes," he pushed out.

Sean and Kelsey stepped up from their chairs, bringing the two simple silver wedding bands Andy's mother had bought last-minute at a pawn shop in D.C. Bishop Gene blessed the two rings and then picked up Andy's hand. I bent forward, taking Andy's hand from Bishop Gene's.

"Andrew, please receive this ring as a symbol of my abiding love."

I pushed the band onto his frail finger.

Bishop Gene then handed Andy the ring he would put onto my hand. I extended my arm. Andy gently held my hand with his left hand as he slowly pushed the band onto my ring finger with his right.

"Sarah." He gasped for breath. "Please do the same."

With outstretched arms, we held on to each other as Bishop Gene proclaimed, "And as much as Andy and Sarah have exchanged vows of love and fidelity in the presence of God and family, I now pronounce them bound to one another in the holy covenant of marriage as husband and wife. Now and forever."

A smile crossed Andy's face. Holding my hand, he looked up from his wheelchair and softly whispered, "I love you."

The drums of "Safe and Sound" cued. And as the song from our first date played, my heart swelled, and I leaned in to kiss my husband.

# CHAPTER 11

# Righteous anger.

The first thirty-six hours of our marriage were exactly like the preceding thirty-six: a lot of sleeping on Andy's part and a lot of pushing him to eat on mine. He experienced two or three more fainting episodes like the one he'd had just before our ceremony. Each time, moving from his recliner to the wheelchair, his eyes would roll back into his head and his face would go white. Those of us around him would start yelling his name while frantically increasing his oxygen.

After each episode, in typical Andy fashion, he'd look up at me and say, "I'm sorry. Are you mad at me?," ashamed that he couldn't make the move and worried he was letting me down by not having the strength to do so.

"No, Beanie, I'm not mad at all. I love you very much," I'd say, trying to reassure him.

The second full day of our marriage was a big day for Andy. He was scheduled to begin the chemotherapy that we all hoped would prolong his life. Somehow we managed to make it from our apartment to Hopkins in Baltimore without another fainting episode.

Before we left, Sean had pulled me aside and warned, "Don't be surprised if they decide to admit Andy."

When the oncologist entered the exam room, it was obvious he was shocked by Andy's decline and the clear increase in oxygen through his nasal tubes. He didn't yet know about Andy's episodes, but blood work had already come back that showed troubling numbers. And despite my best attempts, Andy was significantly dehydrated.

"We may not be able to proceed with treatment today," the doctor informed us.

Andy looked so defeated. With the wedding in the past, all he wanted was to live as long as possible. Seeing Andy's response, the doctor continued: "But I'll tell you what, how about we send you up to the infusion center for some liquid and we'll see where you are. Maybe we can start with some lower doses of chemo." The doctor would also order a new blood test and meet us in the infusion center when the results came back. There was still some hope.

Up in the infusion center, they switched Andy from oxygen through his nose to a larger, clear mask that covered both his mouth and his nose. The change meant an increase in oxygen, which satiated Andy's need but further signaled his internal decline.

Waiting in a curtained-off area in the infusion center for the doctor to return, I heard some nurses discussing the need to admit a patient. I had a feeling who they were talking about, so I excused myself from Andy's side and stepped up to the nurses' counter.

"Um, do you all have an update on Andy?" I asked the three assembled women in scrubs, already knowing the answer.

He would have to be admitted, they informed me. *This is it*, I thought. *This is the end*.

"I'll go tell him," I offered, knowing the news would crush him. Both of us knew that, once admitted, the chance of treatment would evaporate.

The nurse followed me as I opened the curtain and went back to Andy's side. I tried to break the news as gently as possible. He knew what the news meant, but he held out hope that perhaps they'd stabilize him again and then, down the road, he could start treatment. But just as Andy gave me a wink, trying to assure *me* not to worry, the oncologist from earlier returned with even worse news. The concerning numbers had already jumped even higher.

Even with the new mask, Andy's thirst for oxygen continued to increase rapidly, each time requiring the nurse to turn the knob just a little higher, increasing the rush of air through his mouth and nose and into his lungs. As he had been for the last few days, Andy was drifting in and out of consciousness.

With Andy fading in and out, the oncologist asked to have a word with me outside of Andy's curtained area. We stepped out into the hallway, and the doctor turned to me with a pained look on his face.

"Have you two talked about intubation?" he asked, referring to the process of a breathing tube being inserted. The urgency of the question was obvious in his tone.

He didn't have to tell me what that meant for Andy. The fly-killing doctor two weeks before had made it crystal clear. If a breathing tube were to be introduced, Andy would never be able to be weaned off of it. If intubated, Andy would also need to be sedated to do it. And if sedated, Andy would likely never wake up again.

"Can I give him some time before we talk about it?" I requested. After all, he had just gotten the terrible news that he would be admitted.

"Unfortunately, no. You need to have the conversation as soon as possible."

We were immediately given an "upgraded room"—as I tried to jokingly put it during the admittance process—and I sat down with Andy for what would be the first and only extended conversation of our marriage: whether or not he wanted his life continued in a persistent vegetative state.

I was scared to broach the subject. I knew I would be crushing his hopes once again. I told him that for "precautionary reasons" we needed to talk about intubation. My hands shook as I held an advance directive given to us by the nurse.

"Can. It. Wait?" he asked, still straining to speak, but not quite as breathless, given the increased oxygen.

"No, I'm sorry, Bean, it can't."

His eyes widened and he sat up a bit, surprised at the rebuff and the message that it carried with it. I began paraphrasing the advance directive, asking which option he preferred.

"Don't patronize me," he shot back, upset that I was trying to simplify and shorten the language. The increase in oxygen, coupled with the seriousness of the topic, had given him a little extra energy. "I'm still a lawyer. Give me the document."

He stared at it for ten minutes, eventually picking up the pen I had put by his side and marking the box next to the option that read "If my doctors certify that I am in a persistent vegetative state . . . and there is no reasonable expectation that I will ever regain consciousness . . . keep me comfortable and allow natural death to occur."

He knew it was over, that he was in the definite twilight of his life. He didn't have to say anything; it was clear that in checking that box his last bit of hope disappeared.

I called our family and friends and told them to come to Baltimore. His father, his mother, his stepfather, and my mom came immediately. Bishop Gene and our friends, who had been by our side the previous few weeks now, made their way to the hospital.

On Sunday, they had sat in a semicircle around our white tent as Andy and I wed. But now, on Tuesday, that same group stood in a semicircle around his hospital bed, a collection of loved ones—transgender and cisgender; gay and straight; family, both blood and chosen—bound together by our love for Andy.

Some came up each day, but most stayed overnight. "Andy's Fun-Time Cancer Sleep-Away Camp for Adults," he had humorously called it earlier in his treatment. The hospital waiting room became the sleeping quarters for the fifteen who spent each night on the tile floor or on the waiting room's hard chairs, including his parents.

I spent the night in Andy's hospital room, sleeping in a chair next to his bed and holding his hand. My mom slept in a chair next to me, holding my other hand.

With each passing hour, Andy slept more and more. He'd occasionally wake up to squeeze our hands, give us a smile, or signal to us that he needed more oxygen. He'd raise his hand and rotate his fingers with a look of desperation in his eyes. Each time we'd have to tell him, "I'm sorry, it's as high as it can go."

That Wednesday—his second day in the hospital and three days since our wedding—was the last day Andy was awake. When his eyes opened in the late afternoon, I had a feeling it would be the final time I'd see his beautiful blue eyes and he would see mine. Somehow, without knowing how, I just knew. I leaned in and held his hand.

"I love you," I said with the knowledge that it would likely be the last time he'd hear the words.

He looked up at me, raised his eyebrows, and managed to say four words. They would be the last words Andrew Cray would ever speak.

"I love you, too."

His eyes closed and his head fell to the side as he drifted off. I knew instantly that he wouldn't be waking up again and that those would be his last words.

*I love you, too.* He wanted to say it just one more time. Just like with the wedding, he had rallied to express that love. It was perfectly Andy. His final words would not be ones of anger or pain but of love and commitment.

With Andy asleep again, I asked to be alone with him. I had remained stoic throughout the hospital stay, taking command and conferring with doctors, attempting to shield myself from my own emotions. But I needed to let it out.

As the door closed, I sat back down by Andy's side and exploded with tears, wailing as I buried my head into the side of the bed by his hand. *I don't know that I can do this without you,* I thought, crying into the sheets. My relationship with Andy had been a constant since coming out. So much of my confidence and comfort came from him, from our relationship, and from his reassurances. It's hard to live in this world as a trans person, and Andy had been my safe harbor, my safe space. We were supposed to spend the rest of our lives together.

I looked up from my crouched position toward Andy's head, covered with the oxygen mask. "I'm so sorry. I'm so sorry. I'm so sorry," I cried, as I crawled into bed with him. I lay there next to him, feeling his heartbeat, his chest rising and falling.

By the next morning, Thursday, August 28, it was clear that it was only a matter of time, and echoing a conversation I had with one of Andy's best friends the evening before, a nurse told us that sometimes patients need permission to pass away.

*That's so Andy*, we all thought.

One by one we all leaned in to give Andy permission to die.

I was the first and last person to convey that message to him. "I love you, Beanie. I'm going to miss you every day, but it's okay for you to go. No one is going to be mad at you."

I had to say it for him, but I also had to say it for myself. I had to remind myself that it was okay for him to go. That I was going to be fine. That he would be with me forever and ever.

As he grew weaker, the remaining energy and heat focused itself in the core of his body. I kissed the top of his head and slipped a handwritten note into his now-cold clinched fist. "You are loved," it read.

Within minutes, his breathing became more labored, his breaths fewer and deeper. His oxygenation levels began to drop—95 to 85. I called for everyone to come into the room—85 to 75.

We gathered around Andy. His dad held one hand and I the other. I sat next to his mother, and his stepdad stood behind her. My mom and Helen, who'd remained at the hospital for the preceding two days, put their hands on my shoulder.

Everyone was holding on to one another or on to Andy. Everyone was connected, hoping that somehow we could transfer love from the outermost person in the circle to Andy. The collective energy was palpable—75 to 65.

His breathing slowed even further. We continued to hold on to one another and to him. The room was silent but for the slowing beep of the heart monitor and the occasional sounds of quiet sobbing. We stood there for a few more minutes, waiting for the inevitable. I put both my hands around his left hand, which bore our new wedding band.

And then, at three-thirty p.m. that afternoon, Andy passed away.

No one moved for a few moments. No one said anything. No one knew what to do. A few erroneous beeps of the heart monitor cruelly startled us. We almost expected him to come back to life.

The silence continued, interrupted again thirty seconds later. *Beep*.

Frustrated, I silently stood up, the rest of the room looking at him. I walked out and asked a nurse to turn off the monitor.

"Please, just turn that damn thing off."

The room eventually cleared out and I was left alone with Andy again. I sat by his side like I had done right after his last words, this time holding his completely cold and stiff hands.

I stared at him, noticing that the color had evaporated from his face in the last few minutes. Tears began to run down my face. No more sobs like before. Just an exhausted silent release of emotions.

"I love you, too," I whispered, as I kissed his hand.

Over the next few hours, it all felt so unreal. The sadness mixed with exhaustion and disbelief clouded the hours after his death. Later that night, we met at a hotel conference room in Baltimore to decide on next steps. We were all still in shock. Here we were, the same group that had planned the wedding, now meeting to plan the funeral.

We had to answer questions that none of us knew the answer to, like whether Andy wanted to be buried or cremated. We racked our brains for comments or observations that he may have made at some point on the subject, eventually deciding on cremation so that all of us could have part of Andy to honor and remember.

Bishop Gene was tasked with finding a funeral home that, despite the plans to cremate, would ensure that any treatment of Andy's body would respect his gender identity. Frequently, after a trans person dies, we see their lives desecrated. One more indignity on top of the ultimate injustice. Trans people are often misgendered, misnamed, and sometimes even "de-transitioned" in their presentation by funeral homes, dressed up as their sex assigned at birth rather than their gender identity. One last cruel and tragic rebuke of the life they had fought to build for themselves.

"We can't let Andy be disrespected," I instructed Bishop Gene, who was clearly surprised and maddened to learn that this was something that trans people had to even think about. With some research and detective work, we managed to find a funeral home that assured us that they would honor Andy and his gender identity.

After two days of planning, on a humid August Saturday, six days after our wedding, three hundred friends, coworkers, family members, and even some strangers—people who never met Andy, but who benefited from his work—joined together for a funeral service just a few blocks from our apartment.

The funeral would be the first time in more than a month that I would not be rushing around, taking care of someone or something. My mind was finally clear of a to-do list—of responsibilities and others' needs—and the thought of actually having to grapple with my own emotions frightened me. The funeral would be the beginning of my own grieving process.

Like the weekend before, Bishop Gene presided. He wore the same white, red, and gold vestments from the wedding ceremony, declaring that both gatherings were a celebration of life and love. We sang "Here I Am Lord," a Presbyterian hymn that Andy and I both discovered a year before had been our favorite hymn growing up as active members of our local Presbyterian churches.

I asked three of Andy's best friends to eulogize him. His friend Fitz spoke about the preservation of energy, that matter is neither created nor destroyed, and that Andy continued on within the universe for eternity. Kelsey talked about the unique and binding journey that had joined them as "brothers," together struggling with their gender identity, coming out, and transitioning in college. Kellan, one of Andy's best friends and his "partner in crime" in all things LGBTQ health–related, talked about the lifesaving legacy Andy left behind and his selflessness through it all.

In one of the most jarringly moving moments, Kellan invited the entire sanctuary to stand up and applaud the small picture of Andy in front of the stage. During his life, Andy had never gotten the recognition for his game-changing work, but as the crowd rose from their seats and proceeded to applaud and cheer for five minutes straight, I knew that Andy was watching, both cringing and appreciating it all at the same time.

*Andy isn't gone*, I thought. *He lives on in the change he brought to this world.*

Andy's humility was so great in life that it took his death for me to fully understand the breadth and depth of his contributions to the community. Tributes came flooding in from elected officials and city councils across the country praising Andy for his help in expanding health access for LGBTQ people in their communities. Legislation protecting LGBTQ youth from discrimination in federally funded homeless shelters was introduced in the U.S. Senate, with the prime sponsor crediting Andy for making the bill possible.

Transgender people from across the country sent me messages and stories of their interactions with Andy. One transgender woman from Colorado whom I met at a conference had been able to transition, much like me, because Andy had helped advocates in her home state secure protections from discrimination in health insurance. She began crying as she described Andy, someone she barely knew, as an almost godlike figure in her life.

During the first two weeks after the funeral, everything still felt "temporary." I expected Andy to come through the door at any moment. But eventually the shock gave way to the grief that comes a few weeks in, when you fully realize the person is not just away on a trip. That they are gone and never coming back.

The smallest things would set me off. Random daily tasks would instantly trigger memories, particularly of the last month of pain and chaos. The flashbacks would leave me breathless and shaking. I never knew what would do it. It could be the purr of our cat Waffles, who still lived with me, or something as small as getting on the elevator in our apartment building.

He felt so present and so far away all at the same time. While our friends had cleaned out our closets of many of Andy's clothes, Waffles slept every night on a pile that remained. I'd hear Andy's voice calling from around the corner in our apartment for me to come because dinner was ready. I'd hear his breathing as I went to sleep.

I started texting daily with Andy's mom. Through my relationship with Andy, and his battle with cancer, I had gained a family. As difficult as it was for me, my heart ached for what his parents had to go through. No parent should have to watch their child pass away. And I worried that I would be a reminder of what they had lost. But in the days after Andy's passing, his parents made clear to me that I would forever be their daughter.

With time, they also made it clear that they'd understand if I moved on. When they talked about me remaining their daughter, they increasingly included the addition of any future partner. They didn't want me to feel any pressure or worry that I'd have to choose between my new family and a new partner.

When my friends would ask me about dating again, I'd flippantly say, "I'm twenty-four, transgender, and a widow . . . that's a lot for someone in this society to handle." But the truth is that I really wasn't interested. Even as time passed, new love was the one thing I wasn't in a hurry to find.

I've never believed that there is only one person in this world for everyone; chance wouldn't allow all of us to find that person in a world of five billion people with varying cultures, geography, and languages. But I did feel like I had experienced more love in my two years with Andy than most people do in several decades. My heart was totally full (and then some), and I genuinely felt blessed for it.

And Andy's friends made sure I continued to feel the love that Andy had for me even after he was gone. Before his illness, I hadn't been incredibly close with Andy's friends, but through it all, we made lifelong bonds. They had personified amazing grace, demonstrating the goodness of their hearts in the ways they encircled Andy with support.

The months following his death continued to be a roller coaster of emotions as I made my way through the different stages of grief. Disbelief and, later, depression, followed by anger: a quiet but significant anger.

I'm not an angry person by nature. Petty anger, the kind we feel when we are slighted by a friend or feel underappreciated, seems like a waste of time and energy to me. But petty anger isn't the only form that exists. There's also righteous anger, the kind of anger that, when checked with hope and mixed with a cause, can help change the world.

I find it very hard to be angry unless blame is clear. But where was the blame here? I couldn't be mad at Andy's cancer because it was a collection of cells. I couldn't be mad at the bad luck of terminal cancer because no one caused the cancer to happen.

No, I was mad at society. Andy had the courage to come out to a hateful world at a relatively young age. He was supposed to live three-quarters of his life as his authentic self. Instead, because cancer cut his life short, he had less than a quarter. Some people have even less time than that.

Even with a supportive, progressive family, hate had kept Andy inside himself for what turned out to be the majority of his life. None of us know how long we have, but we do have a choice in whether we love or hate. And every day that we rob people of the ability to live their lives to the fullest, we are undermining the most precious gift we are given as humans.

As I said to that state representative in Delaware who had admonished us for moving the trans equality bill too quickly, each time we ask anyone—whether they are transgender, Black, an immigrant, Muslim, Native American, gay, or a woman—to sit by and let an extended conversation take place about whether they deserve to be respected and affirmed in who they are, we are asking people to watch their one life pass by without dignity or fairness. That is too much to ask of anyone.

I was furious at society for taking that time and truth away from Andy. I was angry that people were dying after being denied the right to pursue happiness and wholeness in whatever life they lived.

And in that anger, a deeper fire was lit and a lesson was learned. Every day matters in this fight. Dr. King called it "the fierce urgency of now." Hope can be limitless. Inspiration can always be found. Ideas are endless. But time, that is one resource none of us can afford to waste.

And so I jumped back into *our* work. My weeks were filled with my work at CAP, and increasingly, my weekends were filled with travel, speaking at events across the country with the Human Rights Campaign. I felt closer to Andy continuing the work that we were both so passionate about. And at the center of that work was the fight for nondiscrimination protections for LGBTQ people in every corner of this country.

Before his death, Andy and I had convinced our colleagues at the Center for American Progress to embrace the idea of a comprehensive LGBTQ civil rights bill, a nationwide law that would not just prohibit discrimination in employment like ENDA, but also in housing, public spaces, schools, health care, stores, shops, restaurants, and shelters.

The same conversations that Andy and I, and later our colleagues at CAP, were having about thinking bigger and bolder in our federal advocacy were simultaneously happening across town at HRC. And to our surprise, as we worked on our report at CAP, in mid-July, just two weeks before Andy was rediagnosed with cancer, HRC came out publicly in favor of a comprehensive nondiscrimination bill in an op-ed by the organization's president, Chad Griffin.

"At the end of the day, full federal equality is the only acceptable option," he wrote in the piece. "Nothing more, nothing less."

I had gotten to know Chad through my travels with HRC. Before moving to D.C. to lead the nation's largest LGBTQ civil rights organization, he had helped lead the successful effort to overturn California's Proposition 8, the state constitutional amendment banning same-sex marriage.

Since Chad's move to HRC in 2012, I had been impressed with his charisma and compassion. But what struck me above all else was his desire to stand up for the most marginalized in the LGBTQ community in his role as HRC's president—one of the most prominent positions in the equality movement—and his clear desire for a bold agenda. His op-ed endorsing a comprehensive LGBTQ civil rights bill demonstrated that, coinciding perfectly with the work that my colleagues and I were doing at CAP.

After Andy's passing, I rededicated myself to the issue with a renewed passion and sense of urgency. With many of the same friends and colleagues who had helped us through the last month of Andy's life, including Bishop Gene, we produced a ninety-four-page report called "We the People: Why Congress and U.S. States Must Pass Comprehensive LGBT Nondiscrimination Protections."

"Throughout the 230-year history of the United States, the nation has slowly but steadily expanded access to every vital facet of daily life—from housing to employment to the public marketplace—for communities of Americans who were once excluded," it opened. "Through exhaustive efforts, each generation has broadened the nation's perception of 'we the people.' But despite this progress, too many Americans are still left behind, excluded from the country's most basic legal protections."

The report recounted many of the sobering statistics and stories I had become all too familiar with during our fight for gender identity protections in Delaware and in the year and a half since. One in four transgender people reported being fired from their job simply because of their gender identity. A quarter of same-sex couples experienced housing discrimination in one survey. More than half of

LGBTQ students reported feeling unsafe in schools because of their sexual orientation, and roughly one-third feel unsafe because of their gender according to the student advocacy group GLSEN.

We released the report in December 2014, four months after Andy's death, at a public event at CAP. The moment marked a clear shift in the broader national progressive movement's approach to LGBTQ equality. No longer would we shrink into incrementalism. No longer would we ask for a quarter of a loaf while our community needed a full loaf. As HRC's Chad Griffin had written several months before, we needed full federal equality.

Being the report's lead author, I joined Chad Griffin, out gay member of Congress Mark Takano, and civil rights leader and Maryland pastor Delman Coates on a panel discussing the report and the need for a new federal LGBTQ civil rights act. The conversation was moderated by Maya Harris, who would later serve as the head of policy for Hillary Clinton's 2016 presidential campaign.

But the highlight of the event was the announcement made by Senator Jeff Merkley, the progressive champion who had taken over as the prime sponsor of ENDA, that in the next Congress he would introduce a comprehensive LGBTQ civil rights bill. It was a historic declaration that forever changed the priorities and approach of the LGBTQ movement, and he did so while standing at a lectern and holding up our report, a document dedicated to Andy's memory.

It was a bittersweet moment. Andy would have cherished it. And as the LGBTQ community continued to make significant steps and historic progress over the next two years, each time I couldn't help but think, *I wish Andy were here for this.* Andy would have marveled at the pace of the change that was happening, a rate of progress that, while never fast enough, soon began to feel like an avalanche of advancements.

More and more states were adopting the policies in health care that Andy had championed in his life. Trans visibility, with role models like Laverne Cox and Janet Mock, increased beyond even the "transgender tipping point" of 2013. A brilliant and hilarious transgender woman, Raffi Freedman-Gurspan, made national headlines when she was appointed the first openly transgender White House staffer. Caitlyn Jenner's coming out, as much as I disagree with her political beliefs, initiated conversations around trans identities in living rooms and around dinner tables across the country. And through it all, the percentage of Americans saying they personally know someone who is transgender rose from single digits to roughly a third.

The LGBTQ community writ large experienced almost unimaginable progress. Support for marriage equality continued to rise and initiated a domino effect within the courts. Almost weekly, marriage bans were falling in states across the country.

Eventually, on June 26, 2015, the U.S. Supreme Court issued their historic decision legalizing marriage equality throughout the country. The specifics of the case hit home for me. The Ohio plaintiff in the case, Jim Obergefell, had lost his husband, John, to ALS, the fatal disease that slowly eats away at the individual's motor skills. Because Ohio still banned same-sex marriage, Jim and John, whose health was deteriorating, flew to Maryland, where same-sex marriage was legal, and married on the tarmac onboard a medically equipped plane.

When John passed away a short time later, Jim learned that, despite being legally married in Maryland, the Ohio government would keep his name off John's death certificate, leaving the category of "surviving spouse" blank. Another indignity imposed on LGBTQ people that extended beyond life and into death.

But in a vote of five to four, the nation's highest court ruled against this injustice in favor of nationwide marriage equality.

No union is more profound than marriage, for it embodies the highest ideals of love, fidelity, devotion, sacrifice, and family. In forming a marital union, two people become something greater than once they were. As some of the petitioners in these cases demonstrate, marriage embodies a love that may endure even past death. It would

misunderstand these men and women to say they disrespect the idea
of marriage. Their plea is that they do respect it, respect it so deeply
that they seek to find its fulfillment for themselves. Their hope is not
to be condemned to live in loneliness, excluded from one of civiliza-
tion's oldest institutions. They ask for equal dignity in the eyes of the
law. The Constitution grants them that right.

The atmosphere outside of the Supreme Court and around D.C.
was euphoric following the decision. Soon, news spread that in the ultimate celebration of pride in this historic moment, President Obama
would light up the White House in rainbow colors. And as the sun
set, I joined friends in Lafayette Park, the square just in front of the
White House, to watch the colors of the rainbow envelop the front of
the home of Lincoln, Roosevelt, Kennedy, and now Barack Obama.

Standing amid a sea of same-sex couples celebrating and LGBTQ
people waving rainbow flags, my mind went back to the previous August on our rooftop. I put my hand on my wedding ring, which I continued to wear after Andy's passing. I lifted my hand up to my mouth
and kissed my ring. *I wish Andy were here for this,* I thought again.

"I love you, Bean," I whispered.

While Andy and I were not a same-sex couple and, therefore, were
always eligible to marry, our relationship underscored for me the importance of marriage equality. The roughly 1,500 rights and benefits
associated with marriage go far beyond taxes and include things such
as leave and medical decision-making. For lower-income and working-
class same-sex couples, without the legal recognition of marriage, the
type of illness Andy faced could easily result in having to choose between being fired from your job and serving as a caregiver.

And while my relationship with Andy and our circumstances demonstrated the practical reasons for access to marriage, it also reinforced
the broader importance summed up in Justice Anthony Kennedy's
opinion of the Court. Even facing death, Andy wanted our relationship affirmed and celebrated by our community and society. He likely

should have passed away days before our wedding, but he held on for that simple but common desire to have our love recognized.

I felt grateful to have experienced the kind of love we were celebrating that night and in awe of the significant step forward we had just made as a country. And as darkness fell in Lafayette Square, the colors projected on the north side of the White House grew in their intensity. It was a moving sight. If the Court's decision earlier in the day had been a tangible embrace of equality by our government, that evening's display reflected a symbolic one.

Somewhere in Kansas, or South Carolina, or Utah, a young LGBTQ kid opened up their computer that night. They may have just heard anti-LGBTQ slurs around the dinner table. They may have just been called names in their neighborhood. But on that Friday night in June 2015, they went to sleep after seeing the White House—the ultimate symbol of our democracy—light up like a rainbow.

The ground was shifting beneath our feet; you could almost feel it.

# CHAPTER 12

# There was that word again.
# "History."

It's not often you know that you're witnessing history when it's happening, but that realization was unmistakable in 2015 and 2016. Our community's progress would have seemed unimaginable just a decade before. But because of the tireless work of advocates and activists and the quiet courage of everyday LGBTQ people, "the arc of the moral universe" was bending toward justice. As broken as our politics can seem, our community proved that we can still do big things in this country, that when we advocate from a place of passion and authenticity, change will come.

In the months ahead, the progress continued to roll in: enhanced protections for transgender students, the removal of the ban on transgender service members in our nation's military, and the release of protections in health care that Andy had fought for throughout our relationship.

In a much-anticipated move, the Obama administration made clear that the Affordable Care Act's ban on discrimination based on sex included discrimination against transgender people, including for transition-related care. For the first time ever, transgender people would be afforded clear nationwide protections in federally funded health-care programs and institutions. And while that didn't impact every single health-care provider, it included most insurance plans and hospitals.

Flipping through the pages of the regulation with my colleagues, our hearts filled with pride as we realized that Andy and his work were referenced by name several times throughout the lifesaving document. When I got home, I looked up at the urn of Andy's ashes and the picture of him that sat right next to it. "I'm so proud of you, Bean," I said. "You did it."

As was the case when Andy shepherded through Washington, D.C.'s local health-care nondiscrimination policy, now, even in death, cancer hadn't taken away his voice. He had passed away, but he was still saving others' lives.

But despite these historic steps forward, we were still a long way from full nationwide equality. Progress isn't always linear and can often elicit a dangerous backlash, one that often targets the most marginalized within a community. Violence against LGBTQ people, particularly trans women of color, appeared to be ticking up. In 2016, at least twenty-two trans people were killed in the United States, the most lives lost on record in a single year up until that point.

I routinely met LGBTQ people facing discrimination, couples like Jami and Krista Contreras in Michigan whose six-day-old baby had been denied care by a pediatrician simply because Krista and Jami were a same-sex couple. People like Diane, a transgender factory worker who was forced to place a humiliating sign outside of the women's restroom if she was using it, as if she was a threat to others.

"People won't even park their cars next to mine in the parking lot," she told me. "I'm completely isolated."

While same-sex couples could now legally marry in all fifty states, D.C., and the U.S. territories, LGBTQ people in a majority of states were still at risk of being discriminated against in the workplace, housing, and public spaces. In a majority of states, gay workers could be legally married but then could potentially be fired for placing a picture of their spouse on their desk. More and more transgender people could gain access to health care to live their authentic lives but could be denied access to even the most basic necessities for doing so. In every case, transgender people, and particularly trans people of color, face the brunt of this discrimination.

Soon enough, Senator Merkley held to the promise he made at CAP to introduce a comprehensive LGBTQ nondiscrimination bill. In an ornate room just off the floor of the U.S. Senate, flanked by the first openly LGBTQ senator, Tammy Baldwin, civil rights leader Representative John Lewis, and other elected officials, Senator Merkley and openly gay Representative David Cicilline introduced the Equality Act.

The room was packed with reporters and activists. Cameras lined the back wall across from a lectern with a sign that read "Equality Forward." The LBJ Room, named after the former president who had signed the Civil Rights Act into law in the 1960s, was filled with light from three big windows that looked out onto the expansive lawn just in front of the Capitol, and right in the middle of the central window was a view of the U.S. Supreme Court.

Empowered by our historic progress, our movement was now shifting to a bolder strategy, demanding full federal equality. The Equality Act would be one of the most extensive civil rights bills introduced since the Americans with Disabilities Act, which passed in 1991, and it was introduced with more congressional cosponsors on day one than any LGBTQ legislation in history, a sign of the rapidly shifting public opinion.

Nowhere was the need for these explicit and irrefutable protections more evident than in North Carolina. As gay people became a less effective boogeyman for anti-equality forces, extreme politicians began to turn their attention to transgender people. In early 2016, the city council in North Carolina's largest city, Charlotte, adopted an LGBTQ-inclusive nondiscrimination ordinance much like the laws passed in Delaware, several other states, and more than one hundred cities.

An important but by no means extraordinary step by the city

council was quickly and disingenuously used by anti-LGBTQ politicians in the North Carolina state legislature and by the state's Republican governor, Pat McCrory, as an excuse to push for a so-called "bathroom bill," legislation that would restrict access to restrooms in public buildings, such as schools, airports, and government offices, to the gender marker on a person's birth certificate.

The practical impact of the bill would be similar to the almost-added amendment we thankfully avoided in Delaware during the fight for our positive nondiscrimination bill. By limiting restroom access in public buildings based on a person's birth certificate, the bill would ban the vast majority of the trans community—most of whom have not been able to update the gender marker on their birth certificate—from using bathrooms consistent with their gender identity in many core areas of life.

In an almost laughably extreme move, the governor called the state's legislature in for a special session specifically to regulate where trans people could pee. Calling a special session is required when a legislature has adjourned for an extended period of time and is usually utilized for emergency situations such as a natural disaster. But these legislators could see that the clock was ticking on their political ability to legislate discrimination against trans people. Soon, public opinion would change so much that it would become politically impossible.

It's no surprise that antitrans extremists have targeted bathrooms. Every fight for civil and human rights over the last several decades has included controversies about restrooms. It's partly because we all feel vulnerable in those spaces, so it is easy to instill fear in people.

But it's also more calculated and sinister than that. Access to a restroom is necessary everywhere: in schools, in workplaces, and in public venues. These so-called bathroom bills are nothing more than an attempt to legislate transgender people out of public life.

In March 2016, the North Carolina legislature met in their special session and, in a matter of hours, passed the antitransgender bill, which Governor McCrory signed into law that night. The law, infamously known as House Bill 2, or HB2, wasn't just a bathroom bill; it also included a laundry list of harmful policies. Cities could no longer pass any LGBTQ nondiscrimination protections. Civil rights protections for other identities were undermined. And localities were forbidden from setting their own minimum wages.

The reaction from around the nation was swift and furious, particularly in regard to the section of the law that required state facilities to discriminate against transgender people. Businesses began to boycott. Conventions and concerts started to pull out. Athletic associations made clear they wouldn't locate events in the state. And within weeks, North Carolina was hemorrhaging jobs and economic activity.

But more than anything else, the bill hurt real people. Transgender public school students, many of whom were already using restrooms consistent with their gender identity in school, were now faced with being in violation of state law if they continued to do so.

Just a month after passage of the law, I flew down to North Carolina with a film crew from CAP to interview an eighteen-year-old transgender boy about HB2. Finn Williams lived just outside Durham, North Carolina, and had come out to a supportive family a few years before. After coming out, Finn had gone to four different schools trying to find one that would both allow him to use the boys' restroom and combat the bullying he experienced. In denying Finn access to the boys' restroom, he was told that he would make the other students uncomfortable.

"Just being me shouldn't make other people uncomfortable," Finn told us.

He eventually dropped out of high school entirely instead of facing the constant bullying from peers and humiliation by his school. And now the North Carolina legislature had mandated effectively the same treatment Finn had experienced for the thousands of transgender students statewide.

After finishing up with Finn, we traveled to Charlotte and met with a member of the city council, a trailblazing out lesbian woman named LaWana Mayfield who had helped lead the charge for the city's now-banned LGBTQ nondiscrimination ordinance. After wrapping up our discussion, and just before we left for the airport, I popped into the women's restroom at the Charlotte government center, where we'd interviewed Councilwoman Mayfield.

I had avoided public restrooms while in the state, but I couldn't hold it in any longer. I went in and, just like everyone else, peed. After washing my hands, as I stood alone in the bathroom, I took out my phone and snapped a selfie.

I posted the photo on Instagram and Facebook with the caption:

Here I am using a women's restroom in North Carolina that I'm technically barred from being in.

They say I'm a pervert.

They say I'm a man dressed as a woman.

They say I'm a threat to their children.

They say I'm confused.

They say I'm dangerous.

And they say accepting me as the person I have fought my life to be seen as reflects the downfall of a once great nation.

I'm just a person. We are all just people. Trying to pee in peace. Trying to live our lives as fully and authentically as possible. Barring me from this restroom doesn't help anyone. And allowing me to continue to use this bathroom—just without fear of discrimination and harassment—doesn't hurt anyone.

Stop this. We are good people. #repealhb2

I posted the picture and caption to underscore for my own friends the simple fact that this wasn't an abstract issue. This was a law banning real people like me from public restrooms. I didn't think much of it as I set my phone to airplane mode and took off for Colorado, where I would be speaking at an HRC event in Denver.

As we took off, I looked back at North Carolina knowing I could return to my supportive bubbles, but for so many transgender North Carolinians like Finn, HB2 was an everyday reality. They couldn't escape it.

By the time we landed and I turned on my phone, my Facebook notifications had exploded. At first hundreds of people had shared my photo. Then, a few hours later, thousands. Then ten thousand. Twenty. Thirty. Forty. Then fifty thousand shares.

Soon the media started calling. *BuzzFeed* posted a viral piece: THIS TRANS WOMAN POSTED A SELFIE TO CHALLENGE NORTH CAROLINA'S BATHROOM LAW. Mic.com called it the "Best Selfie Ever," a story Yahoo News reposted. Another article called it an "illegal" selfie. *Teen Vogue* described it as a "powerful political move." MSNBC featured the picture and read the caption on Chris Hayes's primetime television show.

The post filled with comments. Some were great, with the initial wave reinforcing the harm of HB2 and the points I made in the text of the post. Other supportive comments, though, missed the point and began to focus on my appearance as, at least in the picture, a "passable" trans woman.

When I first posted the selfie, thinking that it was going to be limited to my friend network, I posted the picture along with the text to reinforce the realness of the law. But as it spread, the post soon became less about the text and more about the picture itself. Several comments read variations of the same thought: "Of course you belong in the women's restroom, look at you."

I had seen this and tried to push back on that same narrative in Delaware.

And now I tried to use the platform I was given to stress that this wasn't about how I, or any trans person, looked. It was about who we are. Civil rights shouldn't depend on appearance. And the fact of the matter is that those most impacted by laws such as HB2 are the trans people who aren't like me, particularly gender-nonconforming trans people and trans people of color.

Part of me considered stepping back from the stories, but I worried that my message was being lost. I feared that my words were being drowned out by the "vulnerable cuteness of [my] doe-eyes accented with white eyeliner," as one writer put it. I certainly wouldn't be the first woman to have her thoughts overshadowed by her appearance and femininity. So I decided to try to counter that takeaway, to utilize the opportunities for interviews to provide nuance to the reactions. But of course, participating in the stories only perpetuated the attention.

Each story pointed people back to my personal social media accounts. The positive comments were quickly overwhelmed with a flood of hate.

I had witnessed firsthand in Delaware the emotions that the bathroom conversation stirred up in people, but nothing I had experienced quite prepared me for this. The topic of trans bathroom access was contentious, but the actual sight of a trans woman in a women's bathroom was explosive. For many who viewed my picture, it was the first time they had ever knowingly seen any kind of image of a trans woman in a women's bathroom. The political climate and increased violent rhetoric had only ratcheted up the passions.

My social media accounts were filled with threats. The dark web, the underground websites that have become home to "alt-right" trolls, filled with conversations about gang-raping me or murdering me. In the days after the post, my workplace was forced to heighten their security protocol because of the threats that were coming my way.

The most common message wasn't a threat so much as a violent request, frequently appearing as three letters: "kys."

Kill yourself.

Message after message told me to take my own life. My phone would illuminate every three seconds with the same message. Again and again.

"kys."

"kill yourself."

"fucking die u ugly monster."

"kill yourself."

"kys."

"kill yourself you look like a man."

"it."

"kys."

"it."

"you are disgusting and worthless."

Eventually, I turned off the notifications, but every so often I would log on to report and delete some of the most violent and hateful comments. I didn't want young trans kids who followed my social media accounts to see them. I even thought about taking down the picture or setting my accounts to private, but then the haters would have won. I resolved to keep it all up, even if I was miserable.

My parents were instinctually nervous about all the attention, but given their limited use of social media, they had no idea of the hate that was coming my way. I couldn't bear to tell them. I felt completely alone, and honestly, I just wanted Andy. I just wanted him to say "I love you." I just wanted him to hold me, to reassure me. I wanted him to tell me that I was beautiful and that he was proud of me.

The thought of suicide had never crossed my mind. Even in my harshest or hardest moments, I always felt lucky to be alive. Watching Andy fight to live only reinforced how lucky I felt to be alive and to be continuing to fight. But as the messages continued flooding in, I just wanted to escape it all. I couldn't take it anymore.

Standing in my hotel bathroom in downtown Denver, just an hour before I was set to speak before five hundred people at the HRC Mile High Dinner, my heart began racing and I started to hyperventilate. I knew the stories would diminish in a matter of days and the negativity would cease, but after being told to kill myself thousands of times for days, the thought of suicide somehow became a rational thought in my mind for the first time ever. It was a way to end it right now, to escape the deluge of hate. Wrapped in my bath towel, I sat on the edge of the bathtub and began to cry.

*Get it together. Get it together. Get it together.*

I never in a million years would have thought strangers telling me to kill myself would have had such a significant impact on my own psyche. I thought I was too old. Too jaded. With so many privileges and such amazing support structures, how could these words on a screen even begin to shake me to my core?

But they did. And they do for so many. Thinking about the constant bombardment of bullying in schools, I wondered, *How on earth does anyone survive this?*

Across the country, there are young people for whom the glimpse into harassment that I experienced was an everyday reality, both online and in person. And for them it won't go away in two or three days. They won't be able to walk out on a stage in a room full of affirming, loving people like I was set to do that night. Hell, they may not even be able to go home to a family who accepts them. Change cannot come fast enough for the students who must build up so much strength and perseverance to merely make it through the school day.

In the days and weeks after the harassment, I worried about my reaction and what it meant for my future in this work and movement. If I couldn't handle a damn selfie, how could I do more?

The thought plagued my thinking for several weeks. As passionate as I was about the work that I was doing, I wondered whether I was strong enough for it. I worried that I didn't have the confidence for it. I just wanted to curl up into a ball and give up what little platform I had developed.

The kind of hate I experienced was an occupational hazard. At least for the time being, it was a reality of the world we live in. If I were to continue, I'd have to figure out a way to get past it or be miserable. And then one day, after listening to a story about a reporter who had embraced her weight publicly and faced a serious online backlash because of it, something clicked.

It's trite to say that many of the biggest bullies are often LGBTQ themselves and in the closet. It may be true in some cases, but it glosses over a more universal truth that underlies the pervasiveness of anti-LGBTQ hate.

Surely, not everyone who bullies is in the closet. But everyone does hold some kind of insecurity. Whether it's your sexual orientation, your gender identity, how you look, what you sound like, what you do for a living, or any multitude of characteristics, everyone struggles with something that society has told them is wrong. But as LGBTQ people, we have had the courage to embrace something that many think we should be ashamed of; we have stood up and decided to live our truth, not just from a place of authenticity, but so often from a place of pride. We have exercised our own individual agency and power to overcome what was once an insecurity to hold our heads high and proclaim: "This is who I am and there is nothing wrong with me."

And the bullies see that. They see our power and they are jealous of it. They envy the agency we have been able to exercise and the clear power we hold. So often that is where their hate and vitriol come from.

We *are* powerful. In Delaware, I had to learn the power of my own voice. Now I needed to understand the power of my own identity—of LGBTQ lives—to move forward. Society can't make me feel voiceless when I know the power of my own voice. And society can't make me feel weak when I know that I am powerful just for being.

Suddenly, the comments started to hurt less. I was still cognizant of my safety, but I was no longer bogged down by the insults. I was ready to be at the center of the fight.

After three educational, empowering, and emotional years at CAP, I accepted a job at the Human Rights Campaign as their national press secretary. I had been traveling to and speaking at their events, so it seemed like a natural fit to join the organization in a spokesperson role.

It was hard to leave my job at CAP, since it carried with it so many memories of Andy, but I knew that the day would come sooner or later. And as the nation's largest LGBTQ equality organization, HRC was at the forefront of the movement that was already transforming America for the better.

So much of the LGBTQ community's progress was made possible because we had a steadfast defender and supporter in the White House. Barack Obama had done more for LGBTQ rights than all of his predecessors combined. But all of that progress—and the potential for more—was on the line in the 2016 election.

When it came to LGBTQ equality, our country would choose between Hillary Clinton, who, like President Obama, supported and embraced equality, and Donald Trump, who, despite empty claims of being a "friend to the LGBTQ community," had endorsed nearly every single anti-equality position possible. Throughout the election, Hillary Clinton had run the most trans-inclusive campaign in history. She had endorsed all of the major policy goals of the trans community, lifted up trans people and voices, and consistently included trans people, explicitly, in her vision for a kinder, more welcoming country.

I was passionate about continuing the White House's support for trans equality and I knew I couldn't sit on the sidelines. Too much was at stake. Together with two other trans activists, Mara Keisling and Babs Siperstein, as well as an unrivaled ally, Lisa Mottet, we cofounded Trans United for Hillary, a national volunteer effort to mobilize transgender people in support of Hillary Clinton.

In the spring of 2016, Hillary clinched the Democratic nomination and the party began preparing for her formal nomination in

Philadelphia that July, a convention that promised to be historic. Trans United for Hillary and the Clinton campaign were intent on making the DNC the most inclusive major party convention ever. We wanted to set a record for the number of openly transgender delegates and even toyed with the idea of a transgender speaker.

Then, just after July 4, I got a call from Roddy Flynn, the executive director of the LGBT Equality Caucus in Congress, a collection of members of the House of Representatives committed to LGBTQ equality and cochaired by the openly LGBTQ representatives. Roddy, an openly gay man, had joined the staff about a year before and had worked tirelessly to expand the caucus's work on trans issues.

"The caucus cochairs have committed to dedicating half of our six minutes onstage at the Democratic National Convention to having a trans person speak, and they have decided that the caucus will be submitting your name as our speaker."

Roddy continued: "I wanted to let you know, but I also want to make clear that this is just a request. And it's still subject to approval from the Clinton campaign and the DNC, so it's not definite yet."

My head was spinning just at the possibility. On the one hand, I was scared of the hate that would inevitably come my way on such a major stage. On the other hand, speaking at the Democratic National Convention would be a dream come true.

At thirteen, the same age that I began to get involved in Delaware politics, I was glued to the 2004 Democratic National Convention on C-SPAN. Sitting on the floor of my bedroom, I had been introduced to a little-known Illinois state senator who delivered a barn burner of a keynote address. *Barack Obama,* I thought then. *I hope I can vote for him for president someday.*

I was so excited and inspired by the convention proceedings that I built a replica of the convention stage—replete with the Democratic Party donkey flag—in my bedroom, constructed however poorly from plywood and boxes I found in our basement. There I'd deliver my favorite speeches from the week's proceedings. Throughout that summer, my parents must have heard me recite then–state senator Barack Obama's keynote ten or twelve times.

In 2012, I was working at my tiny desk in the White House when President Obama accepted renomination for president of the United States. I could never have imagined that just four years later, in 2016, I would stand on that very same stage and address the Democratic convention and the millions of viewers at home.

A few weeks after the initial call with Roddy, on a Sunday afternoon in late July—a week and a day before the convention was scheduled to begin—I finally got the definitive word.

"Give me a call," Roddy texted me coyly.

I had been on the edge of my seat for the last three weeks, waiting for any kind of news. My gut is usually right, and I just couldn't imagine that I would really speak at the convention. Something would get in the way.

"Roddy! What's up?" I anxiously asked after he picked up the phone.

"I just got word from the campaign. You've passed vetting and are confirmed."

"OH MY GOD! This doesn't feel real. Are you sure?!"

Almost in disbelief, I called the LGBTQ liaison on the Clinton campaign, who confirmed the news. As the call ended, he closed with a question: "Are you ready to make history?"

"History"? That's a big word. I knew it would be a "first," but history didn't seem to fit. *I'm twenty-five,* I thought dismissively. *I don't "make history."*

Over the next week, I worked with friends and colleagues to draft my remarks. I had only three minutes, and there was so much to talk about. How would I narrow down everything to 180 seconds?

I knew I wanted to stress two points. The first was that, despite our progress, a lot of work remains in the fight for LGBTQ, and specifically trans, equality. The second point, and, frankly, the main one, was to remind people that behind this national debate on trans rights are real people who love, fear, laugh, cry, hope, and dream just like everyone else. So often we lose sight of the humanity behind these issues. If I was going to be the first, I wanted to use this opportunity to reinforce the almost absurdly simple point that transgender people are, first and foremost, human.

The Democratic National Convention assigned me a volunteer speechwriter. Veteran communications staffers from offices on the Hill typically volunteer their services for the convention. It's an all-hands-on-deck operation for politicos. I had the option of writing my first draft or talking with the speechwriter on the phone for a bit and allowing her to put something together. Protective of my story and cognizant of the nuances of discussing trans identities, I chose the former.

"Three hundred sixty words, though," I was instructed. "That's your limit, and they are strict."

I wrote out a first draft, utilizing material I had used in the past, and looked at the word count. Six hundred words. Cutting a few words here and there was easy. Trimming more than a third of an already brisk speech was nearly impossible. Sitting at my computer at my desk in the Human Rights Campaign's Washington headquarters, I thought back to the night in May of 2012, sitting in the AU student newspaper's office, trying to cut down my coming-out note by more than half.

Given the urgent and numerous challenges facing the community, my 360 words could have easily been filled with a litany of important and necessary policy goals. But as I reworked my speech, a friend reminded me of the Maya Angelou quote that had guided much of my advocacy: "At the end of the day people won't remember what you said or did, they will remember how you made them feel."

There were certainly policy goals that I felt a responsibility to include, such as passage of the Equality Act and combating violence against transgender women of color, but I also knew that I needed to be vulnerable and to invite the audience into my own journey, my hopes and my fears, my love and my loss. I needed to heed the lessons

I had learned three years earlier while fighting for the Gender Identity Nondiscrimination Act in Delaware: Vulnerability is often the first step on the path toward justice. Vulnerability breeds empathy; empathy fosters support; support leads to action.

I decided that I'd talk about my fear of coming out, my relationship with Andy, and some of the important reforms so needed by the community. And I'd end on an optimistic note: that since coming out as trans, the experiences in my life have demonstrated to me that change is possible.

I submitted my draft to the speechwriter, who made only minor changes before sending it off to the Clinton campaign and the Democratic National Committee. A quick approval returned from the decision-makers . . . along with the news that I would be speaking on Thursday night, the final night of the convention, and just a few hours before Hillary Clinton would take the same stage to become the first woman to officially accept the Democratic nomination for president.

When we found out I was on Thursday's program, my colleague nonchalantly commented, "How amazing. Hillary Clinton won't be the only woman making history Thursday night. Sarah will be, too!"

There was that word again. "History."

On the day before the convention, as I was preparing to head up to Philadelphia with my boss, Jay Brown, my participation in the DNC was announced publicly. As the news broke, driving up with Jay, a transgender man and father of two, we braced for the backlash.

*Am I ready for this? Surely this would be the same as the hate from that damn selfie. Only multiplied by ten.*

But the negativity was far less than I'd feared. Instead of death threats, my social media filled with messages of support, inspiration, and excitement. I had thought people would be excited for me and for the momentous occasion, but it became obvious quickly that people were also excited for themselves, for the message it sent to trans people across the country.

The next four days were a whirlwind of little sleep, less food, and lots and lots of interviews. *ABC News,* PBS, *Time* magazine, the *Washington Post,* the *Huffington Post,* NBC, MSNBC, CNN, MTV. In total, I did about forty interviews during the course of the convention.

Really big interviews were done on the private skybox level of the arena. Walking between interviews in different skyboxes, you'd run into senators and governors, celebrities and other speakers clearly as dazed and exhausted as I was. Each skybox was transformed into a small studio, the sound so overwhelming within the arena that the journalists and interviewees were forced to wear massive headsets to hear each other just a foot away.

While I was a little nervous during my first few interviews, the repetition of the same questions and answers soon alleviated my butterflies. Still, each interview was exciting, particularly when I got to sit down with reporters I watched every day.

Growing up, I had watched Katie Couric on *Today* every morning, but now I was sitting across from her in the Yahoo skybox as she announced in her familiar voice, "On Thursday they'll be making history again when Sarah McBride speaks."

It was a lot to take in, but that was probably a good thing. The constant stream of back-to-back interviews kept me distracted and consumed, unable to think about my big, short speech.

Each morning I'd wake up thinking that it had all been a dream, a good dream this time. But then, as I'd look around my hotel room, I'd realize, *No, wait, that was all real. I'm speaking at the Democratic National Convention.*

Thursday came in a flash, and before I knew it, I was in the car on the way to the Wells Fargo Arena. I rode with Congressman Sean Patrick Maloney, a handsome, openly gay second-term congressman from New York who looks like he came right out of central casting, along with his two beautiful kids and an equally handsome husband. Maloney would be speaking first and then introducing me. As our black SUV weaved through security checkpoint after security checkpoint, Maloney sensed my nervousness and spent the car ride trying to distract me with small talk.

When we arrived, we made our way through a maze of hallways beneath the hustle of the delegates, media, and attendees now arriving for the final and premier night of the convention. For a few hours, we waited in a freezing locker room that had been converted into a waiting room for speakers. The walls were draped with dark blue curtains and the room was filled with IKEA-brand white couches. The only sign that it was a locker room was the big blue carpet with a massive 76ers logo stitched into the middle of it. I anxiously waited, hanging out with the other speakers, including my friend and boss, HRC president Chad Griffin. I reviewed my speech a few times and waited for them to call my name to get ready. I could hear the roar of the arena from backstage, but it still seemed so unreal, as though it were just a TV on full-blast in the room next door.

As I waited backstage, my parents arrived, along with Sean and Blake. I had managed, in a surprisingly complicated arrangement, to get my parents passes to the final night of the convention. Unfortunately, even for guests of speakers, the tickets weren't great. My parents found themselves sitting way up in the nosebleed section, just a few rows below the ceiling of the arena.

In a twist of fate, they happened to sit just a few seats behind my old boss at the White House, Gautam Raghavan. "You shouldn't be up here when Sarah speaks! You should be down on the floor," he said, referring to the space reserved for delegates. Working his magic, he managed to secure them two passes, and as the convention gaveled in for the final evening, my parents walked out onto the floor of the cavernous arena.

About an hour into the proceedings, a young staffer with a clipboard walked into the green room backstage and called my name. "Sarah McBride, it's time for you to get ready to go onstage." And just like that, my nerves shot through the roof. I put on my heels, stopped by for a few touch-ups in the hair-and-makeup room, and then walked down a sterile corridor toward the darkened, cramped area just off the stage.

During the weeks prior to the convention, workers had assembled an impressive stage and display with massive screens. To those in the audience, and to anyone watching on TV, it looked like a permanent feature of the arena. Backstage it looked like a hodgepodge of walls, beams, cords, and screws that I legitimately worried would buckle at any moment. The vibrations from the occasional roar of the crowd and the speakers only enhanced that sensation. My heart felt like it was beating out of my chest as we waited.

In the days leading up to this moment, several people had given me important advice. "You are not speaking to the people in the arena, you are speaking to the camera, the people watching at home, and those who watch a video in the days or years to come," they told me. "While you speak, particularly since it's in the first half of the program, people will be milling around and talking. It's going to feel loud in the arena, and some speakers try to win the crowd over with their charisma and by shouting their speech. Don't fall into that trip. It will appear terrible to anyone watching on television."

Sage advice, no doubt, but as I stood backstage I worried I wouldn't be able to strike the balance. And then it was time. The announcer's voice boomed, "Please welcome Congressman Sean Patrick Maloney [. .] and Sarah McBride."

"Go, go, go," the handler backstage whispered to us.

CNN and MSNBC, which hadn't been covering speeches except for each night's headliners, interrupted their panels to carry the speeches live on national television.

BREAKING NEWS read CNN's banner. SARAH MCBRIDE IS THE FIRST OPENLY TRANSGENDER PERSON TO SPEAK AT A MAJOR PARTY CONVENTION.

Chuck Todd interrupted an interview on MSNBC: "I want to go to this. I want to go to this. Let's take a look here, the first transgender person to ever address a national convention. Her name is Sarah McBride."

As we stepped onto the stage, the crowd erupted in applause. *Oh my God, they care,* I thought as I walked out. And making my way across the stage to stand behind Congressman Maloney, I began to hear chanting.

"Sarah! Sarah! Sarah!"

I didn't know what to do with myself. I tried waving a few times but felt a little foolish. Finally, Congressman Maloney started speaking and the audience was, for the first time that night, quiet. They realized this was a special moment, that they were witnessing a first.

As he spoke, I tried to keep my eyes on him but couldn't help looking around. And because the arena was so well lit, while standing onstage I could see every single person in the crowd, all the way up to the rafters. It was a sea of tens of thousands of faces staring at me.

Eventually, my eyes caught my parents. The Delaware delegation was seated just to the right of the stage and I could see my mom and dad standing, smiling, next to our state's junior senator, Chris Coons, and just under the tall, vertical sign—one of many that filled the arena—that read our state's name.

And then I imagined Andy standing right next to them, watching me and looking as smooth and dapper as he was on our very first date. My mind returned to a conversation that was seared into my memory from the final month of his life.

We were sitting on our big brown couch, Andy scrunched into a ball, crying his eyes out. I remember being taken aback by just how visible the fear was in his eyes and, also, just how blue they appeared through the tears.

"I'm so scared," he cried. "I'm so sad that I won't be around to tell you that I love you, to tell you how beautiful you are, and to tell you how proud of you I am."

It was one of the most emotional conversations I had with him. But because of that, it was also the most vivid—a conversation that had stuck with me as though it had occurred yesterday. And standing on that stage, almost perfectly, I could hear Andy saying those words like he was next to me.

"I love you and I'm so proud of you."

I was no longer nervous. Finally, my train of thought was interrupted when I heard my name.

"I want to introduce Sarah McBride. Sarah McBride is a courageous young leader, and she is right now the first trans person ever to address a national convention. Sarah . . ." The audience began screaming, applauding, and chanting. Maloney paused, not wanting to speak over the cheers. Joining in the audience's excitement, he went off script. "It's about time," he said.

Ten seconds later, he continued: "Sarah, it is an honor to make history with you, because we are stronger together."

*Speaking at the convention was a huge honor and a massive responsibility, but it wasn't about me. It was about all the transgender people seeing our identities affirmed and celebrated on such a large platform.*

I walked up to the lectern and got ready to begin. I didn't want to yell over the cheering crowd, so I paused. I knew time was short, and while they wouldn't throw me offstage Oscars-style, I didn't want to go over my time. I improvised a short thank-you line to Congressman Maloney to signal that it was time to start.

I paused for a few more moments to let the cheers die down and then I started my speech: "My name is Sarah McBride and I am a proud transgender American."

The convention erupted. The screams and chants returned. Delegates and attendees started standing up, cheering.

As I struggled with my gender identity throughout college, I had tried to say the words "I'm transgender" to my mirror. The shame would engulf me and I'd shake my head. "No, I'm not. No, I'm not."

Now I was standing onstage at the Democratic National Convention as my authentic self, having just declared before the nation that I am a proud transgender American. But as much as that single sentence represented my own transformation, it was really a celebration of the moment. Everyone in that arena knew that with that sentence, a small but important barrier had just been broken.

Little did I know while standing on that stage that online communities of parents of transgender children were posting pictures and videos of their kids watching the speech. As a community, trans people have witnessed a slow but steady embrace of us by Hollywood and the entertainment world. It's an important milestone, but it also comes with the understanding that it is an industry known for being on the cutting edge of social change.

Politics, on the other hand, almost by definition, is a cautious field. Now, though, watching on television, these young kids were witnessing an arena full of people standing up and enthusiastically applauding the dignity and equality of transgender people. These parents were watching a mainstream political party acknowledge their families in the most explicit way yet. The convention wasn't applauding me, they were applauding all of us.

As the crowd quieted back down, I continued. "Four years ago, I came out as transgender while serving as student body president in college. At the time, I was scared. I worried that my dreams and my identity were mutually exclusive.

"Since then, though, I've seen that change is possible. I witnessed history interning at the White House and helping my home state of Delaware pass protections for transgender people."

Summing up both the question in the election and our fight for equality, I asked, "Will we be a nation where there's only one way to love, only one way to look, and only one way to live? Or will we be a nation where everyone has the freedom to live openly and equally? A nation that's stronger together?"

And then I got very personal. Speaking about Andy, his work, and our relationship always feels like a powerful and comforting way to keep him with me and to keep his legacy alive. I wanted the world to know about my Andy.

"For me, this struggle for equality became all the more urgent when I learned that my future husband, Andrew, was battling cancer. I met Andy, who was a transgender man, fighting for equality and we fell in love. And yet even in the face of his terminal illness, this twenty-eight-year-old, he never wavered in his commitment to our cause and his belief that this country can change. Andy and I married in 2014 and just four days after our wedding, he passed away.

"Knowing Andy left me profoundly changed. But more than anything else, his passing taught me that every day matters when it comes to building a world where every person can live their life to the fullest."

I spoke about the unfinished work of the movement, the need to pass nondiscrimination protections for LGBTQ people, violence against transgender women of color, and the continuing HIV and AIDS epidemic.

As I finished my speech, I could still see my parents smiling. Beaming, really. The reception at the end was as warm as at the start, and I walked offstage emotionally and physically exhausted. I had been going nonstop for the previous week and nearly collapsed into the arms of the mayor of Los Angeles, who greeted me backstage as he waited for his turn to speak.

"You were amazing!" he exclaimed as he hugged me.

I walked back into the maze of hallways and stopped. People were swirling around me. A seamstress working the convention approached with tears in her eyes. She put her arms around me, said how proud of me she was, and enveloped me in a hug.

As she walked away, I continued standing motionless in the hall and I began to cry, partly out of relief, partly out of exhaustion, but also because of the love that had just filled the hall. It was overwhelming.

I made my way out onto the convention floor where all the delegates were seated. As I passed the Pennsylvania delegation, an older transgender woman, Joanne, whom I had met earlier in the year, stood up and walked toward me. Joanne looks like your quintessential grandmother, and exudes the warmth of one.

We were both smiling as she pulled me into a hug. We held on to each other for a couple seconds, and when we pulled away, both of us were crying. She kept her arms at my sides and held me about a foot from her face and said, "I can't believe I'm seeing this in my lifetime."

Standing there, I couldn't help but think of all Joanne had seen. The years of invisibility followed by the years of feeling like a liability. Now she was attending a major party convention with a record number of openly transgender delegates—twenty-eight in total—and she had just witnessed an arena full of people affirming our dignity and celebrating our lives.

For Joanna, it took decades for it to happen, but change came. She saw it in her lifetime.

It's impossible to describe how powerful that can feel after years, or even decades, of feeling unseen at best and hated at worst. Those of us in the D.C. advocacy world had witnessed over the previous two years the appetite and desire by many elected officials to work on and fight for trans equality. But the rest of the transgender community, let alone the rest of the country, hadn't.

After wading through the crowd, I finally reached my parents. As I approached, I could see them crying, too. It takes a lot for my dad to cry, so seeing the tears in his eyes really hit me in the gut.

They were so scared when I came out. They were so worried that I'd be rejected by friends and denied opportunities. *I hope they know that they don't have to worry anymore. I hope they know that, at least for me, everything is going to be okay,* I wished. With cameras trained on us, I fell into my parents' arms and broke down. I could barely get the words out without sobbing.

"Did you see that?" I asked them, referring to the reception. "Did you see that?"

At that very same moment, in suburban Maryland, a mom was sitting with her ten-year-old child, watching the convention on television in their family room. Her child had been miserable for years. As she grappled with answers, she kept coming back to one gut feeling, *My child is transgender.*

Holding on to the child she had assumed was a girl at birth, the mom asked the same question I had just asked my parents. "Did you see that?

"A transgender person just spoke in front of the nation," she continued. "You can be transgender and be anything you want to be. Transgender people can reach their dreams, too." She looked down at her child and asked, "Is there anything you might want to tell me?"

The child exhaled, burying their face into the mom's shoulder.

"I'm a boy, Mom."

Back in the convention center, I sat down to watch the main event of the evening, the undeniably historic moment when Hillary Clinton accepted the Democratic nomination for president of the United States.

In her speech, she acknowledged the history of the moment, "Tonight, we've reached a milestone in our nation's march toward a more perfect union: the first time that a major party has nominated a woman for president. Standing here as my mother's daughter, and my daughter's mother, I'm so happy this day has come. Happy for grandmothers and little girls and everyone in between."

The next day, with Hillary Clinton's words about her historic and empowering accomplishment still reverberating in my mind, I opened a forwarded email from a woman named Ramsey.

I want to personally thank Sarah McBride for her wonderful speech. Below I have included a picture of my seven-year-old transgender daughter watching in awe. She was very inspired and exclaimed "she's beautiful" when she saw Sarah on TV. It was life-changing for her to see a beautiful, accomplished, intelligent role-model with whom she can identify. I am so grateful that she was given such an important moment at such a young age. I am hoping this email can be forwarded to Sarah so she can see the personal impact she had on one young trans girl.

Attached to the email was a picture of her seven-year-old transgender daughter with long, red wavy hair watching CNN on the family's TV. And there I was on the screen.

*Maybe I had made a little history, too.*

# CHAPTER 13

# Our voices matter.

Two weeks after the convention, I met the little trans girl from the photo, after inviting her and her mom to the HRC office.

"Hi, Lulu, I'm Sarah," I said, kneeling in order to be eye level with the seven-year-old, who was clearly nervous and a little shy. "What do ya say we go get some juice and your mom and I can have some coffee?"

The three of us walked to a coffee shop a few blocks away and Lulu pulled out a folded piece of paper with a few questions written in big block letters.

"Lulu prepared some questions for you," her mother explained with a smile.

"Oh, wonderful!" I exclaimed. Lulu adorably smoothed the paper flat to get out the creases. She cleared her throat and began reading her questions.

"Ms. Sarah," she started, with a slight lisp. "What's your favorite part about being transgender?"

*My favorite part?* Growing up, that sentence wouldn't have made sense to me.

Since coming out, I had been so used to hearing questions about survival or hardship, about negativity and hate. We are inundated with messages that being trans is bad, gross, and a burden for ourselves and others. But Lulu's question turned that negative perspective on its head. It took more than twenty-five years for me to hear that question for the first time.

I paused and thought about it.

"I think I have three favorite things about being transgender," I began with a smile. "The first is that it led me to meet my husband, Andy. The second is that I think it's made me a stronger, better, more compassionate person. And the third? The third is that I get to meet amazing people like you. People who are brave, brilliant, and beautiful."

Her eyes lit up. Lulu represents the first generation of trans people who, in many cases, have been allowed to grow up as themselves. These youth are insistent, consistent, and persistent in asserting their gender identity, and when coupled with supportive parents and a health-care provider versed on the most up-to-date medical consensus, they are allowed to live practically their whole lives, no matter how long, as their authentic selves.

And despite the hate and pushback they receive from the world, the pride so many of them feel in themselves still leads them to ask that simple but radical question: "What's your favorite part about being transgender?"

Following the convention, my life changed dramatically. My travel doubled. I was on the road almost constantly, speaking to groups large and small. Two days in New York, two days in Jacksonville, and another two in Miami. Three days in Seattle, a day in Los Angeles, and another in San Francisco. Two in Dallas. One in Virginia. And too many to count in North Carolina, where the state's incumbent Republican governor, Pat McCrory, was up for reelection. And at each stop along the way, parents would come, bringing along their transgender children.

Each time, I'd ask the trans kids Lulu's question.

"It means I'm a strong person," one sixteen-year-old gender-nonconforming youth responded, echoing one of the sentiments in my own answer.

"Trans is beautiful," proclaimed a fifteen-year-old trans teen in Northern California, quoting Laverne Cox.

"I don't have to hide anymore," a nine-year-old trans girl in Fort Lauderdale answered.

In Durham, North Carolina, an eleven-year-old trans boy didn't beat around the bush. "My favorite thing? That I'm me," he announced through a big grin.

The parents I met would recount their journeys. In many cases, they had endured horrific bullying from neighbors for embracing and loving their children. Often, they had to fight with their schools for their children to have access to even the most basic necessities, like being called the correct name or being allowed to use the restroom. They'd share their stories through tears, but one common thread existed in each one. They all were hopeful. "Things are changing," they'd say.

And then November 8, 2016, arrived. I was in North Carolina on Election Day. The Human Rights Campaign had put unprecedented resources—staff, volunteers, and money—into the state, intent on defeating McCrory and sending the message that targeting transgender people for discrimination is not just morally wrong, it's also bad politics.

The night before, my HRC colleagues and I had joined thousands of fired-up supporters, Lady Gaga, and the Clinton family for the final rally of the 2016 presidential campaign. Hillary walked onto the stage at midnight, just as Election Day arrived, one final time to "Fight Song," the pop melody that had become her campaign theme song. In the bleachers above her, supporters held up massive letters that spelled "H-I-S-T-O-R-Y."

The United States was not only about to elect a woman to the highest office in the land, but someone who had laid out the most progressive and inclusive platform of any nominee in history. For the LGBTQ community, her election would solidify all of the federal progress we had seen in the preceding eight years and provide a platform to continue to push our much-needed policy goals forward.

Within twenty-four hours of the rally, the cheers, the excitement, the H-I-S-T-O-R-Y sign all felt like a cruel dream. As the results came in on the night of November 8, it slowly became clear that Donald Trump would win the Electoral College.

Trump had run the most divisive campaign in modern American politics. He had staked his candidacy on bluster and bigotry, on fear and discrimination, and our electoral system had rewarded him with the most significant honor society can bestow on a person: the presidency of the United States.

Almost immediately, I started thinking about all those parents and kids whom I had met over the previous three months. For many of them, President Obama and his administration had been their one source of protection from discrimination. Their bosses, school boards, local governments, and state governments were all either apathetic to their plight or actively hostile to their interests.

Throughout the campaign, Donald Trump had disingenuously claimed to be a friend to the LGBTQ community while endorsing nearly every anti-equality position thinkable. He had endorsed the ability of states such as North Carolina to discriminate against transgender people. He had committed to nominating judges who opposed marriage equality and trans rights. He had promised to sign legislation that would provide a license to discriminate against LGBTQ people nationwide. And as a sign of things to come, he had picked in Mike Pence a vice president whose entire national profile was built on attacking women's rights and LGBTQ equality.

That the most qualified candidate in modern history—a woman—had just lost to the most unqualified and unfit candidate in all of American history only added insult to injury. Hillary's loss perfectly encapsulated the nearly impossible double standard facing any marginalized person in politics or the workforce.

As a woman, she was required by our society and structures to work two, three, four times harder than any white man to get to the cusp of the presidency. To exert that degree of effort, to navigate a world designed against your success, requires a degree of commitment, intentionality, and determination that cannot be hidden behind the false humility we so often demand of our political candidates.

We reward candidates, particularly for the presidency, who seem almost apathetic to the possibility of being elected. We love the idea of a candidate who seems to stumble their way into the Oval Office. We put effortlessness on a pedestal, which in turn punishes the marginalized for working twice as hard to get half as far. The very perseverance and determination that we require to succeed is then held against the marginalized, particularly women, as self-interested ambition.

The sexism in Hillary's loss and the racism that laced Trump's win were clear. But the biggest tragedy was the hate and discrimination that would be further thrust onto everyday people—Muslims, people with disabilities, immigrants, women, people of color, and LGBTQ people—throughout America.

The morning after the election, many in the LGBTQ community and beyond woke up fearful about what the results would mean for them. The Human Rights Campaign and other civil rights organizations were inundated with questions and concerns. People were genuinely terrified about what the future would hold. The Southern Poverty Law Center would later report roughly four hundred hate-based attacks and incidents in the immediate aftermath of the election. Calls to LGBTQ suicide hotlines skyrocketed. Educators were reporting a dramatic increase in bullying toward their Muslim, Latinx, and LGBTQ students.

Those last two reports—the bullying and the calls to suicide hotlines—struck me the most. It was clear that in the aftermath of the election, a lot of youth were likely feeling completely alone and vulnerable and questioning whether things really were changing.

Amid the troubling reports, my colleagues and I decided that it was important to film a short video message to LGBTQ, and particularly trans, youth across the country. I had not had time to fully digest the results and wrap my mind around the coming abrupt and significant shift from a presidency of progress to a presidency of prejudice. I didn't really know what to say.

Just two days after the election, still feeling like the wind had been knocked out of me, I recorded a three-minute video message to the transgender youth who were facing fear, uncertainty, and increased bullying. Slowly and somberly, I began to talk directly to the camera.

"As a transgender person, I want to speak directly to all the young transgender people and your parents who are wondering if the heart of this country is big enough to love you, too, and who worry that the results of this election have emboldened bullies in your classrooms and neighborhoods," I opened, feeling the weight and urgency of the moment. "But know that no election, no presidency, can change these simple and constant truths: You are worthy, you are beautiful, and you are loved."

I recounted the lessons I had learned from the online harassment I had faced. "And the bullies, they see that. They see our power and they're jealous of it. You are powerful . . .

"We need each other now more than we have in a very long time. We need each other to fight against whatever attacks come our way. And we need each other to stand up to anyone who thinks that they can bully anyone because one of the biggest bullies just became president. We have to have each other's backs. When we see bullying, whether it's against LGBTQ people, Muslims, people of color, immigrants, women, or people with disabilities, we must call it out."

I took a breath and continued. "There is one more simple and constant truth that remains unchanged. We—HRC and advocates in D.C. and around the country—we're here for you, we care about you, and we are going to fight like hell to make sure that every single one of us is treated with the dignity, respect, and fairness we all deserve."

HRC released the video on the Sunday after the election, just as students were getting ready to head back to the first full week of school after the election. I didn't have answers that early—no one did—but it was important to make clear to that LGBTQ youth isolated in a life where it seems that no one sees them and loves them that someone did: that they were seen, that they were loved, and that they were not alone.

Sifting through all the bad news of the 2016 election, there was one bright spot. In North Carolina, McCrory had lost his reelection bid. In a state that went for Donald Trump in the Electoral College, McCrory was the only incumbent Republican governor to lose reelection that year, and he lost largely because of his support for HB2 and the ensuing harm it caused to the state.

His loss reinforced that all was not lost: that when diverse voices are heard, when the progressive community stands together, when allies speak out, there is still a way to make the politics of fear and division, of discrimination and misinformation, no longer effective.

And as the dust from the presidential election began to settle, the sadness gave way to preparations for the fight ahead. A quiet determination set in as we anticipated the policies that were likeliest to be rolled back. The trans community was disproportionately impacted, as so much of our progress had been achieved through President Obama—and what comes from one president's pen can often be struck by the next president's pen.

Late that November, transgender people from across the country convened at the White House for an event to mark Transgender Day of Remembrance, an annual nationwide commemoration dedicated to the transgender people who had lost their lives to hate and violence during the preceding year. Events around Transgender Day of Remembrance are always rightfully somber, but this event was even more emotional than usual: It was the final time representatives of the trans community would be in the White House for the foreseeable future.

One of our staunchest supporters, Attorney General Loretta Lynch, was scheduled to speak to the room of about one hundred local, state, and federal advocates. Lynch had made history as the first African American woman attorney general, and during her two-year tenure trans rights had become a cornerstone of her legacy. The previous spring, she had brought suit against her home state of North Carolina after passage of HB2, a challenge that would later be rescinded by the Trump administration.

I was asked to introduce the attorney general at the gathering. But before we went onstage, I met with her privately backstage. The white walls were still filled with the "jumbo" photographs of President Obama. Within a few weeks, the frames would remain but the images would be replaced with ones of Donald Trump.

I waited alone until Attorney General Lynch entered through large double doors that led to the West Wing.

"Sarah." She walked toward me with her hand outstretched. "It's an honor to meet you."

"The honor is all mine, Madam Attorney General." I thanked her for joining our community for the event. And then I thanked her for the speech she had given in the spring when she announced the lawsuit against HB2. "I hope you know how much that meant to our community. It was the first time that many trans people realized that their federal government was on their side. You saved lives that day."

She grabbed my hand and looked me directly in the eyes. "This administration may be coming to an end, but we aren't going anywhere," she said. "We'll be fighting right beside you outside of government."

And she was right. In all of the talk about what we might lose, the fact remained that most of our progress was irreversible. The hearts we had opened would not close. The minds we had changed would not reverse. The laws we had passed remained on the books. Marriage equality was the law of the land nationwide. And while the Trump administration would likely seek to roll back many of our administrative advancements, they wouldn't succeed on every one. We'd have a new alliance of allies standing shoulder to shoulder with us as we fight back.

And we'd need those allies. As much as Pat McCrory's loss sent a message and offered a strategy, it wouldn't stave off continued attacks on the LGBTQ community. In many ways, Donald Trump's election further emboldened hateful elected officials at the state and local levels, just as many of us feared.

In 2017, more than 130 anti-LGBTQ bills were introduced in thirty states. That year, Texas was ground zero for anti-equality forces, where the legislature was considering a dozen discriminatory bills, including a North Carolina–style bathroom bill. In March, I joined hundreds of trans people and our allies in Austin at the state capitol for a citizen lobby day. Two years before, forty people had shown up. Now it was hundreds, including an influx of allies. People came from across the massive state of Texas to push their legislators to defeat the discriminatory bills.

Scattered throughout the crowd were dozens of transgender kids whose unashamed pride in themselves was undiminished by the incomprehensible hate they were facing from within that state capitol. These nine-, ten-, and eleven-year-old kids entered the Texas capitol, one of the largest legislative buildings in the nation, with their heads held high, determined to fight for themselves and others like them.

Throughout the LGBTQ movement, young voices have been the drivers of change. Sylvia Rivera was seventeen years old when she helped launch the Stonewall Riot. Marsha P. Johnson was twenty-three at the historic rebellion. Marriage equality is a reality today in large part because of younger generations that have slowly but surely moved their parents and grandparents to side with love and equality.

Walking through the intimidating halls of the Texas state capitol with these trans kids, I thought back to just how overwhelmed I was in our fight for nondiscrimination protections in Delaware. I had been twice their age and facing a friendly legislature on a fight for a positive bill. These trans and LGBTQ youth were entering a capitol that was vehemently and viciously hostile to them personally. Many of the elected officials in that building had made clear their disgust with trans kids in the Texas papers and on talk radio and cable news. But that didn't stop these young people from marching into that building to confront their legislators. It didn't slow their pace. They were on a mission and carried with them a gravity that is unique to young voices.

I first began to understand that gravity in Delaware and had seen it since in states like North Carolina and, now, in Texas. When young people participate in politics, they can speak from a place of history. I don't mean the history of the past, but rather the history that remains to be written. Young people will be the ones who write the history books of tomorrow. The ones I was standing with in Texas—and all LGBTQ youth and our young allies—will be the ones that get to decide who was right and who was wrong in this moment. As young people, we carry that perspective with us everywhere, from the safest to the scariest spaces in society.

That is a powerful tool. And if there is one thing I've learned throughout the last few years, it's that our voices matter. My voice matters. Andy's voice continues to matter. These young trans kids' voices matter. Your voice matters. Our voices matter.

People frequently ask me how I remain hopeful in a world too often filled with hate and so often constructed to marginalize. It's simple: I remain hopeful because I know that no matter what obstacles stand in our way, nothing—not even death—can take away our voices and our power. And because of those voices, I've had a front seat to change that once seemed unimaginable.

• • •

Several months after Donald Trump's inauguration, I met a twelve-year-old transgender girl named Stella. Stella absolutely loves history and politics. She was attending an HRC youth-orientated conference that I was speaking at, and when we ran into each other in the hall-way, she couldn't contain her excitement. Her mouth was agape, just like mine had been a decade before when I first met people like Joe Biden and Jack Markell.

As I had with Lulu, I invited Stella and her mom to come to the HRC office a few days later as my colleagues and I were set to protest outside the White House against a proposed anti-LGBTQ executive order. When I met up with Stella that morning, she was wearing flip-flops, blue jeans, a gray T-shirt with "love" written on it in cursive, and a small blue-and-pink button that read "Trans Rights Now." I walked with Stella and her mom to the same coffee shop where I'd talked with Lulu a few months earlier.

We sat across from each other and I asked Stella what she wanted to be when she got older. Without any doubt, she proudly proclaimed, "The first trans president!"

As we talked, I learned just how similar we are. Like me at her age, Stella goes to a Montessori school. Like me, she loves history and politics. Like me at her age, her favorite president is FDR. Like me at her age, she loves movies and filmmaking as a hobby. Like me at her age, her childhood dream is to be president of the United States. Like me, she is trans.

She was just like me at her age in so many ways but one: She was herself.

Sitting there talking with her, I realized that I was looking at a twelve-year-old version of myself, just a more authentic, self-actualized one. I was face-to-face with an alternative past. She was me, had I been able to grow up as myself. If science, society, and awareness had moved just a little bit faster to meet a young me in my own journey earlier.

I told Stella that I felt like I was sitting with the first transgender president and invited her to walk with me a few blocks to Lafayette Square, in front of the White House, where we were getting ready for the protest.

That day was a far cry from two years earlier in that same square, when so many of us had celebrated the marriage equality decision. Now, standing there, Stella got on my shoulders. Her mom snapped a picture of the two of us in front of the White House, Stella smiling and laughing, convinced that she was looking at her future home.

Too often we hear that "politics is the art of the possible," but that belief undersells our power to effect transformational change. Instead, as barrier-breaking leaders throughout history have observed, politics is—and must always be—the art of making the impossible possible. Standing there with Stella on my shoulders, the change was obvious. In one generation, what had once seemed impossible to me growing up was now very real and possible to Stella. She could be herself and still dream.

That progress alone won't save every life. It won't stop discrimination or prevent violence. But the fact that Stella is even a reality today demonstrates how far we've come.

She represents a small but important step toward building a world where you can be trans, you can be gay, you can be Black, Muslim, an immigrant, a woman, or anything that this society says is mutually exclusive with dreaming big dreams—you can be any or all of those things and still be seen, valued, and respected as an equal.

Sometimes it can feel like we're taking two steps forward and one step back. Indeed, in just over a year in office, the Trump administration has rescinded lifesaving guidance promoting the protection of transgender students, reinstated a ban on transgender people serving in the military, and in an action that added insult to injury, taken aim at the health-care nondiscrimination rule that Andy had spent so much of his life working toward. They've attacked the rights and dignity of people with disabilities, immigrants, women, Muslims, and people of color.

I know that it can feel like we're almost lost as a country. But we must never forget that even with all of the hate and all of the challenges, no matter who is president, we can continue to change our world for the better. We've done it before and we can do it again.

It's the change that's allowed a community that was once ignored and later mocked to now stand on the cusp of our chapter in history.

It's the change that's taken a movement from Stonewall to the steps of the Supreme Court and brought marriage equality to every state in the land.

It's the change that has allowed more families and friends, co-workers and classmates, to welcome an LGBTQ loved one with broad smiles and open arms.

It's the change that Andy had dedicated his life to pushing forward.

It's the change that made possible, just one year after the disastrous election of Donald Trump, the historic victories of trans candidates running to serve in city halls, on school boards, and finally, in one of the nation's oldest state legislatures.

And it's the change that allowed me—someone who just four years before couldn't bring myself to say the words "I'm transgender" in my mirror—to stand onstage at the Democratic National Convention and declare before the nation that I am a "proud transgender American."

And we have not come this far to stop now. Not with so much work left to do. In too many places, LGBTQ people are still denied the equal protection of the law. Transgender people, and particularly trans women of color, continue to face an epidemic of violence as 2017 became the deadliest year on record for the trans community. From Texas to North Carolina, hateful laws remain on the books. Barriers still exist. Challenges continue. And through it all, the fundamental truth remains that no one in the LGBTQ community is totally equal until everyone—from the gay Muslim refugee, to the queer undocumented immigrant, to the transgender woman of color—is treated with dignity and fairness.

We must never be pacified by our progress or content with the pace of change. But we must always remember just how far we've come and hold firm to our vision of a fairer, more just society.

Every day matters in this fight. But I remain as hopeful as ever that tomorrow will be different. That someday, generations from now, when our understanding of "We the People" finally includes everyone, a young trans student or a young queer student will grow up and learn about this struggle for justice and equality in those history books. And they'll never have to know what this progress felt like, because they will never know anything different.

That will be because of the courage of the countless LGBTQ people who dared to walk down the street as the person they are or with the one they love. It will be because of advocates and activists who dreamed of a different world. It will be because of the allies who stood up and spoke out. It will be because of our generation.

We *are* powerful. We *are* making history. And, together, I know that we are unstoppable.

# Studies and Resources

CHAPTER 1

Grant, Jamie M., Lisa A. Mottet, and Justin Tanis. "Injustice at Every Turn: A Report of the National Transgender Discrimination Survey." National Center for Transgender Equality and the National Gay and Lesbian Task Force (2011). http://www.thetaskforce.org/downloads/reports/reports/ntds_full.pdf.


CHAPTER 2

Durso, Laura E., and Gary J. Gates. "Serving Our Youth: Findings from a National Survey of Service Providers Working with Lesbian, Gay, Bisexual, and Transgender Youth Who Are Homeless or at Risk of Becoming Homeless." The Williams Institute with True Colors Fund and the Palette Fund (2012). https://williamsinstitute.law.ucla.edu/wp-content/uploads/Durso-Gates-LGBT-Homeless-Youth-Survey-July-2012.pdf.


CHAPTER 3

James, Sandy E., Jody L. Herman, Susan Rankin, Mara Keisling, Lisa Mottet, and Ma'ayan Anafi. "The Report of the 2015 U.S. Transgender Survey." The National Center for Transgender Equality (2016). http://www.transequality.org/sites/default/files/docs/usts/USTS%20Full%20Report%20-%20FINAL%201.6.17.pdf.

"A Matter of Life and Death: Fatal Violence Against the
Transgender Community in 2016." Human Rights Campaign and
Trans People of Color Coalition (2016). https://assets.hrc.org//
files/assets/resources/A-Matter-of-Life-and-Death-2016.pdf?_ga
=2.187411115.226333368.1506486663-1029459558.1454633482.


CHAPTER 5

"2016 State Equality Index: A Review of State Legislation Affecting
the Lesbian, Gay, Bisexual, Transgender and Queer Community and a
Look Ahead in 2017." Human Rights Campaign and Equality Federation
Institute (2016). http://assets.hrc.org//files/assets/resources/SEI
-2016-Report-FINAL.pdf?_ga=2.249603461.226333368.1506486663
-1029459558.1454633482.


CHAPTER 6

Flores, Andrew R., Jody L. Herman, Gary J. Gates, and Taylor N. T.
Brown. "How Many Adults Identify as Transgender in the United
States?" The Williams Institute (2016). http://williamsinstitute.law.ucla
.edu/wp-content/uploads/How-Many-Adults-Identify-as-Transgender
-in-the-United-States.pdf.

Grant, Mottet, and Tanis. "Injustice at Every Turn: A Report of the
National Transgender Discrimination Survey."


CHAPTER 7

James, Herman, Rankin, Keisling, Mottet, and Anafi. "The Report of the
2015 U.S. Transgender Survey."


CHAPTER 8

"When Health Care Isn't Caring: Lambda Legal's Survey of
Discrimination Against LGBT People and People with HIV." Lambda
Legal (2010). www.lambdalegal.org/health-care-report.


CHAPTER 11

"Sexual Orientation and Housing Discrimination in Michigan: A
Report of Michigan's Fair Housing Centers." Fair Housing Center of

Metropolitan Detroit, Fair Housing Center of Southeastern Michigan, Fair Housing Center of Southwest Michigan, and Fair Housing Center of West Michigan (2007). http://www.fhcmichigan.org/images/Arcus _web1.pdf.

Kosciw, Joseph G., Emily A. Greytak, Noreen M. Giga, Christian Villenas, and David J. Danischewski. "The 2015 National School Climate Survey: The Experiences of Lesbian, Gay, Bisexual, Transgender, and Queer Youth in Our Nation's Schools." GLSEN (2016). https://www .glsen.org/sites/default/files/2015%20National%20GLSEN%202015 %20National%20School%20Climate%20Survey%20%28NSCS%29%20 -%20Full%20Report_0.pdf.

McBride, Sarah, Laura E. Durso, Hannah Hussey, Sharita Gruberg, and Bishop Gene Robinson. "We the People: Why Congress and U.S. States Must Pass Comprehensive LGBT Nondiscrimination Protections." Center for American Progress (2014). https://www.americanprogress .org/issues/lgbt/reports/2014/12/10/102804/we-the-people/.

CHAPTER 13

Staff. "More Than 400 Incidents of Hateful Harassment and Intimidation Since Election." Southern Poverty Law Center (2016). https://www .splcenter.org/hatewatch/2016/11/15/update-more-400-incidents-hateful -harassment-and-intimidation-election.

ACKNOWLEDGMENTS

Well, that was a book and a process. I'm so grateful to my family, friends, and colleagues who helped make writing this possible. First, I couldn't have done any of this had it not been for the amazing team at Crown Archetype, my kind, thoughtful, patient, and spectacular editor Jen Schuster, and the stellar broader editorial team of Trish Boczkowski and Jon Darga, as well as Kathleen, Tammy, Julie, Kathryn, and Maya in the marketing and publicity departments. At a certain point in the writing process, it felt like I was in the middle of the ocean, no land in sight, and unsure of whether I was going in the right direction. But Jen (and Trish and Jon while Jen was out) were my North Stars.

A huge set of thanks to my agent, Katie Zanecchia. I don't know what I would have done had it not been for her careful read of so many drafts from the proposal to the final manuscript and her reassurances during my frequent flare-ups of impostor syndrome.

Endless thanks and love to my parents, Sally and Dave McBride, for being the most loving and caring people in the world. Nothing I do in this life would be possible without their love and support. As I say in the book, I lucked out in the parent lottery! A big thanks to Andy's parents, Ardis, Richard, Steve, and Debbie, and the whole Cray-Sweeney crew. A huge "I love you" to my brothers and their significant others,

Sean McBride and Blake Marks Landro and Dan McBride and Jamie Prater. I'm eternally indebted to my friends who have been by my side through so much, putting up with me interviewing many of them about memories and, generously, not rolling their eyes when I updated them on the book: Read Scott, Helen Boyer, Mat Marshall, Harry Berger, Liz Richards, Jaelyn Brown, Sarah Fulton, Alanna Mozeik, Tracey Ross, Sarah Baron, Kendall Bills, Wes Garson, Erin Fitzgerald, Kelsey Pacha, Heather Butt, Jaimie Ermak, Kat Skiles, Kaela Jeffers, Bishop Gene Robinson, Joe Ste.Marie, Erika Zois, Chelsea Babcock, Riley Fujisaki, Taylor Yeates, Eric Reath, Adam Daniel-Wayman, Brett Atanasio, Palak Gosar, Dr. Laura Durso, Sharita Gruberg, Kellan Baker, Rebecca Fox, Jose Morales, Liz Glaser, Mara Keisling, Lisa Mottet, Lisa Goodman, and Mark Purpura.

I couldn't have written this thing and kept my job had it not been for my accommodating, tireless, fearless, and effective colleagues at the Human Rights Campaign, in particular, Liz Halloran, Jay Brown, Chris Sgro, Chad Griffin, Olivia Alair Dalton, David Stacy, and J. Dee Winterhof. I'll never forget my former colleague at the Center for American Progress, Lauren Vicary, who told me years ago to write a book.

I'm so in awe of our former vice president, Joe Biden, for his leadership and compassion, and grateful for his willingness to write the foreword to this book. I can't imagine what my ten-year-old self would say if I had been told then that this would happen. I'm still freaking out. Thank you to Gautam Raghavan and Louisa Terrell at the Biden Foundation. Sonia Sloan is an inspiring advocate in Delaware, and she was instrumental in the beginning stages of the foreword.

Had it not been for the incomparable Roddy Flynn and the LGBT Equality Caucus, who invited me to speak at the convention—with, of course, the permission of Hillary Clinton and her team—this whole adventure would have never been set into motion.

I feel privileged to have been mentored by two amazing leaders, Jack Markell and the late Beau Biden. They took me under their wings, gave unique opportunities to a cringe-worthy seventeen-year-old, and supported me before and after I came out. A quick shout-out to the Great

State of Delaware for being small but mighty, and for always feeling like home.

Finally, to Andy, my bean, I love you forever and ever. I miss you every day. I think about you always. I perpetually ask myself, "What Would Andy Do?" I would give anything to have you back.

I hope I've made you proud.

Sarah McBride is the national press secretary at the Human Rights Campaign, working tirelessly to advocate for LGBTQ equality. She has been featured in the *New York Times*, the *Washington Post*, *Time*, *Cosmopolitan*, *Elle*, *Vogue*, *Rolling Stone*, and *The New Yorker*, and she speaks regularly at national LGBTQ and political events. A native of Delaware, McBride is on the front lines of the progressive movement.

# TOMORROW WILL
# BE DIFFERENT

EXTRA LIBRIS

ESSAYS,
READER'S GUIDES,
AND MORE

# A Reader's Guide

1. Sarah knew that she was transgender at a very young age, but struggled for years to accept her identity because she didn't see herself positively represented in the media. How have things changed since then? What factors do you feel have enabled this shift?

2. What was your experience reading *Tomorrow Will Be Different*? What surprised you the most while reading the book, and about what you learned?

3. Many people don't know where to begin when they start learning about LGBTQ issues, and are often overwhelmed with information. Did you feel this way before reading *Tomorrow Will Be Different*? Why or why not? Did your opinions change after reading this book? If so, how?

4. Which part of Sarah's story were you most drawn to, and why?

5. Sarah writes about the nearly universal desire to be seen. When were some times that you felt unseen, unheard, or marginalized, and how did you go about handling those situations?

6. Sarah's experiences are the main focus of her memoir, but she points out that trans issues are closely linked with many other issues. For example, trans women of color are more likely to experience violence, assault, and even homelessness. What other major issues can you think of that affect transgender people, whether in this book or in the world in general?

7. Throughout Sarah's life, she has sought to bring about change. What do you think of her strategies for making progress? What do you think are the most effective ways to bring about change?

8. Did reading Sarah's story inspire you to want to join the fight for equality? If so, how do you think you might get involved? (Hint: Visit HRC.org to learn more about how to fight the good fight!)

# A Conversation with Sarah McBride

In June 2018, Nora Alice Demick, the co-chair of Penguin Random House's LGBTQ Network, sat down with Sarah McBride and her editor, Jen Schuster, to discuss *Tomorrow Will Be Different*. A portion of their conversation is transcribed below:

**NAD: What did you want to convey with this memoir, and what readers did you want to reach?**

SM: I think that, at the start, I wanted to write this book for two reasons: One, I wanted to reinforce for people that behind this national conversation on transgender rights are real people who love and laugh, hope and dream, fear and cry just like everyone else. So often I think we lose track of the humanity behind the issues that we're debating in our politics, and I think that's true about transgender equality. So I wanted to get past the caricatures and the myths and the fearmongering and demonstrate the humanity behind this issue.

I also—as I talked about at the convention and in the book—wanted to underscore the urgency of this fight. That when you ask marginalized people— whether they're transgender, LGBTQ, people of color, women, immigrants, Muslims—when you ask them to sit by and allow for a slow conversation to take place before you treat them with respect and grant them equality, you are asking those people to watch their own lives pass them by without the dignity and fairness that every person deserves. And so I wanted to make sure that people understood that urgency.

Actually, my editor and I met before the election, and the day that I heard the wonderful news that Jen bid for the book was the day after the election. And I wrote this book from January through June of 2017, and one of the best outcomes for me in that process was that it was a journey back to hope, and it was an ability—at a time when I was demoralized and dispirited—to find my hope again, and to reflect on the lessons of the previous six years of my life and recognize that change is always possible, and that it's oftentimes in the darkest and hardest moments that we take the biggest steps forward in history.

And so my hope in writing this after the election is not just that people could take away more information about trans people, not just that they could empathize with our experiences more, but that they could believe that change is still possible.

**NAD: Jen, when did you realize that this was a story that needed to be told?**

JS: While reading the proposal, it was very clear to me that Sarah was a terrific storyteller, and that her ability to capture love and loss and identity on the page was both universal and relatable to all of us and yet very specific to her experiences. And the timing, as Sarah mentioned, was incredible. We were at the tail end of the campaign election cycle, and it felt to me more important than ever to help give a platform to diverse and marginalized voices; to exceptional storytellers who could put a face and a personal experience to a much larger fight.

NAD: Sarah, was there any part of the process that was particularly difficult or cathartic?

SM: Without question, the part that was the most difficult was writing about my relationship with Andy. But it was also, in many ways, the most cathartic, because I never really let myself truly mourn and recover and process those emotions. Right after he passed, I jumped right back into advocacy. So in writing it, I was able to relive those experiences in a way that helped me process them more deeply, and also to relive the parts of our relationships that weren't just about cancer, and re-recognize just how privileged I was to have Andy Cray in my life, and to learn from him and grow with him. The best part to write and the hardest part to write were one and the same.

NAD: Are there any influences or perspectives or daily phrases that Andy brought into your life that you still recall today?

SM: People say this about those they've lost all the time, but it couldn't be more true about Andy—and it's not just those who were very close to him who think this but anyone who met him. Every day I wake up and ask myself, "What would Andy do?" Because he was truly the most generous, the kindest, one of the funniest people I've ever met. And one of my takeaways from my time with him was that he really taught me how to live the values that I fight for at work and in my daily life. His advocacy was a principled advocacy rooted in compassion and kindness, and I carry that in my own life after Andy.

The phrase that really sticks with me wasn't from Andy but from my brother, and that's "amazing grace." When Andy was dying, my brother—who's a radiation oncologist—was a guardian angel who was there with me every step of the way. And he told me, "This is going to be incredibly difficult, but take stock in the acts of amazing grace that will fill your life." And that grace was truly everywhere, from our friends organizing a wedding for us on the rooftop of our building in five days to Andy surviving long enough to make it to our wedding. And I think it was that perspective shift that allowed me to recognize that that hope only makes sense in the face of hardship.

It was because of Andy that I didn't just learn how to advocate but I learned how to persevere; and I learned that even in tragedy there can be beauty, and even in those darkest moments you can bear witness to acts of amazing grace.

For additional Extra Libris content from your other
favorite authors and to enter great book giveaways, visit
**ReadItForward.com/Extra-Libris.**

**ESSAYS, READER'S GUIDES, AND MORE**